Pay-to-Play Politics

Pay-to-Play Politics

HOW MONEY DEFINES
THE AMERICAN DEMOCRACY

Heath Brown

 PRAEGER™

An Imprint of ABC-CLIO, LLC
Santa Barbara, California • Denver, Colorado

Library of Congress Cataloging-in-Publication Data

Pay-to-Play Politics
Library of Congress Cataloging in Publication Control Number: 2015047219

ISBN: 978-1-4408-5005-9
EISBN: 978-1-4408-5006-6

20 19 18 17 16   1 2 3 4 5

This book is also available on the World Wide Web as an eBook.
Visit www.abc-clio.com for details.

Praeger
An Imprint of ABC-CLIO, LLC

ABC-CLIO, LLC
130 Cremona Drive, P.O. Box 1911
Santa Barbara, California 93116-1911

This book is printed on acid-free paper ∞

Manufactured in the United States of America

Contents

Figures and Tables

TABLES

Acknowledgments

I wrote this book during my first year at John Jay College of Criminal Justice, City University of New York. The support of my new colleagues and resources provided by the college, especially John Jay Research, and the university made the book possible. Much of this book is a synthesis of the excellent work on the topic. Thank you to Christopher Witko, Lee Drutman, Thomas Holyoke, Tim LaPira, Frank Baumgartner, Avi Green, Michael Miller, Zephyr Teachout, Ray La Raja, Brian Murphy, Darrell West, and Michael Malbin for shaping my views of these issues with your excellent scholarship. The project would not have been possible without research and data from the Campaign Finance Institute and the Center for Responsible Politics. Jessica Gribble at Praeger encouraged me to write this book and helped make sure it was of the highest quality.

My family provides me with so much support and editorial assistance. My parents, Muriel Watt and Rick Brown, are my first line of defense against boring prose. I also wrote this book during my first year of marriage to my amazing wife and editor, Kate Storey. She adds the pop to my life and to my writing.

Chapter 1

Introduction

There are two great ironies that define the relationship between money and politics in the United States. One irony relates to the politicians that represent citizens and another irony is for the public-at-large.

The first irony is best illustrated during our most recent campaign. As she announced her candidacy for the presidency in Iowa in 2015, Hillary Clinton said, "We need to fix our dysfunctional political system and get unaccountable money out of it once and for all—even if it takes a constitutional amendment."[1] Clinton's name is synonymous with money and politics, not only because she is the central figure in *Hillary: The Movie*, the documentary at the heart of the landmark *Citizens United* Supreme Court decision that loosened campaign finance laws in 2010, but also because her husband Bill had featured similar themes during his successful presidential bids 20 years earlier.[2]

Clinton was not alone on the issue; her two main challengers at the time, Martin O'Malley and Bernie Sanders, went even further. Senator Sanders declared that the American democracy had come to resemble an oligarchy, and "To restore our one person, one vote democracy, Congress must pass a constitutional amendment to overturn *Citizens United* and move toward public funding of elections."[3] And former Maryland Governor O'Malley was even more specific in his prescription: "While fixing the *Citizens United* decision is important, we can't afford to wait for a constitutional amendment to solve the problem of out-of-control money in our political system. We should start by embracing citizen-funded elections, to reduce the outsized influence of special interests and the very wealthy in our politics. Small donors should have their contributions matched by six-to-one or more, and be rewarded through a refundable tax credit that encourages more people to give and participate."[4] One minor Democratic candidate, Lawrence Lessig, even mounted a campaign based solely on this one issue. From all sides of the party, most agreed about the nature of the problem and even on a set of solutions.

Not to be outdone by their partisan opponents, Republicans entered the money-and-politics fray, though with fewer policy prescriptions. On anonymous political donations, Governor Chris Christie—then testing the presidential waters—said, "I think what is corrupting in this potentially is we don't know where the money is coming from."[5] And South Carolina Senator and then-candidate Lindsay Graham complained, "It's the wild, wild West . . . What I worry about is that we are turning campaigns over to about 100 people in this country, and they are going to be able to advocate their cause at the expense of your cause."[6] Finally, Texas Senator Ted Cruz, the staunchest conservative in the race, summarized campaigning thus: "I've told my six-year-old daughter, 'Running for office is real simple: you just surgically disconnect your shame sensor,' . . . Because you spend every day asking people for money. You walk up and say, 'How are you doing, sir? Can I have money? Great to see you, lovely shirt, please give me money.' That's what running for office is like."[7]

The great irony, of course, was that as each candidate decried the corrupting influence of money on politics, they were each holding major fundraisers to support their own campaigns. Clinton left Iowa for a $2,700-per-person "conversation" at the San Francisco home of Tom Steyer. In the previous election, Steyer alone gave more than $73 million to support pro-environment candidates. And shortly after O'Malley said, "I would hope that in the Democratic Party that all of our candidates might discourage super PACs from being involved," a group of his supporters formed Generation Forward, a *political action committee* (PAC) (or *super PAC*), in order to raise money to support his campaign.[8]

Irony was not lost on the Republican candidates who gathered funds from a constellation of super PACs and at a remarkable rate. Within just a single week of their formation, for example, super PACs supporting Cruz had raised $31 million, and Jeb Bush's super PAC quickly topped $100 million.[9]

A second irony of the rare campaign bipartisanship on the issue of money and politics is the view of the American public-at-large. As the country has grown more polarized, divided, and disagreeable at the start of the 21st century, there was nearly a consensus on money and politics.

While Americans evenly split on partisan affiliations and attitudes toward issues such as abortion, privacy, and the environment, on money and politics nearly everyone—84%—agreed that money had too great an influence on politics.[10] The public was also of the same mind on the need for action. Nearly the same large majority (85%) agreed that major change was needed in campaign finance rules, and more than three-quarters (78%) concurred that spending by outside groups, such as super PACs, should be limited.[11]

Thus, the second great irony: as several presidential campaigns spent multiple billions of dollars to secure the votes to win the White House, nearly all voters deplored that glaring aspect of the process. Hundreds of congressional campaigns followed a similar money-hungry approach, while at the same time routinely passing on the opportunity to change campaign finance laws that would likely decrease the amount of money in politics and greatly please voters. Can a democracy sustain such contradictions? As importantly, should it? In 2016, on the 40th anniversary of the landmark Supreme Court campaign finance decision, *Buckley v. Valeo* (1976), *Pay-to-Play Politics* aims to answer these questions.

WHAT'S TO WORRY ABOUT?

Because money and politics can mean many different things, what one worries about also will differ greatly. The classic concern about money and politics, the concern that motivates federal and state laws, relates to *public corruption* or acts that advance narrow private interests rather than broad public interests. The federal government codifies corruption in statute as when someone outside of government:

> directly or indirectly, corruptly gives, offers or promises anything of value . . . to influence any official act; or . . . to influence such public official or person who has been selected to be a public official to commit or aid in committing, or collude in, or allow, any fraud, or make opportunity for the commission of any fraud, on the United States; or . . . to induce such public official or such person who has been selected to be a public official to do or omit to do any act in violation of the lawful duty of such official or person.[12]

It is also against the law when someone in government demands payments for official acts. To be sure, what is and is not in the public interest is hotly contested, and the country has a long history of associating the private monetary gains of corporations with the well-being of the nation: the CEO of General Motors, Charles Wilson, famously said during his nomination hearing to become secretary of defense, "what's good for GM, is good for America."[13]

Notwithstanding the difficulty of precisely defining what is or is not in the public interest, corruption remains illegal. For example, because elected officials make decisions about how the government will spend its money, a primary concern is that these officials will use this power for personal benefit, what is called *graft*. Rather than choosing the most competitive bid from a private contractor to build a new bridge or public school, graft could lead to awarding contracts to second-rate companies, faulty construction, and government waste. So, when the mayor of New Orleans, Ray Nagin, accepted a half a million dollars in bribes for granting favors during the reconstruction of the city following Hurricane Katrina, he ended up in jail.[14]

Elected officials also have authority over who are given government jobs that pay money. We worry that jobs will be given out as favors, what we often call *cronyism*, rather than based on merit. Cronyism is a problem because the government could quickly grow incompetent as jobs are awarded based on nothing more than close business ties. We associate cronyism with the machine politics that dominated city governments in the 19th century and so incensed the Progressive Movement, but cronyism persists today. After Barack Obama was elected president in 2008, Illinois Governor Rod Blagojevich was charged by U.S. Attorney Patrick Fitzgerald with trying to sell the open senate seat to the highest bidder, a move that ended with a conviction and an impeachment. Interestingly, after serving several years in jail, a group of federal judges overturned some of the charges against Blagojevich because they deemed his actions as a normal part of "logrolling"—the trading of political favors and legislative votes—and thus distinct from bribery and very much legal.[15] Nonetheless, in order to protect us from such self-serving behavior, laws make it illegal to offer bribes to government officials and illegal for government officials to commit graft in accepting or soliciting those bribes.

Corruption, bribery, and graft are all the obvious reasons to worry about the relationship between money and politics, as each could lead to the erosion of public interest and limits on the capacity of government to serve the people. Other, less observable, concerns also must be considered. Even if money is not directly exchanged for favors, which is illegal, there may be more indirect exchanges that could be just as harmful. A large contribution from an interest group to a congressional reelection campaign could be repaid years later in a favorable vote taken by that member of Congress. This type of influence is generally legal, but many worry that since only some interests have sufficient money to make these campaign contributions, legislative votes are harmfully skewed by money. Research, though, has been inconsistent and inconclusive that this worrisome theoretical relationship actually exists in practice. It is nearly impossible to find a causal link between money—whether it is spent on political lobbying or campaign contributions—directly leading to favorable legislative outcomes. It is not always clear that more money even leads to more favorable electoral outcomes or less competitive elections, as little research can support the argument that the candidate that spends the most always wins. I pick up this debate in Chapter 4.

Despite the lack of conclusive empirical evidence, the concern about the indirect corrupting power of money on elected officials remains. One of the reasons for this is a fact we can demonstrate pretty clearly: those in Congress have much more money than the average citizen.[16] While wealth may not guarantee a candidate gets elected, those with limited personal resources, solidly middle-class citizens, rarely run for federal office and seldom win. Your average citizens are almost always represented by someone who is much richer than themselves. Thus, money relates to inequities in political representation: there are very few middle-class members of Congress and almost no members of Congress grew up poor.

We worry about the role of money in the official world of Washington politics but also at the more individual level of politics. Money seems to be related to different political behaviors and attitudes, and that raises concerns about the distorted signals sent to elected officials. For example, the wealthy are more likely than the general public to contact their senator, members of the House of Representatives, White House officials, and even federal regulators.[17] Wealth is also related to other behaviors: wealthier people complete more years of education, donate to charities more frequently, and vote at higher levels than the general public. In each of these cases, the higher levels of political engagement of those with money results in elections and political debates with only a portion of the population taking part.

Not only does political participation differ along class lines, what the rich and the poor actually believe differs substantially. Research shows that the top 1% in the United States view government programs differently from the larger public. In his book, *Billionaires*, Darrell West summarized earlier research that demonstrates these very different worldviews.[18] The vast majority (87%) of the general public agree that the government should spend whatever it takes to have good public schools, compared to just a third (35%) of the top 1%. A majority of the public (53%) agree that the government should provide a job for anyone willing to work but unable to find a job, compared to less than a tenth (8%) of the top 1%. Not surprisingly, nearly six in ten (58%) of the top 1% favor cuts in public programs such as Medicare, education, and highway funding to reduce budget deficits, compared to just a quarter (27%) of the general public. I write much more on the public's view of these issues in Chapter 2.

A society with different beliefs and interests is not itself a problem and should be expected. If elected officials respond evenhandedly to the wishes of those with and without large amounts of money, then the democracy is working and we should not worry. The reality, however, suggests something very different. As Kay Schlozman, Sidney Verba, and Henry Brady concluded, "if votes, campaign contributions, e-mails, lobbying contacts, comments on proposed agency regulations, or amicus briefs come from an unrepresentative set of individuals and organizations, government policy is likely to reflect more fully the preferences and needs of the active part of the public."[19] Research shows that Congress usually passes laws that are favored by the wealthy and interest groups but are unresponsive to the wishes of the general public. Martin Gilens and Benjamin Page found that "Not only do ordinary citizens not have uniquely substantial power over policy decisions; they have little or no independent influence on policy at all."[20] On the contrary, "economic elites are estimated to have a quite substantial, highly significant, independent impact on policy."[21] Perhaps that is not surprising given the affluence of most members of Congress who may then share a common ideology and policy preferences with wealthy voters. Nevertheless, a system of representation fails when elected officials routinely ignore the vast majority of voters who are anything but rich.

These concerns all fall within the category of direct outcomes of the oversized role that money plays in politics and politics plays in money. Over the medium to longer term, however, there are also concerns about the larger legitimacy of the political system. When federal lawyers successfully prosecute a corrupt public official, the legal system has worked, but it is not a total victory for the government. Each cover story of another elected officials being led off in handcuffs further wears away at what the public believes about the democracy. There are reasons to believe that the increasingly prominent relationship between money and politics over the last 40 years is also related to growing distrust in government. Recently, less than a third of the country approved of Congress, down from more than 50% in

2002. And while more than four in five Americans trusted government in 2002; today that number is closer to one in five.[22] Just 14% of the country was satisfied with "the way the nation is being governed" in 2013. Money can lead to corruption, and perceived government corruption likely leads to public distrust, disgust, and disenchantment.[23]

And there are also longer-term problems to worry about. We risk the loss of future generations of public servants, as young Americans today also hold elected office in low regard. Jennifer Lawless and Richard Fox found that 89% of young Americans had little or no interest in running for office; interestingly this same sentiment was held by equal numbers of boys and girls, young Democrats and Republicans, and those from affluent and working-class families. Young Americans have as much—or as little—faith in government as their parents, and this is not simply the result of the perceived low pay of government. When asked whether they would be interested in a series of jobs that all paid the same amount of money, while half of young Americans chose "business owner," "teacher" was the next most popular (35%), hardly a profession known for its high salaries. Just 10% of young respondents most wanted to be a town or city mayor. The same pattern emerged when the choice was between "business executive," "school principal," and "member of Congress"; just 13% chose the elected office. These attitudes are not simply the result of the political apathy of the young; they likely also relate to a political system that is widely perceived to be corrupted by money.

The potentially negative results of an unchecked relationship between money and politics are numerous and profound, short, medium, and also long term. These results cannot be addressed with a series of FBI stings and federal prosecutions. Corruption, real and perceived, can poison the populace to democratic institutions, depress voter turnout, and drive away the next generation of leaders. The stakes, thus, are quite high.

AIM OF THE BOOK

The primary aim of this book is to figure out whether this situation is simply an expression of the paradoxical wisdom or a great indictment of the foundations of the American system of representative democracy. Can honest politicians denounce super PACs one day and rely on them to win the next? Can voters disparage a system flush with money yet regularly reelect those best able to raise the most? Can businesses legitimately celebrate the power of the open and free market and at the same time spend an ever-increasing amount of money to dictate friendly rules and regulations?

The answer to these specific questions and the larger debate about money and politics usually comes down to one of significance. While nearly all of the public hates the role of money in politics, the issue barely cracks the top 20 as a top priority, far below terrorism, jobs, and the environment. For politicians, all may detest raising money, but none will forgo money altogether if they have any hope for a future in office. Whether it is public indifference toward the issue or an "if you can't beat 'em, join 'em" rationale, money and politics has long suffered from a lack of energy needed for change.

One of the reasons for this is that debates about the issue have been diffused and compartmentalized. Conversations about campaign finance reform occur separately from related conversations about lobbying reform. Presidential elections occur just once every four years, and even if campaigns seem to grow longer, public attention strays during off-cycle election and wanes following Election Day. And the direct role of business in electoral or Washington-based politics is often treated quite distinctly from the less direct—and potentially more decisive—roles that business plays in the larger politics of belief, social norms, and taste.

A second aim of this book is to address these dimensions of money and politics by examining a diversity of perspectives on the issue in one place. By analyzing the evolving way that the courts, Congress, business, and the public think about—and act toward—money and politics together in a single volume, I hope to draw stronger connections between these areas of concern and spur a more well-rounded conversation.

DEFINING MONEY AND POLITICS

To say that most of the public and politicians deplore money and politics risks exaggerating the extent of agreement on what money and politics truly means. The public may worry most about headline-grabbing corruption scandals and the influence of shadowy billionaires, while politicians may complain more about the hours devoted to fundraising that takes away from lawmaking. Money and politics means different things to different groups, so some clearer definitions are a first step to understanding the issue.

With the exception of a handful of Supreme Court justices, most people define money in the same way: as a medium of exchange of value. While not everyone has it, most understand what money is in about the same way. Money may be the type you keep in your wallet, store in a safe, or even track in a digital account like Bitcoin. Money can be exchanged, traded, or used for commerce. Money is what permits us to store value that we can later use to purchase what we demand.

If everyone possessed the same amount of money, money would be much easier to define in simple terms. So, a full conception of money must also reconcile differences in who has it. Money, in all its forms, is unequally distributed in the United States, meaning we must pay close attention to measures of inequality or gaps in wealth. And these inequalities—which I delve into more in this chapter and also later in the book—suggest that different people have the opportunity to buy different things and in different amounts.

Politics, though somewhat more ambiguous, can also be defined. Politics is a process of influence, usually associated with influence over what the government does or does not do. Politics is also about power: who holds the most influence is the most powerful. Governments embody politics because different government actors possess varying amounts and types of power, including the power to make the decisions described earlier, such as over government jobs, spending, and contracts. But politics is not reserved for only those in government. Politics relates to the influence that every voter possesses as a constitutional right, such as the power associated with voting, protesting, and lobbying. In the United States, however, not every citizen uses his rights to the same extent. Elections rarely top 90% in voter turnout and many Americans are woefully, and often willfully, ignorant of the basic functioning of the government. To understand politics in the United States, we must appreciate the paradox of a system built on individual freedoms and democratic institutions, with remarkably low participation in either.

While defining money and politics separately is somewhat clear, defining how they interact is much murkier. Money plays a part in a variety of ways in politics, and politics does the same for money. The first way the two are related in a democracy is during increasingly pricey campaigns for elected office. In order to be elected, candidates have to persuade a majority of their fellow citizens through direct and indirect communication. Today, many forms of communications are expensive, so money helps candidates for office pay for communication, including for advertisements on television, for transportation to speak at public events, and for a team of advisers to design a convincing website and other material. For some interested in becoming a candidate, they already have sufficient money for these *campaign expenditures*. If you are rich, you have a clear advantage in politics, and in the United States that advantage often leads to Election Day victories. A majority of our recent presidents, members of Congress, and even Supreme Court justices have been millionaires.[24] Thus, a second way that money and politics are related is the fact that a large majority of those in politics have money—and a lot of it.

For others, those with somewhat smaller personal fortunes, there are other financial options, including asking for money, which is called *campaign fundraising*. Someone interested in politics can make a *campaign contribution* of money *directly* to a candidate to be used on the campaign and increasingly can also give *indirectly* to support the candidate through contributions to political parties and to the private super PACs mentioned earlier. One can argue that this money is simply a financial expression of the political rights of the contributor. As certain means of communication, such as broadcast television, have grown more important and expensive, it takes more money to express political support or opposition. In fact, over the last 20 years, the cost of winning a seat in the House has increased by 70% to $1.4 million and by 35% to $9.6 million in the Senate.[25] While there are some limits on how much one can give, the Supreme Court has, since the 1970s, viewed campaign contributions as a type of political speech and consequently provided ever-stronger protections for contributions and expenditures based on the First Amendment. So, a third way that money and politics are related is that candidates for office can raise money from other people to win political races, and those interested in political races can be the ones to give.

A fourth way that money and politics are related is through the legislative process. The same person who gave money to the candidate for office can also give money to someone else to convince other elected officials how to legislate. This is the process of lobbying, and lobbying involves an ever-growing amount of money—$3.24 billion in 2014—as businesses, nonprofit organizations, and individuals give money to lobbyists.[26] So if you want a member of Congress, the president, or a judge to support your cause, you can pay money to someone to make that case on your behalf. The more powerful the lobbyist, the more likely you will get that vote. This type of lobbying is legal, particularly when you abide by federal reporting requirements. Paying money for votes, though, is not. It is generally deemed against the law—considered bribery—to directly pay money (or give something valuable) in exchange for an official act, such as a vote or a governmental decision. So when New Jersey Senator Robert Menendez travelled to the Caribbean on the private plane of a Florida doctor, while at the same time seeking a favorable ruling from the Department of Health and Human Services, the Department of Justice took notice and soon indicted the senator on corruption charges. Yet, maybe this was simply a case of the senator vacationing with an old friend whom he happened to share a view on the proper regulation of health care. While there is ongoing judicial debate about how to interpret cases like these, in general, federal and state law prohibits explicit *quid pro quo* agreements involving money, whether that money goes directly to an official or to support an official through a campaign. In short, money used to pay for lobbying is legal; money used to pay for favors is not.

These are four of the many direct ways that money and politics are related. There are also less direct ways that warrant attention. Businesses and individuals can give money to charities and philanthropic foundations that are involved in politics. Large foundations, such as the Ford Foundation, Coors Foundation, and Open Society Institute, all participate at the fringes of politics and rely upon money to do so. For example, the Ford Foundation—established by the family associated with the car company in the early 20th century—gave a $700,000 grant to the Center for Nonprofits and Voting to help "increase voter participation, and to increase Latino civic participation in the Southwest."[27] Without this money, the Center would not be able to help register new voters, inform voters about where their polling station was located, or provide translated voter information for those unable to speak English. Numerous other foundations provide millions of dollars to organizations working on similar voting issues or to other organizations to conduct research on political issues, hold conferences on policy problems, or disseminate information to the public. Many think of money spent in this way as advancing the broad public interest and that it is not only legal but also something to be encouraged with favorable tax incentives. Money and politics, thus, are not always related in such troublesome ways; sometimes the influence of money on politics is viewed in quite positive terms.

Business, too, can shape politics in indirect ways through the products it sells and the way it sells those products. For example, businesses can influence political decisions by threatening to move production to states or countries with different and more advantageous laws. The loss of the money from business can change the mind of government officials who might fear the loss of jobs or revenues from taxes. Businesses can also shape public opinion about political issues through the product advertising they pay for in magazines and newspapers and on television. And individuals and organizations can influence politics through boycotting—or not paying money for—the products sold by businesses, such as the boycott of companies that did business in apartheid South Africa during the 1980s.

There are dozens of other ways that money can be used to influence politics, but politics also influences money. While not always the focus of discussions of money and politics, to be sure, political decisions about tax rates, government spending, and federal interest rates all relate to the availability of money to companies, organizations, and individuals. As Larry Bartels wrote, "Economic inequality clearly has profound ramifications for democratic politics . . . politics also profoundly shapes economics."[28] Since at least the 1970s, the country has grown increasingly unequal, as the rich have become richer at a faster and faster rate. The growth of extreme wealth has much to do with the ingenuity of those with money but also has to do with political decisions that have made it easier to make and retain money. Deregulations of major industries, great reductions and caps on certain taxes, and friendly rules for the financial sector have contributed to inequality and what some characterize as the *1% problem*. Recently, nearly a quarter (23.5%) of national income went to the country's top 1%, an 80-year high.[29] Real income of those at the very top has also grown more unequal. Over the last 30 years, real income for those in the top 1% has doubled while income for the top 0.01% has increased "fivefold."[30] As described earlier, the problems associated with this division of wealth are not isolated to finance; they also relate to politics. The wealthy are more likely to vote, donate to campaigns, and run for office, meaning the voice of the affluent is heard loudest when political decisions are made.[31]

Money and politics is a big subject, involves many multidirectional relationships, and is ever evolving because of changes in law and public policy. I describe these direct and indirect ways that the two are related as just an entrée into the complexity of the subject. Throughout the rest of the book, I explore these complexities from different perspectives to clarify rather than to simplify. The hope is that this clarity will lead to a better understanding and appreciation for the complexity of money and politics.

Thus far, several terms have been defined, but some additional terms also need clarification before we go any further. At the national level, the Federal Election Commission (FEC) regulates the role of money during elections. The FEC was established by Congress in the 1970s, and its commissioners are chiefly in charge of implementing aspects of the Federal Election Campaign Act (FECA). The FEC regulates the amount of money that individuals, businesses, and other organizations can give—what we call a *political campaign contribution*. When those contributions are given directly to candidates for office, associated political parties, or certain political organizations, that is called *hard money*, to indicate the money may only be used for particular campaign-related purposes regulated by federal law. Hard money contributions are capped at specific amounts to certain candidates and parties. When that money is given more generally to a political party, not associated with a particular campaign, and it falls outside of the limits of federal law, we call that *soft money*. Soft money has been largely banned since reforms in the early 2000s.[32]

Broadly speaking, contributions can be given to candidates directly, to a leadership PAC associated with an elected official, or to a PAC associated with a company or organization. PACs provide a legal way for companies and interest groups to directly support candidates with money. For this reason, the FEC regulates the amount of money that a PAC can contribute to a candidate. Since the 1970s, the number of PACs has grown sixfold from 600 to 5,431, mostly from businesses.[33] More recently, the Supreme Court has opened the opportunity for a new type of PAC, a super PAC, which can receive an unlimited amount of contributions, including from the treasuries of businesses, as long as the names of the contributors are reported to the FEC and the money is not directly given to candidates. Super PACs also cannot coordinate with parties or candidates, but they can make unlimited independent expenditures to advocate for and against those running for office separate from the campaign. A final category of organization, called a *501(c)(4)* for its IRS designation, operate as nonprofit organizations, but because of their political goals, the donations they receive are not eligible for tax deductions like other charitable nonprofits. These 501(c)(4) organizations are nearly unregulated by the FEC, are not required to report the names of donors, and have few restrictions placed on the type of political or campaign activities in which they can engage, as long as those expenditures remain below approximately half of the organization's total expenditures.[34]

In subsequent chapters of the book, the importance of each of these terms will be described in greater detail and with more clarity. Clarity alone, though, is not sufficient for a subject with profoundly negative possibilities. If there is simply too much money, maybe there should just be less? If there is too much money from certain sources, then maybe spending limits should be targeted and specific? Or maybe it is not the amount of money but rather the secrecy that matters most? Spending caps and limits, public financing of elections, donor and organizational transparency, and new regulation of communications all must be considered in a thorough vetting of money and politics.

On the contrary, there are thoughtful commentators who contend quite the opposite. The problem, as they see it, is not too much money but too little.[35] The total cost of the 2014 election was around $4 billion, about the same as how much Americans spend each year on Halloween candy ($3 billion), perfume ($4.2 billion), and St. Patrick's Day festivities ($4.14 billion).[36] If only we spent as lavishly on politics as we did on green beer, maybe politicians would be more responsive to the public.

Or, as Jonathan Rauch argued, efforts to limit corruption may be associated with the exact political gridlock that stymies progress and turns off the American public to politics. Money, according to this take that Rauch dubbed *political realism*, acts as the grease needed to make the Washington machine run smoothly. When the grease is in short supply, the gears slow. Money for pet congressional projects in a home district, for example, can help adversaries come together and agree on complex budget deals and how to run the country. Take away the money, and one-time compromisers become unwilling opponents. Instead, Rauch postulated, a return to the machine politics of the late 19th century or even the 1980s would bring compromise and negotiation back to Congress. Rauch wrote, "Back-scratching and logrolling (the practice of legislative vote trading) are signs of a healthy political system, not a corrupt one."[37] Rauch did not call for making graft and bribery legal but rather for a return to the type of secret deal making that today lands members of Congress in Citizens Against Government Waste's annual "Pig Book" or the Federalist Society's "Wastebook."[38] If we just let a little bit of the informality of the past back into the system, permit horse trading to happen behind closed doors, and allow a bit of money to be legally exchanged, then our dysfunction Capital might be made functional again. A provocative thesis, to be sure, as it runs counter to decades of political idealism, idealism that hardly stripped money from politics. Instead, idealism and political reforms have made slow and steady gains, particularly in transparency and the openness of government to the public. To Rauch, as well as to Raymond La Raja and Brian Schaffner, these reforms, while well meaning, are politically naïve and lead to political paralysis, party polarization, and policy stagnation.[39] Rauch's realist viewpoint must be addressed, not only for its unconventional take but also because of the implications of what a return to machine politics might look like.

OUTLINE OF THE BOOK

As any book about politics should start with the body politic, Chapter 2 begins by delving more deeply into what the American public thinks and does about money and politics. Attitudes and actions often do not align, and the public has as complicated and as confused a relationship to money and politics as it does to politics in general.

If money and politics were up for a popular vote, we would likely see great change in federal and state laws, but the United States is governed by a constitution. So, Chapter 3 examines what the courts think of money and politics. Over the last several decades, it has been the Supreme Court that has issued the strongest and often most radical judgments about money and politics. The chapter explains how those rulings have shaped the issue since the 1970s and will into the future.

Court decisions have corresponded with a major overhaul in the attitudes and behaviors of American business. Chapter 4 answers the question: What do business leaders think of money and politics? In answering the question, we can view the dramatic change in how business has interacted with the political realm, growing ever more active, thorough, and bold.

Congress has not stood by idly during the dramatic changes in the Court and Corporate America; rather, Congress has had a fraught relationship with money and politics. Chapter 5 looks at the dozens of federal corruption cases that have exposed the inherent flaws in a political system so reliant on money. At the same time, Congress has passed quite ambitious, and often bipartisan, laws to reign in money and politics.

As the start of this book suggests, presidents and presidential candidates have become more and more embroiled in the issue of money and politics. For an office that aims to be above politics and certainly above the tawdry politics of money, the White House has become the center of debates about the proper role of money and politics. Chapter 6 shows how candidates and presidents have wrestled with the issue.

If nothing else, a book on money and politics owes its readers a set of recommendations and reflections on the future. In the concluding chapter, I try to answer: What can and should we do to address money and politics? Borrowing handsomely from recommendations from across the political spectrum, the final chapter evaluates what could work and what could be implemented in the years to come.

Chapter 2

The Public and Political Money

Life in many parts of California is expensive, from the southern California beaches to the northern California wineries. State politics, too, has grown increasingly pricey. Take one of the most unusual and expensive races in 2014—not the Senate contest or the race for the governorship but for the position of *state superintendent of public instruction*. This nonpartisan election pitted the incumbent, Tom Torlakson, a Democrat, against his rival, Marshall Tuck, also a Democrat. While the elected office has little authority over state education policy, the race attracted more than $30 million in campaign spending, three times the amount as the contest for governor ($10.1 million).[1] The individual candidates spent a small portion of that total, less than $5 million combined. The majority, more than $25 million in independent expenditures, came from a variety of outside groups, including $7 million from the California Teachers' Association supporting Torlakson, and $7 million from Parents and Teachers for Tuck for State Superintendent (PTTSS). Major philanthropists and donors, including Eli Broad and former NYC Mayor, Michael Bloomberg, contributed mightily to PTTSS.[2] In the end, Torlakson narrowly won the contest.

If the position of superintendent has little authority to spend public monies or award public jobs, then maybe we shouldn't really worry about how much money there was in this campaign. An elected official who has no favors to give might be immune to corruption and an unlikely target for bribes. But why, then, did the race attract so much attention? And what were campaign contributors supporting the two candidates trying to get for their money?

In particular terms, the race drew attention because of the large size of the state and substantial conflict over the direction of an important policy area. Torlakson and Tuck represented two competing and philosophically distinct ways forward for the state on education, one adhering closely to the wishes of the teachers' union and the other to the wishes of pro-market reformers. Though the winner of the election might not decide whether the state would create hundreds of new charter schools or hire thousands of new teachers, he would at least have a seat at the table for such decisions in the largest education system in the country. At stake was $75 billion in education spending and the jobs of 300,000 teachers.[3] As I noted in the Introduction to the book, money drives decisions about politics and politics drives decisions about money. Donors with interests in either side of this reform debate saw the superintendent race as a way to challenge their opponents and influence the future of schools, even if other state officials held more real authority.

Influence, though, has proven an unpredictable bet. This expensive race saw money nearly evenly split, and some of the richest donors backed the loser, Tuck. Knowing that the donations did not guarantee influence over the final vote, we must ask: what exactly was going on in the mind of the political donors? What motivates them to give millions of dollars to support candidates who are likely to lose?

The vast majority of the public, the students, the teachers, and the parents, though, made just a tiny share of the campaign contributions. It could not have been that they were unconcerned about the quality of schools and future education policy decisions. So, we also should ask: What does the rest of the public—the vast majority that never spends a dime on politics—think about making political contributions, specifically, and money and politics, more generally? This chapter tries to answer these questions by delving into what people, both the very rich *and* the rest of us, think *and* do about the relationship between money and politics.

HOW DO BIG MONEY CONTRIBUTORS GIVE?

As outlined in the Introduction to the book, there is a variety of ways citizens use money to influence politics. The primary ways are to give money to support candidates for elected office and to organizations to advance their preferred position on policy issues during elections. Citizens also can hire lobbyists, but that is usually done through businesses and business associations, which I return to in

Chapter 3. For now, I focus on how the wealthy legally give money to support candidates and issues.

Citizens with considerable money have long given directly to candidates. Famed 19th-century banker J. P. Morgan gave lavishly—and with few limitations—to William McKinley's campaign for the presidency. He gave, in part, because of the candidate's support for the gold standard that Morgan and his business interests strongly supported.[4] Most recently, the amount one could give was restricted by the FEC to no more than $2,700 per candidate per election cycle.[5] For this reason, a wealthy donor interested in politics could give the maximum amount to multiple candidates. And following a Supreme Court ruling in 2014, there were no more limits on how many candidates a contributor could give to. In theory, a contributor could give the $2,700 maximum to every candidate running for office and not violate any federal election rules.

Once a large contributor has given directly to a candidate or candidates, they may also support indirectly through donations to political parties and to political organizations. These contributions are regulated by ever-evolving federal and state law, which I delve into in more detail in the next chapter. In the most recent election, FEC restrictions meant that a donor could contribute up to $33,400 to a favored national political party and $10,000 to state parties, which then can spend that money on behalf of the contributor during the election. A contributor can also give a maximum of $5,000 to an official PAC and can give almost limitless amounts to other political organizations. Of late, the most popular way to do this is either by giving to a super PAC, which can raise and spend unlimited amounts but must disclose contributor names, or to a 501(c)(4) nonprofit, which faces many fewer regulations, particularly on disclosing the names of donors.

If we combine the various ways contributors might give during an election, we can get an idea of how many large contributors there actually have been in the past. In 2014, there were just 1,281 individuals who gave greater than $95,000 to candidates, parties, and super PACs. That is a fraction of a fraction of the total American population and even a small percentage of all political contributors. This elite group of major contributors gave $192 million in total; much more to Republicans (59%) than to Democrats (38%), and, in 2012, more to Romney than to Obama.[6] Romney had 721 contributors who gave more than $80,000, resulting in nearly $55 million, whereas Obama had 536 contributors of this size, resulting in a little more than $40 million.[7]

These mega-donors are often neighbors. Public Campaign found that half of the largest contributors in 2012 lived in the richest 1% of neighborhoods in the country. They also work together: a quarter of the big donors worked on Wall Street or in the financial sector (9% were lawyers; 7% worked in communications), meaning that there were more big political contributors in the state of New York than 32 other states combined.[8] And these large contributors are quite obviously rich. A quarter of the richest 100 Americans were also on the list of big money political contributors.

WHAT DO BIG MONEY CONTRIBUTORS THINK?

Michael Bloomberg, the former mayor of New York City, was one of the contributors to the Turk campaign in California. Bloomberg was not a newcomer to campaign contributions in 2014; he had spent his own money lavishly throughout his public life—to help him get elected mayor three times and to influence other races and pet issues, such as gun control. In 2014, in fact, Bloomberg was the second largest individual contributor to national campaigns, giving $28.3 million to advance mainly moderate to liberal interests. Bloomberg was not alone; Tom Steyer gave $73 million to similar causes, while Sheldon Adelson and Charles Koch gave more than $10 million combined to support conservatives.[9] Bloomberg, Steyer, Adelson, and Koch also gave money through organizations, including super PACs, which then supported or opposed candidates without directly coordinating their activities, a legal distinction lost on most observers. Some also donated to 501(c)(4) nonprofits, though the lack of disclosure requirements means we know little about the specifics of this dimension of mega-donor political activity. Nevertheless, we know there is a small cadre of very wealthy Americans who contribute large amounts of money to influence politics, but why do they do it? What do they expect to get from these multimillion dollar expenditures?

While it is impossible to know exactly what motivates any given person, we can rely upon what contributors say about money and politics to gather some initial impressions. Based on a reading of these interviews and public statements, major political contributors seem to be motivated by at least three factors: (1) specific influence over policy—single-issue contributors; (2) general ideological interest in politics—ideological contributors; and (3) very simple partisan competitiveness—partisan contributors. Bizarrely, some mega-donors also agree that there is too much money in politics, and regulations should change to limit campaign donations, but they continue contributing nevertheless.

One type of large donor seeks influence over particular policy issues, what we might call *single-issue contributors*. Tom Steyer, the hedge fund manager who held the fundraiser for Hillary Clinton mentioned earlier in the book, falls into this category. Asked by the *Los Angeles Times* what he got for his $75 million in campaign expenditures in the 2014 election, Steyer explained that the money allowed him to raise the salience of environmental issues among candidates and voters—including concern for addressing climate change and preventing the federal government from approving the construction of the Keystone oil pipeline. Steyer said, "Our mission is to prevent climate disaster and preserve American prosperity. In states we were in, we made climate a first-tier issue maybe for the first time ever."[10] Much of Steyer's money, around $67 million, was funneled through a super PAC called NextGen Climate Action. NextGen bought political advertisements to oppose Senate candidates (mainly in Colorado, Iowa, Michigan, and New Hampshire) deemed hostile to the environment. (Steyer-supported candidates won in Michigan and New Hampshire but lost in Colorado and Iowa.)[11] Steyer went on to claim that the money also influenced public opinions: "We probably have 350,000 people across different states who said they would be climate voters."[12] So, while Steyer may have had many goals, his central reason for spending money on politics relates to his particular concerns about the environment and specific ways he would like politicians to address the issue.

Michael Bloomberg, too, has talked openly about particular issues he has used his money to influence. At the end of his terms as mayor of New York, he told *New York* magazine about the role of his wealth: "there's some things you couldn't have done. I couldn't have given $30 million and got $30 million out of George Soros and then have $60 million for this Young Men's Initiative to help young minority males."[13] Bloomberg, both a billionaire and the mayor, believed he could improve the living conditions for a part of the city, but only with his money and what his money would encourage from other donors on single issues.

Billionaire donors supporting liberal causes are not alone in focusing on single issues. Missouri's $37 million mega-donor, Rex Sinquefield, hated the state's tax system. Sinquefield claimed, "I have never given money to a candidate or an officeholder in the belief that they're going change their position on something," but he believed strongly that elected officials should "Get rid of your personal tax, get rid of your corporate taxes, don't punish work, don't punish profits, don't punish productivity."[14] So, rather than try to use his money to change minds, he explained that "I only give it to people who we already support, who we know support our positions . . . And, frankly, the purpose is so their lives become easier. They don't have to spend all their time raising money." Sinquefield's millions have gone to tax-cutting candidates and support-ive political organizations, such as Let Voters Decide, Grow Missouri, and Missouri Club for Growth.[15]

Not all single-issue contributors prefer to work with allies; some see money as a way to persuade. Paul Singer, the hedge fund CEO of Elliot Associates, advocated for gay rights with Republican candidates through the money he contributed. For a party that has frequently opposed gay marriage and other LGBT-related social issues, Singer hoped to use his contributions to convince candidates to change their positions or at least to be more outspoken in their support. He wrote that "Our job is to let them know they have plenty of like-minded friends, activists, and party leaders who will stand with them."[16] Singer funded American Unity PAC (a super PAC) to give nearly $5 million to pro–gay rights Republican congressional candidates in 2014.[17]

Other political donors explain what they get from their money in less specific policy terms and broader, philosophical, or even patriotic ways—what we might call *ideological contributors*. Texas chemicals bil-lionaire Harold Simmons, who supported Newt Gingrich's presidential aspirations in 2012, summarized his motives in simple terms: "I've got the money, so I'm spending it for the good of the country."[18] Others have agreed but been more expansive in their explanations. Asked about what he expected in return for candidate donations, billionaire hedge fund CEO Ken Griffin told the *Chicago Tribune*, "I want the person that I am supporting to go to Springfield (the state's capital) and put into place regulations, laws and policies that will create a vibrant jobs market and create a state of fiscal sustainability, where we pay our bills on time."[19] In addition to influence in the state of Illinois, Griffin also hoped for influence at the national level, first with Barack Obama in 2008, then later with Mitt Romney in 2012. Griffin's wishes were for influence, but much broader influence over a wide range of issues than Steyer and other single-issue donors. Griffin also believed that those with money have a special burden to spend money on politics. He said, "I think [the ultrawealthy] actually have an insufficient influence. Those who have enjoyed the benefits of our system more than ever now owe a duty to protect the system that has created the greatest nation on this planet."[20]

A set of billionaires that has long taken up Griffin's plea have been members of the Koch family, who have overseen an empire of chemical, energy, and other industrial products for 50 years. Charles Koch, whose brother David ran for vice president in 1980 with the Libertarian Party, framed his political donations in similar terms to Griffin: "Somebody has got to work to save the country and preserve a system of opportunity. I think one of the biggest problems we have in the country is this rampant cronyism where all these large companies are into smash-and-grab, short-term profits, (saying) how do I get a regulation, we don't want to export natural gas because of my raw materials . . . well, you say you believe in free markets, but by your actions you obviously don't. You believe in cronyism."[21] For those who assume money and politics often leads to corruption and cronyism, Koch's large political contributions must sound counterintuitive. Nevertheless, Koch explained how his multimillion dollar contributions to the super PAC Americans for Prosperity helped advance these issues: "We contribute and we helped start it, so we have some influence. We try to push them on things that will help people make their own lives better and policies that move in the direction of well-being for everybody and fighting cronyism."[22] Americans for Prosperity spent $36 million during the 2012 election to thwart cronyism, advance pro-market policies, and elect ideologically conservative candidates.[23] So, for Koch and Griffin, money helps to influence politics on broad ideological terms, in each case advancing a conservative philosophy about low levels of government regulation and pro-market policies.

Another category of donors frame their political giving in terms of the political process itself, often as an antidote to giving from the other side—*partisan contributors*. Jeffrey Katzenberg, the CEO of DreamWorks, gave $3 million in 2012, primarily to the super PAC Priorities USA, which backed President Obama. In return for his donations, Katzenberg told CBS News, "My only expectation was that President Obama and other like-minded candidates would benefit by being able to compete on a more level playing field."[24] Katzenberg contrasted his giving with those supporting conservative candidates and causes. He said, "I hope my donation will draw attention to the amount of money being raised by the extreme right wing and serve as a catalyst for other Democratic donors."[25] Katzenberg may have been referring to Sheldon Adelson, the billionaire casino owner and conservative supporter, who framed his donations in similar terms. Adelson explained, "I do whatever it takes, as long as it's moral, ethical, principled, and legal."[26] And he clarified the seeming contradiction of his political giving to

Politico: "I don't believe one person should influence an election . . . So, I suppose you'll ask me, 'How come I'm doing it?' Because other single people influence elections."[27] We can assume Adelson was referencing Katzenberg and his liberal donor allies. Or perhaps he was referring, as Harold Simmons did, to the money from interest groups often associated with Democrats. Simmons explained that his political contributions would combat the "unlimited amounts from labor unions."[28] But the competitive instinct spans ideological boundaries. Steyer, one of those opposed to Adelson and Simmons on most issues, shared Simmons's pragmatic views on money and politics. He said, "We don't believe outspending your opponent is the way to go since we don't believe we will be ever outspending our opponents!"[29] This category of donors conceives of their money as a countervailing weight against the influence of other people's money. While each side may vehemently disagree about political and policy outcomes, this group of large donors seems to agree that money is a necessary evil to thwart their foes and that the current system invites competition.

Those from the Left and Right also share a peculiar view of the landmark *Citizens United* Supreme Court case (which I take up in more detail in Chapter 3). Seth Klarman, who gave $3 million in 2014 to mainly conservative super PACs and was the 16th largest outside donor in 2014, said to the *Boston Globe*, "I agree that Citizens United was a terrible decision that I am not in favor of."[30] The more liberal Katzenberg agreed: "I thought the Supreme Court decision paving the way for the current campaign finance system was a terrible one."[31] And fellow liberal Steyer said, "We agree that Citizens United is a very bad decision."[32] In many cases, though, the same large donor who disagrees with the wide donor latitude permitted by *Citizens United* believes that little can be done other than spending more money. Katzenberg argued that despite his opposition to *Citizens United*, "it is the law of the land, and it would be foolish for one side to unilaterally disarm. Until the law changes, we have to mount as vigorous a defense as possible."[33] Steyer concurred: "We oppose Citizens United. But at the same time, the political time frame for repairing the Supreme Court's decision and the timeline we have to take on the urgent issue of climate change means that we have to accept the post-Citizens United world as it is, and until a different and more effective system is adopted, we will work within it."[34]

Not all big donors agree. Simmons, for one, argued, "There shouldn't be restrictions of any kind on political contributions."[35] And the opposition expressed by Katzenberg, Steyer, and Klarman to the Supreme

Court decision must be weighed against the actual behaviors of donors that continue to give. Notwithstanding these somewhat contradictory views of current regulations, if we accept the personal accounts of contributions, we are left with a rosy picture of what motivates the wealthy to donate. Far from shadowy figures out of a comic book, mega-donors present their ambitions as patriotic, selfless, and open. Griffin said, "The rules that encourage transparency around [super PAC donations] are really important." And Steyer concurred, "We are committed to using our resources openly and transparently . . . We are trying really hard to be transparent."[36] Not only are donors willing to be open, they don't even want anything in return from the candidate. Simmons said, "You never talk about what you want when giving money."[37] And Adelson recounted how he said to then-candidate Mitt Romney, whom he had supported, "I'm not looking for an ambassadorship. I'm not looking for anything, except if I'm fortunate enough to be invited to another [White House] Hanukkah party, I want two potato pancakes, because last time I was there, they ran out of them."[38] Another Romney donor, hedge fund billionaire Julian Robertson, agreed: "The last thing I want him to think—and I know he doesn't think that—is that he is beholden to me . . . I don't think that he will do the X or Y or would do X or Y because I called and pushed it."[39] All Robertson wanted was "a great president of the United States."[40] At face value, these big money donors are simply expressing what others believe but lack the bank accounts to express in dollars.

As all readers might suspect, the situation is a bit murkier, and we shouldn't take these personal statements too literally. What a donor claims in public may be different from the reality of their deeper, private ambitions. For example, despite nearly a century of reforms to the way government jobs are awarded, there remain numerous political appointments to be given out at the discretion of the president, what is called *patronage*. These jobs do not necessary have to go out to big money donors but they often do, thereby pushing patronage to the edge of cronyism. In just one area of the government, the evidence of such patronage is striking. Presidents have wide latitude to decide who is given an ambassadorship, one of the most prestigious jobs in the U.S. Foreign Service. There are often hundreds of career civil servants qualified to take these positions, but the attractiveness of a post in an exotic city abroad proves tempting for many wealthy donors. At an increasing rate over the last 30 years, those jobs are given out to wealthy friends and donors rather than to career diplomats. President Obama awarded 32.9% of the ambassadorships he filled to political friends, up from the percentage for the two previous administrations, and in his second term that figure rose three percentage points to 35.3%.[41] And sometimes those political friends are large donors. Prior to being confirmed as ambassador, Noah Bryson Mamet collected—what insiders call *bundling* to refer to the way political supporters pool together campaign contributions—$500,000 for the president's campaign. Despite never having travelled to Argentina, Mamet was later named ambassador to the country.[42] Patronage and cronyism occur along a continuum of acceptable governance. When elected officials tilt toward the latter, the quality of government performance may suffer, and trust in government further eroded.

Katzenberg, Koch, Steyer, and Adelson have never been awarded a prestigious job in government, but it does not take much looking to discover that each has a pet project or two, and sometimes these projects align closely with their bottom line. For example, the Koch family has given widely to conservative organizations and candidates but also paid lobbyists to oppose solar and renewable energy programs with which the family business, Koch Industries, competes.[43] For Charles Koch, this opposition to government subsidies for wind and solar companies may fit with his pro–free market, anti-cronyism philosophy, but it is not entirely selfless; it also aligns closely with his company's competitive position in the marketplace as a supplier of natural gas and petroleum services.

Koch has not been alone in mixing business with politics. While Adelson claimed to want nothing more from Mitt Romney than a couple of latkes, he was an active financial supporter of efforts to ban online gambling, a potential financial threat to his empire of casinos. According to the *New York Times*, Adelson used his money to sway the positions of trade associations and to influence the introduction of new legislation by politicians to whom he had donated.[44] The paper claimed that Adelson threatened to remove his support for the American Gaming Association (AGA) if it refused to oppose online gaming. The AGA soon grew quiet on the issue. He also funded the operations of the Coalition to Stop Internet Gambling, which advocated that "Congress must protect United States residents and citizens by restoring the longstanding federal ban on Internet gambling."[45] And Adelson later hired a lobbyist, Andy Abboud, who helped write the legislation to ban online gambling that was later introduced by Senator Lindsey Graham, a beneficiary of Adelson's campaign donations. In response to the new friendship with Adelson on the gambling issue, Graham said, "I would say that Sheldon has aligned himself with most Baptists in South Carolina . . . I am on solid footing in South Carolina with people I represent. The fact that Sheldon is on board is a good thing."[46]

And Katzenberg's donations, which he claimed came with no strings attached, may have resulted in an invitation from Vice President Joe Biden on a visit to Los Angeles.[47] Biden was travelling with Chinese Vice President Xi Jinping and meeting with representatives of the entertainment industry to discuss Chinese quotas on the importation of foreign films. Katzenberg lobbied Vice President Biden to push for better access for American movies in China, particularly for the large-format films that are the specialty of Katzenberg's company, DreamWorks. Before Xi left the country, the two countries struck a deal to allow 14 additional 3D movies into China per year, a resolution that must have pleased Katzenberg.[48]

Were these cases of the fortuitous common cause formed between successful businessmen and conscientious elected official who shared worldviews on the evils of renewable energy, gambling, and trade restrictions? Or were these cases the sort of legalized corruption that defines the American democracy and the relationship between money and politics? Perhaps, a bit of both. To be sure, similar anecdotes can be found for each of the other contributors mentioned at the start of the chapter or, in fact, for any political supporter of a government official. The causal link between money and politics, between donations and votes, though, is exceedingly difficult to prove. I return to examine this point and the excellent research on the subject in greater detail in Chapter 3. Until then, there is another reason to be worried about the size and growth of large political contributors, specifically how discordant they are with the views and behaviors of the public-at-large. How often do voters contribute to candidates and how much do they give when they do? The quick answer is *rarely* and *not much*.

The mega-donor views summarized above also reflect an entirely male perspective, and this is not a coincidence. Among large donors, most are men: three-quarters of donors giving greater than $95,000 in 2014 were men.[49] In recent elections, particularly at the national level, only a handful of mega-donors, those in the top 100 of total donations, were women: Amber Mostyn, Amy Goldman, and Anne Earhart were notable exceptions. [50] Polling in 2000 of mid-sized donors (those who had given at least $5,000) also found that three-quarters were men and most were older.[51] This is a pattern that has held steady for at least the last 20 years, motivating the formation of new groups, such Emily's List and Susan B. Anthony List, which aim to encourage women donors and support women candidates. And in addition to being small in number, women mega-donors give more evenly to Republicans and Democrats, splitting their large contributions 49%/49% in 2014.[52] There are many reasons and competing explanations for these patterns, but most would agree that it implies that rich women and men may view money and politics differently, and attention should be paid to how these attitudes differ in the general population.

DOES THE PUBLIC-AT-LARGE CONTRIBUTE?

As the start of the chapter suggested, the number of mega-donors to campaigns is a tiny percentage of the overall population. This is hardly surprising given that those donors regularly spend twice as much on politics as the typical American family earns in a year.[53] In fact, in 2014, a fraction of 1% (0.31%) of the adult population in the country—or 722,619 Americans—contributed more than $200, the minimum amount tracked by the government. Those contributions totaled $1.6 billion given to various candidates, party committees, and super PACS. That may sound like a lot of money, but it has to be viewed in the context of the enormous number of campaigns in an average electoral cycle. Jennifer Lawless and Richard Fox estimated that there are more than 500,000 elected positions in the United States, and while not all of them hold elections on the same day, citizens have nearly limitless choices of where to give.[54] In need of money to run a campaign, there are dozens of candidates for the presidency every four years, 435 House races with at least two candidates competing in each race every two years, and nearly 20,000 statewide offices.[55] Citizens have plenty of options, but few choose to contribute.

Of those that do choose to give, we know that they tend to give somewhat more to Republicans (55%) than to Democrats (45%), but if we remove from that pool the larger donors, the patterns change somewhat. For example, small donors ($200–$2,599) have leaned toward Republican candidates but only slightly more than Democrats: 37% compared to 34%. And, in the 2012 presidential race, according to the Campaign Finance Institute, President Obama received a larger portion of support (about 20% of his contributions) from very small donors (those giving less than $200) compared to Mitt Romney, who raised less than 10% from very small donors.

Based on these statistics, what is clear thus far is that (1) the general public donates little overall to candidates; (2) when they do, Republicans benefit slightly more; and (3) among the class of small contributors, the partisan distribution is more even. There are several obvious relationships driving who gives money to political candidates. First, those who earn less, give less. Research has long demonstrated that, whereas the rich and poor have about the same amount of free time to devote to politics, spare money for politics is quite unevenly distributed in favor of the affluent.[56] Of those who give, very few are middle income. In 2014, less than a fifth (17%) of the pool of political contributors earned under $30,000 a year, and when this middle-income group gave, they usually contributed less than $100. This compared to half (48%) of the pool of contributors who made more than $75,000; nearly two-thirds of whom gave greater than $100.[57] Second, the same pattern holds for age and education: a much smaller share of under-30 donate than over-30, and a larger share of those with a college degree donate compared to those without at least a college degree. These demographic patterns are not surprising, as they relate to numerous other class, age, and education differences in related political and nonpolitical behavior, such as voting or running for office.[58]

Third, it is also the case that those who are most engaged in politics are more likely to give. The Pew Research Center studied the relationship between engagement and political behaviors, such as contacting public officials, volunteering on campaigns, and contributing money.[59] What Pew found was that only 21% of the public were strong ideologues, either consistently liberal (12%) or consistently conservative (9%). These two extremes were much more active than those in the middle, what might be called political moderates, in most political activities, including contributing money. Despite making up only a fifth of the population, close to half (41%) of those who contributed money were strong ideologues. Put another way, a majority of consistent conservatives and consistent liberals made political donations, a considerably higher percentage than any other more moderate ideological segments of the public. And this finding fits with other evidence that showed most political contributors give based on ideology (69%) rather than partisanship (31%).[60] Passion for ideas, rather than party affiliations, drives certain members of the public to participate in politics, and contributing money is one of the ways they do so.

Fourth, we also know that where you live seems to matter for political contributions. Though around a third of the public in all four of the regions of country give to candidates, the most money comes from urban dwellers. Republicans and Democrats raise money from donors living in the same areas: city centers along the coasts, including the New York area, Southern California, and the Great Lakes cities of Chicago and Detroit.[61] Even though states may vote as solidly red or blue, there are enough wealthy partisans in the major cities for the two parties to raise money in Boston, Atlanta, and Houston. And this effect has extreme consequences for the concentration of contributors. In the last election, residents of just ten zip codes in San Francisco, New York City, Washington, DC, and Chicago gave a total of $271 million to national candidates.[62]

Finally, the same gender differences between women and men megadonors also show up in donations among the general population of men and women. Men far exceed women donors and have for several election cycles. In 2008, 2010, and 2012, women barely topped 30% in the percentage of contributors and percentage of total contributions.[63] Women also typically make smaller contributions than men. On average, women donors gave $2,347 in 2012 compared to $2,949 for men; interestingly, not that much different than the national pay gap between women and men.[64] As women and men now make up nearly equal portions of the working population and women control a growing portion of wealth, it is not altogether clear why these disparities persist. One reason has to do with the perceptions of politics. Research suggests that women view political contributions quite differently than men. Women typically do not view donating as a way to show support for a candidate and do not see contributing money as a civic virtue, as they do voting or volunteering.[65] While women may view other forms of charity and philanthropy in quite positive terms, it seems that women do not make that same judgment about the financial side of politics.

WHAT DOES THE PUBLIC THINK ABOUT MONEY AND POLITICS?

These demographic factors (wealth, location, education, and gender) explain certain aspects of money and politics for the general population: if a person lives outside of a major city, hasn't graduated from college, and is a woman, chances are she isn't going to be asked for money, and if she is, she probably isn't going to give. In addition, other, more subtle attitudinal factors explain more about why someone will give to a political candidate, including trust and efficacy. Believing in a candidate who is asking for money (trust) and a feeling that contributed money will advance some valued belief about politics or policy (efficacy) increase the chances of giving a donation.[66]

Trust and efficacy also relate to other fundamental beliefs the public holds about the larger issue of money and politics. Given what we know about how few Americans trust politicians and believe that Washington can effectively solve problems, it then makes further sense why so few people contribute. For example, since the 1950s, distrust of government has increased from around 20% to nearly 60% of the population in the early 2000s.[67] In 2015, less than a third of Republicans, Democrats, and Independents trusted Congress, down from a majority of each group just a decade earlier. And when asked to estimate how much of each dollar spent by the federal government was wasted, the public said more than half (51 cents), interestingly much more wasteful than the public perceived state or local government.

So another reason why so few Americans contribute to political candidates is that people tend to contribute when they are trusting, and most are anything but trusting of politicians. The low levels of trust also likely relate to other widespread feelings about politics, especially the growing role played by money. For example, the *New York Times* and CBS News commissioned a poll in 2015 that asked detailed questions on attitudes toward money and politics and beliefs about what should be done. The major finding was that the vast majority of the public, six in seven respondents (84%), said that money had "too much" of an influence on politics.[68] And two in three (65%) believed that the wealthy also had too much influence in politics. It is striking, in a country that is evenly divided along partisan and ideological grounds, that there was this level of agreement on these two aspects of money and politics. And the *New York Times*/CBS News poll was not the first to discover this. Nathaniel Persily and Kelli Lammie culled evidence from 50 years of national survey research on public opinion and found growing distrust of government and special interests. In 1958, for example, around 30% of the country believed big interests ran government; by 2002 greater than 60% believed that.[69] Furthermore, other research focused just on political contributors in the 1990s—those who willingly participated in financing campaigns—found a majority believed the campaign finance system was broken. Worth noting is this research was completed a decade before several major campaign-finance Supreme Court rulings, especially *Citizens United*, loosened campaign finance regulations and raised even more pressing questions about the campaign finance system. Nonetheless, Clyde Wilcox et al. found that 78% of congressional campaign contributors believed the campaign finance system was "broken" or had "problems" in 1996, and 69% of presidential campaign contributors felt the same in 2000.[70]

Polling also reveals what the public thinks about what should be done about money and politics. Public Citizen found, in 2014, that nearly eight in ten respondents (78%) told pollsters that "reducing the influence of money in politics and elections" was an important issue.[71] Two-thirds (61%) opposed the *Citizen United* case, with similar percentages of Democrats (61%), Republicans (58%), and independents (62%) in agreement. A large majority (85%) of the public said that "the political money system needs fundamental changes or a complete rebuild." A similarly large percentage (78%) seemed to oppose super PACs, agreeing that "outside-group money spent on advertising in political campaigns should be limited." And half (54%) disagreed with the notion that political donations should be protected as free speech by the Constitution.[72] These findings corroborated earlier findings from another poll conducted by Rasmussen Reports that showed a majority (54%) of likely American voters supported more regulations on the size of campaign donations.[73]

Polling even demonstrates that most Americans are willing to vote for new restrictions on money and politics. In 2013, Gallup showed that nearly eight in ten respondents would vote for "a law that would put a limit on the amount of money candidates for the U.S. House and Senate can raise and spend on their political campaigns."[74] Men and women expressed identical views, as did similar percentages of Democrats (82%), Republicans (78%), and Independents (78%). Interestingly, the greatest differences emerge by age group: younger Americans (18–29 years) were the least likely (71%) to concur with the statement, a much smaller percentage than the 84% of middle-aged (30–64 years). Nevertheless, the vast majority of the country would vote for new campaign finance restrictions.

What this polling suggests is a clear signal to elected officials that large segments of the public oppose the current system of politics that permits such a strong role for money. The public thinks there is too much money in politics, the wealthy have too much influence, and current regulations are insufficient. Why then has there been so little momentum for change? The answer lies in the idea of salience or priority. While there is near-consensus on the problem, there are other issues that seem to matter more to the public. For example, when asked by the Pew Research Center about top priorities for the president and Congress in 2015, most of the public said terrorism (76%), the economy (75%) and jobs (67%), or social issues such as education (67%), health care (64%), and social security (64%). Money and politics ranked far down on the list, attracting just 42% of respondents, and only slightly more for the influence of lobbyists (43%). Moreover, some of the widest partisan gaps emerge when we move from attitudes to priorities. Half of Democrats (51%) listed "dealing with money and politics" as a top issue, compared to a third (33%) of Republicans and 43% of independents—an 18-point partisan gap. Whereas there is wide partisan agreement on jobs, global trade, and crime reduction, Republicans place strengthening the military and national economy, reducing budget deficits and crime, and defending the country against terrorism as much more important problems than money and politics. There are also differences by age group. Younger Americans (18–29 years) and older Americans (+65 years) rank money and politics as a higher concern (43% and 48%, respectively) than middle-aged Americans (30–64 years: 40%).

Additionally, while there are increasing concerns about money, politics, and corruption, and colorful anecdotes to point to regarding particularly egregious cases of public malfeasance, public corruption has not been increasing over the last 20 years. As Figure 2.1 shows, at the federal level, convictions for public corruption have dipped from consistently above 400 a year during the late 1990s to under 400 since 2010. At the state level, there has been a slight increase in convictions, but the total has rarely topped 100 for a state workforce of several million. To be sure, these statistics count just convictions, and many cases of corruption may never be discovered. Nevertheless, it is hard to argue that there is an epidemic of

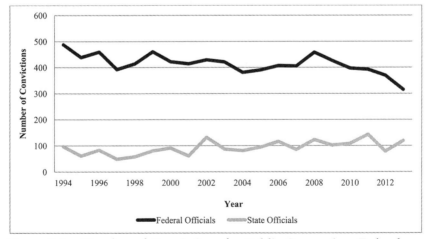

Figure 2.1   Number of Convictions for Public Corruption, Federal and State Officials (Public Integrity Section, Criminal Division, U.S. Department of Justice)

illegal public corruption in the country, possibly an explanation for the disconnect between public concern and public salience.

Low levels of issue salience and partisan disagreement on salience explain part of the lack of movement on changing campaign finance laws, but low levels of *efficacy* also likely matter. As noted earlier, efficacy relates to whether someone believes their political acts (i.e., voting, protesting, or contributing) will have an effect (such as whether one's vote can tip an election). Low levels of efficacy may relate to cynicism about politics, a feeling that politics is simply a game played with rigged rules. Persily and Lammie showed that decades of polls conducted by Gallup revealed that the public has been concerned about money and politics but also believes little can be done. Less than a third (28%) of the public believed that major changes in campaign finance laws would reduce the powerful influence of special interests.[75] Most (67%) of the public believed that special interests would remain just as powerful, even if laws were changed.[76]

That the public does not seem to rationally connect strongly negative feelings to empirical realities of corruption in the country may overstate how well we understand public opinion. Most of what we know about public sentiment about money and politics comes from public opinion polls, including those referenced earlier in this chapter. These polls provide a general understanding of public's discontent but little deeper on what exactly drives these sentiments. Shaun Bowler and Todd Donovan overcame this gap in the literature with a series of experiments that varied information about campaign finance.[77] They found that the public was sensitive to details about the sources, amount, and how funding entered a campaign. The public judged large campaign contributions from corporations and unions used to support negative advertising as *much more* corrupt than small financial contributions from individuals used for campaign advertisements. Partisan differences also emerged: Democrats judged contributions from corporations as much more corrupting, while Republicans judged contributions from unions as much more corrupting. These are not necessarily surprising findings, but they do suggest that sentiments about campaign finance are not uniform and that the public differentiates between different forms of campaign finance in a sophisticated fashion. It is also another reason why public pressure to change campaign finance may not be as strong as we might anticipate.

A final reason—one that brings this chapter full circle to its start— that explains many paradoxes between how most Americans feel and act toward the issue of money and politics is how wealth relates. I've already established that wealthier Americans are more likely to contribute to campaigns and to contribute more than middle- and lower-income Americans. This much is obvious. What is less obvious is that perceptions of the system also differ. Wealth seems to relate to how you feel about the government, and this had held over time. Persily and Lammie showed that in the late 1950s, most Americans of all levels of wealth basically trusted government, though the wealthy saw the government as much less corrupt than others. Just 10% of those in the top income bracket believed that the government was "crooked," compared to around a third of those in the lowest income bracket. Fifty years later, both income groups grew more suspicious of government, but the very poor continued to view the government as more corrupt than the wealthy. This finding reinforces the circular relationship between demographics, money, and political attitudes. Those without very much money have little to spare on politics and tend to get the least attention from politicians. This reinforces distrust, which further reduces the likelihood of future participation in contributing to candidates or even in voting. The wealthy, on the other hand, seem to trust government more, are courted by politicians to a much greater degree for money, and often get something for it, even if it is just the feeling that the contribution made the world a better place. These positive feelings likely lead to future political giving, more attention, and better political outcomes in the future. And over time, as the system has grown ever more open to money and politics, the belief and behavioral wedge between rich and poor on the issue grows wider too.

HAS TECHNOLOGY CHANGED MONEY AND POLITICS FOR THE PUBLIC?

There are plenty of reasons to be deeply concerned about the state of the American democracy, whether you focus on the largess of megadonors or the deep cynicism of the general public. Technology, though, has offered a glimmer of hope. If part of the difficulty of giving a campaign contribution is the time associated with attending a fundraiser and completing an in-person transaction, then perhaps digital innovations could offer to broaden participation in campaign finance. A simple website or cell phone application could make contributing as easy as downloading a movie. And several companies have developed these very products. You can now give a donation through PayPal, Twitter, and Click&Pledge. Those less inclined to give can also use the BuyPartisan app to see the candidates and issues that companies who sell products give political contributions.[78]

While digital products have been around since the 2000s, the evidence that technology has changed who contributes is limited at best. One consulting firm, Greenberg Quinlan Rosner Research, claimed that there was a positive and significant correlation "between the number of likes a candidate has and their fundraising totals" as well as between Facebook likes and successful fundraising.[79] However, claiming that online tools can increase fundraising is not the same thing as saying those tools increase the number of donors or diversifies the pool of donors. The Pew Research Center found that in 2012, one in eight (13%) of those polled had made a contribution to any of the presidential candidates.[80] The largest portion, though, had contributed in offline ways: two-third (67%) of contributors gave in person, on the phone, or by mail. Interestingly, half contributed online or by email, and 10% used their cell phone to contribute. Pew also showed that while contributors were evenly split between Republicans and Democrats, it was Democrats that were using technology to a greater extent. More than half (57%) of Democratic contributors gave online (15% via cell phone app) compared to a third (34%) of Republican contributors (6% via cell phone app).

Technology might also change the money and politics equation if it can help lower the cost associated with running for office. Since the mid-2000s, candidates for office and political organizations have begun to use technology to communicate with potential voters at a much lower cost than other traditional modes of technology such as television advertising or direct mail.[81] Stephanie Stamm estimated that online advertising jumped from less than $1 million in the 2000 presidential campaign to $74.5 million in 2012.[82] Technology has also permitted fundraising at a decreasing direct cost to the political organization. Dave Karpf described the innovative ways that the organization MoveOn changed the nature of political fundraising in the early 2000s. Karpf contrasted traditional paper-mailing-list fundraising with newer electronic mail lists: "The distinction here lies in the dramatic reduction in transaction costs online. When organizations communicate with their membership through the mail, a large, disorganized list consumes too many resources." On the contrary, "The infinitesimal marginal costs of e-mail" permitted MoveOn to make much more direct contact with its donors and also introduce more innovative and effective fundraising strategies.[83] These types of low-cost technology innovations have enabled a new set of political actors to emerge that would have been shut out in the past.

It has also made possible some new campaigns. When he had few of the money advantages of other candidates in the Democratic race, the upstart campaign of Vermont Governor Howard Dean in 2004 was feasible because of low-cost technology.[84] Technology, though, is not cost free. President Obama's victories in 2008 and 2012 were credited as much to his ability to raise money as to the efficiency with which he spent that money on technology.

Newer research is slowly emerging to fill some of the gaps in what we know about online fundraising, and the initial findings are hopeful for addressing some of the concerns raised earlier about gender disparities. Comparing online to offline donors, David Magleby, Jay Goodliffe, and Joseph Olson found that, though more men than women contribute offline (just 36% of offline contributions in 2008 were from women), more women than men donated online in 2008 (52% online contributors were women), and men and women were on par in 2012 (50% online donors were women).[85] While income did not differ between online and offline, online contributors were somewhat younger (in 2012: median age of 52 online compared to 67 offline) and made smaller contributions (2012: median donation amount $100 online, median donation $150 offline). What these findings suggest is that technology might change the tendency for political contributors to be male and older and empower new donors, including women, younger voters, and small contributions, to participate in much greater numbers than in the offline-only past.

CAN THE PUBLIC CHANGE THE RELATIONSHIP BETWEEN POLITICS AND MONEY?

The vicious circle of unequal participation in politics, leading to greater public distrust and further widening the gap in participation, greatly diminishes much hope for change. Rulings by the Supreme Court and the actions of the business community, Congress, and candidates for the presidency over the last 50 years further dampen the possibility of change from the top. But in at least two cases, the Tea Party and Occupy, recent mass-based social movements have included at least some concern for money and politics in their respective calls to action. While each failed to translate that agenda item into a successful policy proposal, the activism on the issue points to the pent-up frustration and potential enthusiasm among the public for change.

First, the Tea Party, which burst onto the political scene in 2009 on an anti-tax, anti-government, and anti-immigration conservative agenda, also showed some concern for the influence of big businesses and the role of money in politics.[86] To be sure, certain Tea Party organizations, such as FreedomWorks and Tea Party Patriots, benefited handsomely from the financial support of mega-donors, including the Koch family.[87] And other Tea Party organizations, especially Tea Party Express, have been major campaign contributors as well. But the rank-and-file members of the Tea Party expressed more mixed views of the issue of money and politics, possibly aligning with the populist ideology in the movement. Polling indicated that in 2010 nearly half (49%) of Tea Party supporters favored a proposed law to limit corporate and big-donor influence in elections called the Fair Elections Now Act. And 63% agreed that outside groups harmed democratic elections and the work of Congress.[88] Even Tea Party-affiliated candidates for office have successfully run on the issue. Dave Brat famously defeated Virginia Congressman Eric Cantor in a 2014 Republican primary by attacking Cantor's relationship with big banks and donors. In his victory speech, Brat said, "what you proved tonight was dollars don't vote—you do."[89] In Congress, Tea Party-affiliated members have mounted their most ambitious legislative battles on money issues, first pushing to shut the government down because of the size of federal spending, and later blocking funding and appointments to the Export-Import Bank because of concerns about cronyism.[90]

Second, while sharing little in the way of ideology and few policy preferences, Occupy also focused on money and politics, especially the influence of Wall Street in Washington. The Occupy Movement—or Occupy Wall Street (OWS)—saw thousands of people descend on city centers to protest the power of corporate America, international austerity policies, and the limits of contemporary democracy. Occupiers famously rallied in Zuccotti Park, steps from the Lower Manhattan center of financial power in the United States. Deep concerns about money animated many of the rallies and drew protesters from across the country. Unlike the Tea Party, though, the movement behind Occupy never showed any real interest in electoral politics. According to Michael Gould-Wartofsky, some Occupy activists believed both political parties were "beholden to the interests of billionaires," meaning that rallying voters in the name of Occupy would be self-defeating.[91] In subsequent elections, Occupy played an insignificant role in supporting candidates or mobilizing voters, relegated to a memorable social movement with little political power to advance an agenda opposed to influence of the financial sector in politics.

In the end, the energy behind Occupy faded away, while the Tea Party grew distant from its grassroots and increasingly became institutionally tied to the Republican Party and money. As a result, the opportunity for diverse members of the public to participate in a movement that opposed the corrupting role of money and politics and the outsized influence of large corporations on politics disappeared. The country was then left with just memories of what motivated liberal, conservative, and libertarian Americans to rally and protest and an assortment of elected officials with few pressures to fight for change.

CONCLUSION

Few of us can claim the fortunes of Koch, Katzenberg, or Adelson. A tiny fraction of the country has the spare money to contribute to genuine charitable causes, let alone distant candidates for office. But the reasons for these disparities in giving do not merely relate to how much money you have in your bank account. There is a deep divide in the country between those who contribute and those who do not. The difference seems to relate as much to an attitude toward politics as to wealth. The vast majority of non-contributors have grown deeply cynical about politics, distrustful of elected officials, and unconvinced that much can be done. For mega-donors, it appears they believe quite differently. Whether they hope to influence single issues, the ideological direction of the country, or just which party holds power, large contributors seem endlessly optimistic about their power—a power that is denominated, not in votes, but in hundreds of thousands of dollars in campaign contributions.

For these reasons, we face two different problems. First, if large contributor optimism is right, can we allow such a legalized form of political corruption to persist? Can the democratic system hold up to a small number of supremely powerful individuals, eagerly waiting to sway an election every two and four years?

Second, and perhaps equally as worrisome, if non-contributor pessimism is right, how can we hope to maintain a functioning democracy as generation after generation grows distant from many of the ways to participate in politics? Can the deep cynicism be reversed without concerted efforts to reform the current system of politics to equalize representation and balance power across a larger segment of the population?

These problems, though, must be tested against other dimensions of the relationship between money and politics. Mega-donors may have deluded themselves into thinking they have nearly the influence over elections and policy making that they actually have. Other features of Washington politics, including the power of incumbency, the status quo, and countervailing institutional pressures, may weaken the power that a dollar of political spending has on electoral or policy outcomes. And for the public-at-large, if the relationship between money and politics is much weaker than it appears, better information about how policy making actually works could serve as an antidote to the current antipathy most hold toward Washington.

As a result, additional perspective must be added to this treatment of money and politics, including a better historical context with which to understand how we have ended up in our current circumstance. The next chapter builds this historical case and then shows how the courts have interpreted the Constitution over time. The changing view of the judicial branch toward political money and corruption explains a large part of how our system of government and politics currently operates.

Chapter 3

Cash, Courts, and the Constitution

While much of the public has developed a deeply suspicious view of money and politics, the courts have eyed this relationship from a very different perspective. Of late, a laissez-faire philosophy has colored major court rulings, emphasizing concerns about freedom of speech over historic worries about corruption. Much attention has been paid to the more recent court rulings on the issue, including major decisions in 1976, 2010, and 2014. These decisions, though, build on a much longer constitutional, legal, and political tradition in the country that must be understood to better appreciate our current state of affairs. Tracing this history helps make sense of how the country has regulated corruption, campaign donations, and money in politics more generally. Better appreciating this history also helps us understand the way the courts shape social norms about money and politics and the way the Court is itself shaped by changing social mores. This chapter sets out to survey this history, not as a definitive legal critique or full history of the political economy of the country but as a way to mine important decisions for how they relate to our contemporary political system and democratic life.

MONEY AND POLITICS IN THE EARLY REPUBLIC

It is a truism that *all* politics is about money and has always *been* about money. That much seems obvious but not particularly revealing. The history of the founding of the United States is often portrayed in equally formulaic and uninteresting terms, as an unambiguous victory for individual rights, democracy, and freedom. The actual story is much more complicated and the role of money and politics prominent. And even if we put to the side the great limitations of the conventional portrayal of the founding of the country that ignores the plight of African Americans, women, and those without land and education, there is still room to unearth ways that money influenced the politics of the founding of the country. Historians teach us that money and politics were profoundly intertwined in the late 18th century, as was the concern for establishing a functioning representative democracy and stemming corruption. Money and politics mattered in the early Republic because the relationship represented something vital and disturbing about the colonial past as well as something critical about the uncertain independent future. The way that early leaders of the country treated the relationship between money and politics, negotiating the past and the future, helped dictate the direction of the country. In the start to this chapter, I explore several aspects of this earlier period. My hope is to establish some themes that permit a better understanding of the Constitution and later court rulings that so greatly affect our world today.

The earliest days of the country—the period after the 1776 Revolution but before the crafting of the 1789 Constitution—were fraught with many pressing concerns about the structure and form of government. Just recovered from life under the reign of the king, the fear of concentrated power dictated many aspects of the Articles of Confederation, the loose legal arrangement between the former colonies. The central government was to be small in size and weak in power, with the understanding that the new states would have authority over most of the affairs within their borders. The thought of creating a new, powerful central authority that might mimic the anti-republican monarch was anathema to most of the former revolutionaries.

Centralized power shaped many of the decisions of that time, as did deep concerns about corruption, real and apparent, that were held over from the recent past. Too close a relationship between money and politics was exactly what the Founders were trying to prevent. Self-interest, bribery, and avarice, be it of the British or French variety, were to be replaced by a political culture based on virtue, statesmanship, and advancing the public interest. Constitutional scholar Zephyr Teachout examined the way that these worries manifested themselves in the laws and practices of the time. She argued in her book, *Corruption in America*, that the Founding generation of Franklin, Madison, and Hamilton cared so deeply about the threats posed by bribes—particularly from foreign governments—that they treated corruption much more seriously than we do 200 years later.[1] For example, the commonplace diplomatic practice of exchanging gifts or gift giving, a norm at the time within British and French trade circles, was viewed as unseemly and potentially corrupting. Teachout wrote, "Americans started their experiment in self-government committed to expanding the scope of actions that were called corrupt to encompass activities treated as noncorrupt in British and French cultures . . . Americans felt the need to constitute a political society with civic virtues and a deep commitment to representative responsiveness at the core."[2] One way they did this was to include a strict ban in the Articles of Confederation on national and state public officials receiving gifts. The document stipulated, "nor shall any person holding any office of profit or trust under the United States, or any of them, accept any present, emolument, office or title of any kind whatever from any King, Prince or foreign State; nor shall the United States in Congress assembled, or any of them, grant any title of nobility."[3]

And the ban was not simply a hollow gesture; it was enforced by Congress and adhered to by those in government. Teachout recounted how John Jay, then negotiating a trade agreement as the county's ambassador to Spain, requested permission of the Spanish envoy to purchase a prized Spanish horse for himself.[4] Rather than grant that permission, the Spanish King offered a horse as a gift, likely a gesture of gratitude to Jay but also in violation of the gift ban. Jay, having witnessed colleagues face great public criticism for accepting similar gifts, said he could not accept the horse without the permission of Congress.

To be sure, after deliberating on the request, Congress later granted Jay permission to accept the gift. But what seems most important, and what Teachout emphasized, was the regard Jay showed to the concerns about corruption and to congressional authority to oversee this type of exchange. There was little indication that the gift of the horse was offered in exchange for any specific favor in the trade negotiation, what we would call *quid pro quo*, but social mores of the time—and also the law—prohibited even the appearance of trouble. Jay's deference to the prevailing rules on public officials showed the severity of apprehensions about corruption. So an act that for many of the period would be accepted as an inconsequential aspect of international diplomacy took on deeper and more significant meaning.

According to Teachout, corruption was broadly defined at the time as "excessive private interests influencing the exercise of public power."[5] Rather than our current narrow legal definition of corruption (which I

will return to later in the chapter), during this time period, public officials were expected to act virtuously and to avoid even the suggestion
that they conformed to the potentially corrupt traditions of Europe.
Teachout concluded that for this significant time period in the history
of the country, the Jay horse-gift case (and others) "reflected a broad
view of what constitutes corruption, a broad view of the importance
of protecting against even the slightest temptation, and a commitment
to using absolute, prophylactic rules to support a civic society in which
people put public interests first in their public roles."[6] Recall, also, that
this was a period when active and costly campaigning for office was
nearly nonexistent, even strong political party affiliations were frowned
upon. Many of the obvious concerns that exist today, including the effect
of accepting campaign contributions on the virtue of an elected official,
were absent from the political landscape of the 18th century. Despite
this political environment with few of our high-dollar worries, even the
hint of political malfeasance and the appearance of corruption were
verboten.

Many of these concerns about corruption persisted through the
Constitutional Convention that reshaped the country. As those drawn
to Philadelphia in 1787 sought to perfect their union and to bind the
states together in a more centralized democratic system, defenders of
the new Constitution had to continually demonstrate that corrupting
influences—particularly from foreign nations—would not ruin the new
country. For example, in *Federalist* No. 57, the likely author, James Madison, explained how the new, larger republic that they had designed in
Philadelphia would protect from corruption by choosing better leaders
than a small one. A larger electorate would be better able to sort out the
heroes from the scoundrels. Madison disagreed that "five or six thousand citizens are less capable of choosing a fit representative, or more
liable to be corrupted by an unfit one, than five or six hundred"; rather,
"Reason, on the contrary, assures us, that as in so great a number a fit
representative would be most likely to be found, so the choice would be
less likely to be diverted from him by the intrigues of the ambitious or
the ambitious or the bribes of the rich."[7]

Alexander Hamilton elaborated on this point in *Federalist* No. 68.
He conceded to concerns about corruption as he explained the way the
president would be selected: "Nothing was more to be desired than that
every practicable obstacle should be opposed to cabal, intrigue, and corruption. These most deadly adversaries of republican government might
naturally have been expected to make their approaches from more than

one querter [*sic*], but chiefly from the desire in foreign powers to gain an improper ascendant in our councils."[8] However, Hamilton claimed that democratic protections were in place to address these worries: "But the convention have guarded against all danger of this sort, with the most provident and judicious attention. They have not made the appointment of the President to depend on any preexisting bodies of men, who might be tampered with beforehand to prostitute their votes; but they have referred it in the first instance to an immediate act of the people of America, to be exerted in the choice of persons for the temporary and sole purpose of making the appointment." Through popular elections, the country would be insulated from many forms of corruption. And further: "No senator, representative, or other person holding a place of trust or profit under the United States, can be of the numbers of the electors. Thus without corrupting the body of the people, the immediate agents in the election will at least enter upon the task free from any sinister bias."[9]

Madison went further in *Federalist* No. 55 regarding the potential corrupting power of a government job, what we call cronyism. Perhaps, members of Congress might gain personal fortunes through appointments in the federal government. Madison cautioned not to worry: "The members of the Congress are rendered ineligible to any civil offices that may be created, or of which the emoluments may be increased, during the term of their election."[10] Article 1 Section 9 of the final Constitution, the Emoluments Clause, prohibited members of Congress from serving in appointed governmental positions for which they could use their legislative power to vote a salary increase. The Framers also kept the gift ban from the Articles of Confederation, though in a somewhat more limited fashion than the original.[11]

The essential argument of an extensive republic and divided government rested, at least in part, on concerns about corruption and self-interest. But Madison and others at the time were also optimistic about the virtues of public officials in the country. Despite every opportunity to be disloyal to colonies during the Revolutionary War, many American leaders remained patriotic to the cause. And with what must have been routine offers from foreign nations, Madison held to the belief that few took bribes for personal enrichment. In *Federalist* No. 55, while ensuring that anti-corruption mechanisms had been included in the Constitution, Madison still remained buoyed by a belief in the goodness of those serving in government and of the country-at-large. He reflected on the War: "Yet we know by happy experience that the public trust was not betrayed; nor has the purity of our public councils in this particular ever suffered, even from the whispers of calumny." And even as Madison offered his oft-quoted axiom, "If men were angels, no government would be necessary. If angels were to govern men, neither external nor internal controls on government would be necessary," it is important to remember that he followed it with an endorsement of the primary role of citizens in the new government. He continued, "In framing a government which is to be administered by men over men, the great difficulty lies in this: you must first enable the government to control the governed; and in the next place oblige it to control itself. A dependence on the people is, no doubt, the *primary control* on the government; but experience has taught mankind the necessity of auxiliary precautions"[12] [emphasis added]. Madison showed a concern about self-interest but placed "primary control" in the hands of the citizenry, and only extra control in the ability of varied and competing interests to keep the system in check.

Out of these debates about the design of the new system of government, and concerns about corruption, came eventual state ratification of the Constitution. Madison, Hamilton, and the other Federalists largely won the debate for an expanded federal system with stronger powers held by the national government. Divided government with separate powers, an assortment of public officials bound by elections, and various clauses to prevent cronyism, bribes, and corruption marked the new system of federalism and republican government. Concerns about self-interest driven by money winning over virtuous public interest would be allayed at every turn by a system of government designed with this in mind. The Bill of Rights, too, would offer additional protections. Those first ten amendments to the Constitution gave citizens a set of rights that could counteract a potentially corrupt government. Voting, speech, petition, and association rights all enabled citizens to question public officials and replace the rogues every two, four, or six years. Citizens could associate freely and criticize whomever they pleased based on their First Amendment rights without the fear of congressional interference. The ultimate system of government hatched in Philadelphia demonstrated a deep commitment to a system of government with dozens of internal protections against corruption but external democratic protections as well.

Institutionalizing Partisanship and Finance

Control over money also shaped the political development of the newly formed United States, especially the formation of political parties.

Recall that in negotiating the final details of the Constitution, federal assumption of leftover debt incurred by states during the war was a prominent point of disagreement. Much to the dismay of many delegates whom had met in Philadelphia, Alexander Hamilton ultimately won the debate, and an assumption bill passed Congress in 1790. As a result, Hamilton next sought to convince the Congress of the new republic to authorize a national bank with his *Report on a National Bank*.[13] No longer tied to Britain and British banks, the country's manufacturing and industrial future, so thought Hamilton, hung on the ability to borrow, invest, and finance debt. To his opponents, Hamilton was advancing a dangerous new government mechanism that would be prone to corruption and in service of urban "stock-jobbers" over the interest of the nation. Historian Mike O'Connor, in *A Commercial Republic*, concluded that "To them, Hamilton was at best misguided, at worst dangerously corrupt."[14] Against this vigorous opposition from those who also saw a national bank as unconstitutional, and yet another example of the federal government growing excessively powerful, Hamilton again won, and the new National Bank of the United States was sanctioned by Congress and President Washington.[15]

Part of what permitted Hamilton to push through such controversial measures was a widely held enmity among politicians of the time toward overt partisanship. Parties were seen as a threat to the unity of the nation, and all efforts were made to discourage vicious partisanship. In his Farewell Address, George Washington strongly cautioned the country about parties and organized factions: "they are likely, in the course of time and things, to become potent engines, by which cunning, ambitious, and unprincipled men will be enabled to subvert the power of the people and to usurp for themselves the reins of government, destroying afterwards the very engines which have lifted them to unjust dominion."[16] Statesmen, it was held, should stand above partisan bickering and hold their country and the Constitution above the self-interested unpleasantness so often associated with parties. Even a casual reader of American history knows this period of anti-partisan consensus was short lived, and, according to some accounts, it was money that drove the wedge to split the Hamiltonian Federalists from the Jeffersonian Republicans once and for all.

To understand this development, we must move from Philadelphia to New York City. New York was the center of much of the early development of American politics and commerce, for a time the geographic center of both. What transpired in the city, therefore, set the course for much of the rest of the country. Political historian Brian Murphy's account of the parallel development of banking and parties—of money and politics—in the city is a testament to the city's importance. As mentioned earlier, during this period, political parties were a minor player in national politics, not nearly as prominent as today. While divisions existed, and nascent party apparatus were forming under the Federalist and Democratic-Republican banners, acknowledging that interests broke along predictable political lines was deeply threatening to the fragile nation.

The financial sector was similarly underdeveloped at the time. New York City had just two banks, a branch of the national bank that Hamilton had championed and the Bank of New York, also closely tied to Hamilton.[17] Access to lending and other banking services was greatly restricted by these two institutions, meaning that merchants had few financial options to realize their economic dreams. While not explicitly discriminatory, both banks were maintained by Federalists, many associated with Alexander Hamilton, leaving little room for Republicans. According to Murphy, "During the 1790s, New York Republicans had no meaningful way to participate in corporate banking because the institutions that controlled access to bank credit—the banks and the legislature that could charter and regulate them—had been captured by Federalists and a Federalist way of thinking about banking. Hamiltonian Federalists owned and ran the city's banks and, by extension, made state policy when it came to banking by swaying legislators and shaping public debates."[18] Those not closely tied to Federalist city leaders, especially leading Republicans, were shut out of opportunities to participate in the potential personal and political gains made possible by banking. Yet, according to Murphy, publicly acknowledging this situation was deemed impractical. Federalists, too, were loath to admit that the banking system had tinges of partisanship and thus rejected applications to award government charters to open new, Republican-operated banks. Murphy wrote, "Federalists could not support such an application if to do so meant admitting that banking in New York had become partisan, and even among Republican allies such a petition would have no political legitimacy."[19]

One Republican, Aaron Burr, had a solution, if not an entirely transparent one. As the city grew to fill the island of Manhattan and beyond, residents needed additional services, including basic ones like water. City government itself had little capacity to provide these services, so private groups would petition the state government, as they had for the right to open new banks, to receive a charter. The private group would then be given permission by government to be the provider of that service and keep the monetary proceeds. In a rapidly growing state like New York, with few essential services, private wealth could be made on roads, waterways, and providing water.

Burr saw the opportunity to provide water services in the Bronx and gathered together a group of well-heeled investors, a mix of Federalists and Democrats, to apply. The opportunity was financial and also potentially political but only if Burr's new water company could gain a little financial flexibility. Thus, in the final stages of the application process, Burr added a provision to the end of the water charter application that would permit excess revenues generated by providing water to be used at the discretion of what was dubbed the Manhattan Company. In essence, the provision would grant the Manhattan Company, and Burr, the opportunity to use those profits for any purpose they deemed useful, including financial. The exact wording of the application would permit the Manhattan Company to easily become both a water company and also a bank, Burr's ultimate motivation for the application. With no substantial questions about the clever provision, Burr won the charter and the Manhattan Company was free to begin providing water services, and soon opened that bank.

Through lucrative lending and financing of new business development in the city, the Manhattan Company enabled Burr to enrich himself and his friends and allies. It also allowed Burr to grow his political reputation, influence, and power. Murphy summarized, "By offering patrons and client access to bank credit and by becoming an investor in fellow Republicans' enterprises, the company attached a material benefit to Republican Party membership that could not be replicated by existing Democratic-Republican societies."[20]

So money and politics were tied together during this period by the development of the infant commercial and financial sectors. Without a strong set of political parties to help organize politics, banks provided a way for social elites to pool money and financial opportunities and to build allegiances. Federalists, including Alexander Hamilton, sought to limit these opportunities to those linked to their cause, but his hold was short lived and quickly weakened. Burr's clever maneuvers created a third bank in New York, which would give Republicans equal opportunities to build a financial base and then to use this to broaden its political power.

And this was not just a story of New York money and politics. The rapidly growing Manhattan Company gave Burr opportunities to shape national politics and his own political future. Federalists had controlled city and state politics, but Burr assembled a slate of candidates, nearly all with ties to the Manhattan Company, to take control for the Republicans. If Republicans could win a majority of the New York statehouse, then they would have the electors in place (state legislators had the power to choose the presidential and vice presidential electors) to determine the next president of the United States. Thomas Jefferson, writing to James Monroe in 1800 (quoted in Murphy's book), agreed: "In New-York all depends on the success of the city election, which is twelve members and of course makes a difference of twenty-four, which is sufficient to make the two houses, joined together, republican [sic] in their vote."[21] And with Burr's growing financial and political influence, he organized an electoral strategy to win a majority in the city and thus control for his party and his company.

During this time, money and political were not tangentially related. Money made possible Burr's ascension and soon his shot at the White House. In 1796, the state legislature was dominated by Federalists and had backed John Adams for president. Four years later, thanks to Burr's effective state election strategy, the state electors were all loyal Republicans, and backed Jefferson for president and Burr for vice president. Because of the peculiarities of presidential election voting at the time, Jefferson and Burr both won the most electoral votes and ended in a tie.[22] While the complex politics that resulted in Jefferson ultimately winning the White House are out of the realm of this book, Burr's rise to national prominence, at just age 44, would not have been possible without his clever manipulation of money and politics. Burr built a financial and electoral infrastructure that could unseat the politically and economically powerful Alexander Hamilton in New York City and then the equally mighty incumbent campaign of John Adams in Washington.

So another way that money and politics were linked together in this period was that money and politics each became institutionalized in overlapping and complimentary ways. By the end of 1800, financial institutions grew in number, sophistication, and prominence as the engine of economic growth in the country. This institutionalization happened because of politics and the determination, at first, of Federalists to block the authorization of new banks and, later, Republican efforts to acquire their own banking opportunities. As finance became increasingly institutionalized, it also shaped politics. Political parties, which had been a dubious feature of American politics before 1800, afterward emerged as an increasingly prominent and divisive feature. This would not have happened in the same way if they were not closely tied to finance and the opportunities presented by a changing economic landscape. Brian Murphy concluded, "Put simply, partisanship provided a path to becoming enmeshed in the commercial, civic, and ceremonial life of the city" and also the nation.[23] Partisanship led to increasingly competitive elections and to electoral campaigns that would necessarily cost more. Remember, George Washington did not campaign at all for the presidency in 1789, preferring to wait at home rather than sully his reputation with soliciting anyone for a vote.[24] By 1800, American electoral politics began to resemble the combustible, retail-style partisan contests of today. While it took more than 200 years for elections to grow truly expensive, the mingling of financial opportunity and politics in the early Republic gave rise to a political system soon driven by party machines, which would demand more and more money to survive.

PAYING TO VOTE AND THE CONSTITUTION

Another issue that has tested the Constitution and defined American politics is the relationship between money, politics, and voting rights. And as with so many other uniquely American issues, this relationship has been defined by race and equality.

As politics evolved in the United States, and voting became more universal and important, money was used to restrict who could and could not participate in politics. Once a right restricted to just white, male, property holders, following the Civil War, voting rights expanded to include newly free African American males. While it took another 70 years to expand that right to women, the period after the Civil War witnessed a great expansion in the number of people who could participate in the democracy, and many did in large numbers. At least according to the new Fifteenth Amendment to the Constitution, voting rights could no longer be prohibited based on race or color, and states had already begun to eliminate property requirements on voting, including New York City in 1826.[25] But it did not take long for the emergence of new ways, part of a host of government policies dubbed "Jim Crow," to prevent African American males from realizing their political rights, and many of these ways involved money.

In order to maintain the status quo in many southern states, state officials developed tactics to limit the political and economic power of African Americans. In numerous states across the South, eligible citizens were required to pay a tax, often of $1.50, in order to register to vote.

While not a large sum in today's terms, for farmers of the era, the vocation of most African Americans, a cash payment of even this amount was significant. In the late 1800s, 11 states had adopted this type of tax, which would have the effect of depriving primarily African American but also poor residents, the right to vote. In states like Georgia, election officials perverted existing laws related to property ownership and began to enforce, target, and strengthen their impact. Georgia increased the amount of the poll tax but also made the tax cumulative, so that back taxes would be charged for all those years after the person turned 21.[26] The cumulative tax bill would quickly become too large for a poor citizen in the state to ever pay, effectively disenfranchising them for life.

The effects of poll taxes were swift, dramatic, and racially discriminatory. For example, researchers compared voter turnout in majority black counties in the south.[27] In counties without a poll tax, voter turnout increased from 51.4% in 1892 to 65.3% in 1912. In counties with a poll tax, voter turnout decreased from 33.8% in 1892 to 15.5% in 1912. As disturbing, during that same time period, the number of non–poll tax counties with a majority African American population dropped from 161 to 1, and the number of poll tax counties increased from 115 to 258. As a result, by the 1920s, there were no majority black counties without a poll tax, and voter turnout was down to just 10%. The poll tax, along with related Jim Crow laws such as grandfather clauses and literacy tests, used money and inequality as a tool to disenfranchise most African Americans across the South for nearly 100 years.

Despite these dramatic effects on voting and the democracy, the Supreme Court remained unconvinced that the poll taxes violated the equal protections provided by the Constitution. The Court heard the case of *Breedlove v. Suttles* in 1937.[28] The Court rejected the argument that the Georgia poll tax violated the Fourteenth and Nineteenth Amendments to the Constitution. Instead, the Court argued that poll taxes were forms of taxation, not voting restrictions. The decision read, "To make payment of poll taxes a prerequisite of voting is not to deny any privilege or immunity protected by the Fourteenth Amendment. Privilege of voting is not derived from the United States, but is conferred by the state and, save as restrained by the Fifteenth and Nineteenth Amendments and other provisions of the Federal Constitution, the state may condition suffrage as it deems appropriate."

Through the period of the New Deal, poll taxes remained as a financial barrier to voting. Historian Glenn Feldman wrote, "For Southern whites, the poll tax was the key to black voting, and black voting was the key to a whole Pandora's box of racial and political trouble."[29] Despite passage in the House of Representatives in 1942, filibusters in the Senate blocked passage of anti–poll tax bills in 1943, 1945, 1947, and 1949.[30]

It was not until 1962 that Congress passed the Twenty-fourth Amendment to make poll taxes unconstitutional. With a passing vote of 295 to 86, the ratified amendment read, "The right of citizens of the United States to vote in any primary or other election for President or Vice President, for electors for President or Vice President, or for Senator or Representative in Congress, shall not be denied or abridged by the United States or any state by reason of failure to pay any poll tax or other tax."[31] As a part of a generation of political decisions associated with the Civil Rights Movement, Congress denied states the chance to explicitly use money to deny voting rights.

The era of Jim Crow was defined by many other tortuous aspects of life for African Americans, including the systematic use of the harshest forms of violence. Segregationists also used money to divide society along lines where race and wealth united. Full participation in the democracy for most African Americans was contingent on having enough money to pay to register to vote, spare money that most did not have. As a result, during this era, democratic institutions were corrupted by money in a profoundly new way, much more debilitating to political freedom than the ways the founding generation imagined a century earlier. The Founders placed no protections into the Constitution against this type of corruption; thus it took nearly 200 years to strip this practice from American elections.

VOTE-BUYING AND THE CONSTITUTION

The act of using money to prevent citizens from voting or participating in politics has been unconstitutional for 50 years and unacceptable for much longer than that. Using money to encourage people to vote, though, has a more ambiguous legal history. Political machines in cities like New York and Boston infamously used money, and other items of value, to nearly guarantee party wins. Aaron Burr organized members of the Columbian Order to help get Democratic-Republicans elected in 1800. The Columbian Order was also called The Society of St. Tammany, the political organization that went on to oversee New York City politics for much of the 1800s, using money and other types of payments to reward loyal partisan voters and party members.[32]

Political reforms of the early 20th century, initiated by Progressives, slowly eliminated the corrupt practices of political machines. Today, in almost every jurisdiction in the country, it is illegal to pay someone—in money or something of monetary value—to vote for or against a candidate or issue. At the federal level, Congress has placed stiff penalties, including $10,000 fines and up to five years in prison, for voter bribery.[33] Vote buying is almost always illegal because it fits with our definition of public corruption: a trade of a public good for something of private value. In this case, the holder of the public good is not an elected official with authority over a land deal or government expenditure but a citizen who holds authority over one vote.[34] Just as corruption of public officials by foreign governments was a threat to the early Republic, corrupt vote buying is seen as a threat to free democracies today. Richard Hasen explained that concern for this type of corruption is also tied to issues of wealth. If poorer voters are more likely to be tempted by the payment of money, then economic disparities could turn into political disparities, as many more of the poor might be bribed into voting against their economic interests than might the wealthy.[35] Others contend that voting is a right and thus cannot be sold. Just as you cannot sell your freedom of speech or religion, your voting rights are not transferrable, even for money.

Vote buying is unambiguously illegal among citizens, but Hasen argued that in other settings the practice is generally accepted as normal. In legislative settings, for example, Hasen contended that elected representatives routinely trade votes—sometimes called "logrolling"—to advance separate policy interests but mutual political interests. Parenthetically, this was the basis on which the appeals court overturned certain corruption charges against former Illinois Governor Blagojevich. Few worry when a legislator offers to vote in favor of another legislator's pet project in exchange for a return of the favor on a future vote. And if this practice of legislative vote trading is acceptable to most, why, then, is it unacceptable for lobbyists to participate in that market and offer other benefits—campaign donations, for example—as a part of a vote trade? Conversely, how different is a lobbyist offering to pay an elected official for a vote from an elected official offering to lower taxes if elected or to lower taxes on a certain group of campaign contributors? What distinguishes these cases relates a lot to the specificity and openness of the exchange. The lobbyist cannot personally enrich the elected official in exchange for a vote, but contributions to help a campaign are viewed a little differently. Likewise, a campaign contribution for an unspecified future vote is clearly quite different from a contribution for a specific ruling that will directly favor the lobbyist or her client.

To be sure, the legal distinctions are blurry, and the Supreme Court has offered only vague guidance. Hasen showed that in 1982 the Court ruled in *Brown v. Hartlage* that broad campaign promises were protected by the First Amendment and that much depends on whether campaign promises are made in public or in private. In this view, the appropriateness public promises can be widely judged by the full electorate and are thus acceptable, while private or secret promises of this sort are not. This is much the same argument made for transparency and disclosure policies on lobbying. Also, the Court considered whether promises are targeted to particular voters or broadly based on the normal functions of government. Promising citizens at a local rally that you will fully fund public schools in exchange for their votes is very different from promising to steer a government contract to a specific company in exchange for a campaign contribution.

A related consideration is when money is used to help people vote—*vote facilitating*—such as providing transportation to the polling station or sending stamped envelopes for registering to vote. While it is illegal to pay someone to vote—*vote inducing*—the courts have generally ruled that it is legal to pay for things related to fulfilling one's right to vote.[36] So, as long as the organization or individual paying for the transportation to the polling station or the envelopes for an absentee ballot or other things just related to the act of voting does not require the voter to choose only one candidate, vote-facilitating payments are deemed acceptable to the courts and the FEC.

CAMPAIGN FINANCE AND THE COURTS

From this history, we can now return to the more immediate issue at hand: campaign finance and the Constitution. The start of this chapter demonstrated the paradox of the formation of the country: a tightrope walk over the related concerns about the corrupting influence of money, on the one hand, and varied financial interests that often divide along partisan lines, on the other. The Constitution aims to address these concerns with a system of elections, representation, and checks and balances. Despite the wishes of the Founders, parties quickly formed and grew powerful in American politics, first based on access to money and later able to disperse both political access *and* money. And while for much of the history of the country, money was used to institutionalize racism and disenfranchise millions of African Americans, the country—both the Supreme Court and Congress—slowly came to recognize the inherent problems with this system and abolished poll taxes with the Twenty-fourth Amendment. Political rights, including voting rights and freedom of speech, are now shared by all adults, providing another check on government and corruption. These paradoxes of the American political experience, a political system deeply committed to freedom and equality but also defined by persistent inequalities that often relate to money, shape recent Court rulings on the relationship between money and politics.

Prior to the 1970s laws, Congress had a weak history of addressing the issue of campaign finance, punctuated by the occasional response to a political scandal.[37] Much of the history of campaign reform, in fact, has fit with this pattern of scandal and public outcry, followed by new regulation, then efforts to overturn or outfox the new law.[38] In 1867, Congress passed a law that would limit campaign contributions and campaign spending and require public reporting by candidates. Additional legislation passed in 1907 (the Tillman Act to prohibit banks and companies from contributing to campaigns), in 1925 (the Federal Corrupt Practices Act, which added additional disclosure provisions), and in 1947 (the Taft-Hartley Act, which barred labor unions from contributing) was all largely ineffective because, according to the FEC, "none provided an institutional framework to administer their provisions effectively."[39] Candidates had plenty of ways to evade the rules, and the government had few resources in place to catch them.

During this period, though, campaign spending was relatively meager. President Dwight Eisenhower's 1952 campaign cost $2.5 million, just $20 million in current dollars, a tiny fraction of the millions spent by even minor presidential candidates today.[40] During the 1960s, the cost of campaigning for president began to rise. These rising costs worried President John F. Kennedy so much that he wrote to Congress, "In these days when the public interest demands basic decisions so essential to our security and survival, public policy should enable presidential candidates to free themselves of dependence on large contributions of those with special interests."[41] Congress did not act on the recommendations of Kennedy's Commission on Campaign Costs, and those costs kept rising. Indicative of this, Richard Nixon raised $10.1 million on his losing campaign in 1960 but nearly tripled that eight years later when he had $25.4 million to spend on his winning 1968 campaign. Four years later he was up to $61.4 million.[42]

The increasingly costly price of campaigning resulted in calls for new campaign finance regulations, in part because many of the Nixon contributions appeared and ultimately were judged illegal. The infamous scandal was named for the illegal break-in of the Democratic Campaign headquarters by Nixon officials in the Watergate Hotel in Washington, DC, but the violations were not neatly constrained to breaking and entering. According to Tim Weiner's account of the scandal, President Nixon told his top adviser, "Anybody who wants to be ambassador must at least give $250,000."[43] Many ponied up to this demand and ended up leading American embassies abroad. Following the discovery of the Watergate Hotel break-in, journalistic and federal investigations uncovered the systematic corruption at the heart of Nixon's White House and the illegal use of money and campaign contributions. Dozens of individuals and corporations associated with the President Nixon were eventually convicted of violating existing campaign finance laws.[44] In one egregious case, an ally of the president from New Jersey travelled to Washington with a briefcase full of cash, $200,000 in $100 bills.[45] In another, an executive from Penzoil, Roy Winchester, carried $700,000 from supporters in Texas to Nixon's campaign committee headquarters.[46] Watergate demonstrated the dishonest nature of the Nixon White House and the powerful corrupting role played by campaign fundraising in national politics. Watergate represented the realization of every great fear about money and politics, and triggered a major change in national politics and federal law.

1970s Regulation: FECA

Partially a result of Watergate, the country demanded congressional action. When Congress passed the Federal Election Campaign Act of 1971 (FECA) and further modified the law in 1974, a much more robust, comprehensive, and institutionalized process for regulating campaign finance was in place. FECA established limits on campaign contributions and expenditures. Individuals and certain PACs would be limited to $1,000 campaign contributions under the new law as well as be subject to a $5,000 contribution limit for other PACs and $25,000 annual limits on individuals. The law also capped individual spending to support or oppose a candidate (that was uncoordinated with the campaign) to $1,000.

FECA mandated much more stringent, and enforceable, reporting of campaign contributions and expenditures. Amendments to FECA also established the Federal Election Commission (FEC) to take over execution and implementation of FECA as well as collection of the campaign disclosure data. Finally, FECA established a new publicly funded program to support presidential candidates. If a candidate accepted a series of restrictions on contributions and spending, the federal government would match fundraising and help finance the campaign.

In sum, Congress greatly changed the rules of campaigning in the country by addressing the corrupting influence of money and politics through spending and contribution limits, heightened transparency through new disclosure requirements, and a new independent agency with the authority to monitor and enforce the law. Though his misdeeds were a chief provocation for the passage of the bill, President Nixon endorsed the new law. In his signing statement, he stated:

> It limits contributions by candidates and their families to their own campaigns. It provides for full reporting of both the sources and the uses of campaign funds, both after elections and during campaigns. By giving the American public full access to the facts of political financing, this legislation will guard against campaign abuses and will work to build public confidence in the integrity of the electoral process.
>
> The Federal Election Campaign Act of 1971 is a realistic and enforceable bill, an important step forward in an area which has been of great public concern. Because I share that concern, I am pleased to give my approval to this bill.[47]

1970s Supreme Court Ruling

Despite Nixon's validation of the law, FECA, as it was initially designed, was short lived. The Court, in *Buckley v. Valeo*, sought to apply the First Amendment to the law and treat campaign money as a type of speech. The case involved Senator James L. Buckley, a Conservative Party member from New York, and Eugene McCarthy, a former Democratic senator from Minnesota, against the Secretary of the Senate, Frank R. Valeo. In its final ruling, the Court drew a distinction between FECA limits on campaign *expenditures* and limits on campaign *contributions*.[48] The Court was unconvinced that the contribution limits in FECA violated the First Amendment, whereas they believed the expenditure limits did. The Court wrote, "In sum, although the Act's contribution and expenditure limitations both implicate fundamental First Amendment interests, its expenditure ceilings impose significantly more severe restrictions on protected freedoms of political expression and association than do its limitations on financial contributions."

On expenditure limits, the Court stated, "A limitation on the amount of money a person may give to a candidate or campaign organization thus involves little direct restraint on his political communication, for it permits the symbolic expression of support evidenced by a contribution but does in any way infringe the contributor's freedom to discuss candidates and issues." Therefore the Court found "under the rigorous standard of review established by our prior decisions, the weighty interests served by restricting the size of financial contributions to political candidates are sufficient to justify the limited effect upon First Amendment freedoms caused by the $1,000 contribution ceiling," and, further, "In view of these considerations, we conclude that the impact of the Act's $1,000 contribution limitation on major party challengers and on minor party candidates does not render the provision unconstitutional on its face." The contribution limits of the law essentially remained in place as constitutional.

On the contrary, the Court struck down the expenditure limits (contained in §608 of the law) as a violation of the First Amendment and an unconvincing protection against corruption. The Court wrote, "We find that the governmental interest in preventing corruption and the appearance of corruption is inadequate to justify §608(e)(1)'s ceiling on independent expenditures." Therefore, the Court concluded "that §608(e)(1)'s independent expenditure limitation is unconstitutional under the First Amendment." The Court argued these independent expenditures would not likely lead to corruption or serve as an effective bribe, since they were by definition uncoordinated with the campaign and thus unlikely to directly aid the candidate.[49] Since the law directed expenditures limits at uncoordinated spending, then this was not likely to limit corruption and thus was an unconvincing reason to limit a First Amendment right.

In addition to significantly altering FECA, the *Buckley* case introduced a distinction between political communication that was deemed "express advocacy" and that which was deemed "issue advocacy." The Court ruled that FECA regulations applied only to the communications of non-candidates that used terms such as "vote for," "vote against," "support," or "defeat"—what they called *express advocacy*. If a non-candidate individual or PAC did not use those words and phrases, then the communication was *issue advocacy* and not subject to the regulations of FECA. These special words have become a central feature of the debates about regulating campaign finance since the *Buckley* decision. In practice, then, the Court permitted nearly limitless independent expenditures to be used to say almost anything about a campaign, as long as the communication did not expressly advocate for or against the election of an individual.

To review, the *Buckley* ruling stands out and remains as a seminal part of the history of money and politics in the United States. The Court established that federal oversight of elections was permissible, but only limits on campaign contributions were constitutional as a basis to protect the public from corruption (or perceived corruption); limits on campaign expenditures were not. In the case of expenditures, the Court adopted the view that the First Amendment and the principle of free speech protected an individual or organization's spending on a campaign. To limit an individual's expenditures was tantamount to unconstitutionally limiting their free speech, which is justified only if it protected against direct threats of corruption. As well, the Court accepted other provisions of FECA that remained in various forms for the next 40 years, including disclosure requirements, the FEC, and a publicly financed fund to support presidential candidates.

2002 Regulation: BCRA

In the 1990s, the next round of concern for campaign finance emerged, and a new round of federal policy making commenced. One of the reasons for these concerns was what Paul S. Herrnson called the political "adaptation" to the law as "political parties, interest groups, individual donors, and congressional candidates learned to operate within its confines."[50] It was perfectly legal for political parties to raise and spend what is called *soft money* or money used for issue advocacy and other party-related expenses not directly associated with campaigns. Because the *Buckley* decision drew a distinction between issue advocacy and express advocacy, none of the FECA limitations and disclosure requirements applied to soft money. As a result, clever parties and political groups saw this as a loophole—or what Michael Malbin called "the vehicle"—through which they could indirectly influence campaigns without substantial federal oversight.[51] According to analysis by Herrnson, there was a threefold increase in soft money spending by parties between 1992 and 1996, and a twofold increase by the next presidential election in 2000.[52] While the money could not be used to air advertisements urging voters to "support" or "oppose" any candidate, a violation of the express advocacy communication provisions of FECA, the ads could help the party by shaping the campaign narrative by raising favored policy issues. Herrnson estimated that these communications totaled more than $100 million in 2002.

The rise of soft money raised deep concerns among those worried that money was driving politics and that regulators had few tools to put on

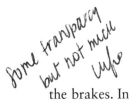

the brakes. In 2002, Congress passed the Bipartisan Campaign Reform Act (BCRA), what has also been referred to by the names of its Republican (Arizona Senator John McCain) and Democratic (Wisconsin Senator Russ Feinold) Senate sponsors, McCain-Feingold. The primary effect of BCRA was to outlaw the use of soft money by parties, one of the primary adaptations that emerged after the passage of FECA. BCRA forbid national political party organizations from raising or spending money that was not covered under BCRA—no more soft money. Parties could only use FECA-covered money—hard money—on communications for races involving candidates for federal office.

BCRA also broadened the express advocacy definition to include an assortment of communications, not just those that use the "vote for" or "vote against" language. If a communication targeted at voters occurred within 30 days of a primary election or 60 days of the general election and mentioned a candidate, it was considered an *electioneering communication* and subject to FEC disclosure of funder names.[53] The law also increased contribution limits of FECA for individuals from $1,000 to $2,000 and doubled the aggregate annual contribution ceiling, a point that comes back in the *McCutcheon* decision several years later. Finally, we can credit BCRA with that tagline that ends each campaign advertisement: "I am _____ and I approve of this message." In many ways, BCRA strengthened and updated FECA for 21st-century politics.

Though not a champion of the bill, President George W. Bush conceded to the merits of its design and primary objectives. He wrote in his signing statement that the major provisions of BCRA "will go a long way toward fixing some of the most pressing problems in campaign finance today. They will result in an election finance system that encourages greater individual participation, and provides the public more accurate and timely information, than does the present system. All of the American electorate will benefit from these measures to strengthen our democracy."[54] But he also raised concerns and rightly predicted future judicial review: "I also have reservations about the constitutionality of the broad ban on issue advertising, which restrains the speech of a wide variety of groups on issues of public import in the months closest to an election. I expect that the courts will resolve these legitimate legal questions as appropriate under the law."[55]

Scholars have attempted to measure the impact of BCRA and found that only some of the act's key provisions had the intended effect. Robert Lowery studied how fundraising changed after 2002 with data up to 2006.[56] He found that various PACs quickly adjusted to the ban on soft money and rechanneled their fundraising and donating to other purposes. BCRA seemed to broaden the geography of fundraising for PACs as well as to shift the focus to wealthier parts of the country. In the end, though, Lowry concluded that "the world of political campaign finance will always adjust to changes in legal regulations."[57] Money, much like water, has a unique way of finding new channels, despite cleverly constructed walls and boundaries.

2000s Supreme Court Rulings: *Nixon v. Shrink Missouri Government PAC* and *McConnell*

Just as FECA met with Court review shortly after its passage, BCRA also faced review within a decade. The first efforts to challenge the law were rebuked by the Court. In *McConnell v. FEC*, the majority opinion, written by Justices John Paul Stevens and Sandra Day O'Connor, upheld the long-standing view of the government's role in stemming corruption. The Court wrote, "Just as troubling to a functioning democracy as classic *quid pro quo* corruption is the danger that officeholders will decide issues not on the merits or the desires of their constituencies, but according to the wishes of those who have made large financial contributions valued by the officeholder . . . And unlike straight cash-for-votes transactions, such corruption is neither easily detected nor practical to criminalize. The best means of prevention is to identify and to remove the temptation."[58] This was a broad interpretation of what constitutes corruption and what then justifies government intervention. Therefore, the Court ruled, "It was not unwarranted for Congress to conclude that the selling of access gives rise to the appearance of corruption. In sum, there is substantial evidence to support Congress's determination that large soft-money contributions to national political parties give rise to corruption and the appearance of corruption."[59] The use of the word *access* here is important. For this ruling, even if campaign contributions resulted in a supporter *just* getting a meeting scheduled or a phone call answered by the elected official—political access—that was enough to warrant concern for the Court. Access need not lead to a demonstrably favorable policy outcomes in order to compel regulation.

The Court went further to affirm that the provisions prohibiting electioneering communication by corporations and labor unions were valid because "they remain free to organize and administer segregated funds, or PACs, for that purpose. Because corporations can still fund electioneering communications with PAC money, it is 'simply wrong' to view the provision as a 'complete ban' on expression rather than a regulation."[60] If a company wanted to influence an election, it could do so by establishing a regulated PAC.

In a related ruling, Justice Stevens also expressed a view on the long-standing question of whether monetary political contributions were a type of speech and therefore protected by the First Amendment in the same way as writing a letter to a member of Congress or addressing those gathered in protest. Stevens declared in a concurring opinion in *Nixon v. Shrink Missouri Government PAC*, "Money is property; it is not speech."[61] Stevens contended that property rights were protected by the Constitution, but "The right to use one's own money to hire gladiators, or to fund 'speech by proxy,' certainly merits significant constitutional protection. These property rights, however, are not entitled to the same protection as the right to say what one pleases."[62] While in the majority in the *Nixon* decision, Stevens's view of free speech protections soon landed him in the minority.

Citizens United and *McCutcheon*

free speech to they should be able to air it no subject to oversight

While initial efforts to overturn the law were rejected by the Court, two significant cases ultimately altered many of the key provisions BCRA and the way the Court would view free speech, corporations, and corruption. The landmark *Citizens United* decision carved new legal terrain for how the government could regulate campaign finance, specifically corporate expenditures on electoral communication. The case pitted Citizens United, a political nonprofit organization, against the FEC. In January 2008, Citizens United released a documentary, *Hillary: The Movie*, that was critical of Hillary Clinton, at the time a candidate for president in the Democratic primaries. The documentary had been funded by corporate donors, and since Citizens United wished to air the documentary and advertisements on television within the 30-day period before a primary election protected by BCRA, they feared the airing of the documentary would be in violation of the law. BCRA specifically prohibited corporations from funding independent expenditures on express advocacy communication. Lawyers for Citizens United argued that these electioneering communication regulations established in BCRA (and ruled constitutional in *McConnell v. FEC*) were in fact an infringement on the First Amendment and unconstitutional.

The Court approached the case on the broad question of political speech, and issued a far-reaching decision on First Amendment

protections. One of the key debates in the case was whether corporations should be afforded the First Amendment protections of individuals. An earlier court ruling, *Austin v. Michigan Chamber of Commerce*,
had upheld electioneering expenditure restrictions on corporations in the
law, and the majority had cited that case in *McConnell v. FEC*. In *Citizens United*, the Court overruled the earlier judgments, stating, "There
is no basis for the proposition that, in the political speech context, the
Government may impose restrictions on certain disfavored speakers,"
and "Because speech is an essential mechanism of democracy—it is the
means to hold officials accountable to the people—political speech must
prevail against laws that would suppress it by design or inadvertence."
The Court's conclusion was that Congress might be able to regulate
corporate contributions, but when it came to expenditures, aspects of
BCRA had the effect of an unconstitutional ban on speech and thus violated the First Amendment.

Based on this argument about extending free speech protections to
corporations, the Court then addressed the issue of whether the government had a justifiable reason to impose restrictions because of concerns about corruption. The Court disagreed with previous judgments
about the appearance of corruption, especially Stevens's interpretation. The decision read, "this Court now concludes that independent
expenditures, including those made by corporations, do not give rise to
corruption or the appearance of corruption. That speakers may have
influence over or access to elected officials does not mean that those
officials are corrupt. And the appearance of influence or access will not
cause the electorate to lose faith in this democracy." So, according to the
Court's opinion, if corporations had speech rights that were protected
by the First Amendment, and the potential that using those rights did
not pose an overwhelming risk to the integrity of the democracy, then
the prohibitions in the BCRA law were unconstitutional. The Court did
not overturn other aspects of the campaign finance system; rather they
tailored the decision to the independent expenditure provisions of the
law. Shortly after *Citizen United*, the Court extended this interpretation
from expenditures to contributions in *Speechnow.org v. FEC*.[63] *Citizens
United* and *Speechnow.org* meant that corporations, still bound by certain candidate and party contribution limits, would now be permitted
to make nearly limitless independent contributions and expenditures on
political communications and be in full compliance with the law.

Citizens United presented a major change in the role of money and
politics, in many ways an invitation to corporations to spend as much

as they pleased on express advocacy communication. The Court decided that campaign spending was equivalent to political speech and therefore could not be regulated as distinct from the speech of individuals. Four years later, the Court deferred again to the First Amendment in ruling on the case of *McCutcheon et al. v. FEC*.[64] In doing so, the Court moved further from the broad conception of corruption that so worried the Founders of the country and toward the more contemporary free speech argument. Recall, for the Founders, there was a public interest in prohibiting explicit forms of corruption but also restricting other practices, such as accepting gifts, that would give the appearance of corruption. In reaching its slim majority decision in 2014, the Court adopted the much narrower *quid pro quo* definition; in many ways retreating from the long-standing view of the government's interest in stemming the appearance of corruption.

The case involved Shaun McCutcheon, a businessman from Alabama. McCutcheon was a contributor to the Republican Party and Republican candidates but grew frustrated that FECA prevented him from giving to more candidates. In 2011–2012, he had given to 16 candidates and wanted to give to an additional 16, but aggregate limits in FECA prevented him from doing so. Lower courts had upheld the aggregate limits as consistent with the overarching goals of the law to constrain the amount of money any individual could contribute during any campaign. McCutcheon sought to challenge those decisions with the backing of many conservative groups that had long disagreed with this aspect of the law.[65]

McCutcheon's legal team, building on the *Citizen United* precedent, argued that much had changed since the 1970s, and the new regulatory environment on campaign finance made the case for aggregate limits much less convincing. Lawyers for McCutcheon wrote, "In the more than 35 years since this Court decided *Buckley*, Congress has substantially altered its regulatory scheme, most notably through the FECA Amendments of 1976 and BCRA, to foreclose the avenues *Buckley* identified for circumvention of per-candidate contribution limits" and continued, "These fundamental changes in campaign finance law have eliminated *Buckley*'s rationale for upholding FECA's aggregate contribution ceiling."[66] As a result, they argued that the government was no longer justified in stemming First Amendment rights. They wrote, "BCRA's aggregate contribution limits impose an unconstitutional burden on core First Amendment activity . . . Because the circumvention problem they were originally designed to target no longer exists, aggregate limits are

now left prohibiting constitutionally protected activity for no permissible reason. They are fundamentally incompatible with the First Amendment and cannot survive any meaningful concept of rigorous scrutiny."[67]

On April 2, 2014, the Court issued its decision. Chief Justice John Roberts wrote, "There is no right more basic in our democracy than the right
to participate in electing our political leaders. Citizens can exercise that
right in a variety of ways: They can run for office themselves, vote, urge
others to vote for a particular candidate, volunteer to work on a campaign, and contribute to a candidate's campaign."[68] In the end, the Court
largely agreed with McCutcheon and overturned the aggregate limits.
The Court explained, "the aggregate limits on contributions do not further the only governmental interest this Court accepted as legitimate in
Buckley. They instead intrude without justification on a citizen's ability to
exercise 'the most fundamental First Amendment activities.'" In reaching
this decision, the Court articulated the narrow view of corruption: "Congress may target only a specific type of corruption—'quid pro quo' corruption . . . Spending large sums of money in connection with elections,
but not in connection with an effort to control the exercise of an officeholder's official duties, does not give rise to quid pro quo corruption. Nor
does the possibility that an individual who spends large sums may garner
'influence over or access to' elected officials or political parties." Not only
did the Court agree with McCutcheon's First Amendment argument, it
also formulated a new and narrower way to conceptualize corruption.

In the end, the *McCutcheon* decision removed the aggregate limits on
annual contributions but upheld the limits on contributions to individual candidates. After the decision, a contributor still could not contribute unlimited amounts to each candidate but now could give to dozens
or more candidates with no ceiling on total campaign contributions in a
given year. One result of the decision was the emergence of *joint fundraising committees* as a legal way that candidates could join together and
allow contributors to write a single large check to be divided up among
the group.[69] Together, *Citizens United* and *McCutcheon* represented a
reinterpretation of the Constitution and historic concerns about the relationship between money and politics. The corrupting influence of campaign donations should be viewed in narrow terms, not the broad ways
of the past. And corporations, like individuals, should be treated similarly when it came to balancing campaign finance regulations against
First Amendment protections.

Not surprisingly, there were dramatic reactions to these decisions.
Shortly after the *Citizens United* ruling, President Obama stated, "With

its ruling today, the Supreme Court has given a green light to a new stampede of special interest money in our politics. It is a major victory for big oil, Wall Street banks, health insurance companies and the other powerful interests that marshal their power every day in Washington to drown out the voices of everyday Americans."[70] Others celebrated the decision, including Senator Majority Leader Mitch McConnell, the plaintiff in *McConnell v. FEC*: "With today's monumental decision, the Supreme Court took an important step in the direction of restoring the First Amendment rights of these groups by ruling that the Constitution protects their right to express themselves about political candidates and issues up until Election Day."[71] With the exception of Senator John McCain, the cosponsor of BCRA, much of the reaction broke along partisan lines, with Republicans elated and Democrats despondent.

PETITIONING FOR REDRESS AND REGULATED LOBBYING

Much of the attention paid to the relationship between money and politics has rightly focused on campaign finance and elections. Money may be most visible during the exchange between a contributor and a candidate. Less visible but no less important is another way money can be used to influence politics: lobbying. Similar to giving a campaign contribution to support a political candidate, the Constitution protects a citizen's right to question or seek the help of government. The First Amendment reads, "Congress shall make no law . . . abridging the freedom . . . of the people peaceably . . . to petition the Government for a redress of grievances."[72] If you have a problem with your taxes, mail delivery, or the size of the nation's military, you have the right to make those concerns heard, and Congress cannot prevent you from doing so.

Over time, the courts have come to accept that, in practicing this right, it is permissible to hire someone to petition government on your behalf. If you are too busy to travel to Washington or believe someone else might make a better case for your concerns, you can pay someone money to do this for you. We call those people lobbyists, and they have been actively seeking redress for clients since the formation of the country.

Lobbyists represent an assortment of interests, from businesses to schools to cities. Congress first acted to define lobbying in 1946 with the Federal Regulation of Lobbying Act. That act, later modified by the courts, essentially defined lobbying as a specific type of political work. A lobbyist's job is to convince a public official to act on policy in the best interest of the client, whether that official is a member of Congress or the president or someone working on one's behalf, such as an appointed official in the executive branch or a congressional staffer. Lobbying then is direct influence. Lobbying is not, however, the same thing as bribery. It is illegal to pay a lobbyist to offer an elected official money to support or oppose some act of government. A good lobbyist should be very persuasive, but they cannot use money to directly influence an official. Moreover, lobbying is not indirect influence, such as influencing government through public relations campaigns, organizing public rallies, and coordinating letter writing campaigns, which generally fall out of the political action that has been defined as lobbying if it is not focused solely on the passage of a specific law or policy.

Unlike giving a campaign contribution, however, there are many fewer regulations on the amount of lobbying expenditures. The primary regulations on lobbyists have been related to transparency. According to the 1995 Lobbying Disclosure Act (LDA), which further defined the act of lobbying, lobbyists are required to report to Congress which issues they have been hired to lobby on, the name of the clients, and amount they have been paid.[73] If the lobbyist is hired to do other work, not directly focused on influencing the public official to act, then that work is not considered lobbying and reporting is not required. Further, a person hired to lobby, who does this work as only a small part of their job (less than 20%), also is not required to report, even though he may be lobbying.

The thrust of lobbying regulations has been that secrecy leads to the public perceptions of corruption.[74] Mandatory reporting by lobbyists and disclosure to the public may reduce the perception of corruption by showing exactly who is paying, who is acting, and who they are trying to influence. Congress has tried to shape the behaviors of lobbyists and reduce the pressure born by elected officials through publicizing what lobbyists do. I return to this point in Chapter 5.

CONCLUSION

Two hundred and forty years after the Declaration of Independence declared that the colonies would form a new union based on equality and the consent of the governed, the nation still faces many of the same philosophical concerns that worried the Founders. How can the people erect a government and system of rules that promote equality and also liberty? How can democratic institutions empower citizens to oversee public officials without the fear, real or imagined, of corruption? The corrupting role of money and influence shaped the writing of the Constitution, the nation's early development of commerce and politics, and the evolution of democratic institutions. Depending on how you view money, it has either been used to express the political rights of those eager to contribute to political campaigns or as a way to restrict political rights by tying taxes to voting or some combination of the two.

Early Republicans in New York City saw their political and economic livelihoods quashed by limited access to money. They maneuvered to create the financial institutions needed to build a political base onto which they could win control of the city, state, and even the White House in 1800. For African Americans, they too had political and economic rights taken away through the racist application of the poll tax but then fought for generations during the Civil Rights Movement to regain those rights and remove these explicit financial barriers in front of political participation. The relationship between money and politics is the story of this country; it always has been and likely always will.

Most recently, Congress and the courts have pushed and pulled between the ongoing concerns about whether money corrupts or empowers. With FECA and BCRA, Congress sought to reign in the outsized influence of money and politics. The Court has consistently pushed back on these legislative efforts, with rulings in 1976, 2010, and 2014, that each eased limits on how individuals, contributors, corporations, and organizations might use money to influence politics. Today, the complex intersection of the Constitution, federal law, and federal enforcement defines the relationship between money and politics.

In Chapter 2, I presented an assessment of the ways individuals participate in this system. Some wealthy donors take every legal opportunity to use money to participate in politics, but the vast majority of the public has few inclinations to spend even a dime on politics and has grown increasingly disenchanted with those who do. But as the Court showed us in *Citizen United*, we are not merely interested in how individuals feel and act. We must ask: how have these laws, and various Court rulings, shaped the way business thinks and acts about politics? Have corporations always acted in ways that confirm the worst fears of campaign finance and lobbying reformers? The next chapter shifts the focus to Corporate America and the ways it has participated in politics.

Chapter 4

Business, Money, and Politics

The first two chapters of the book demonstrated two perspectives on money and politics: individuals and the courts. From each perspective, great contradictions define how money and politics are linked in the United States. The public-at-large holds deep and increasingly suspicious views of how important money is in the democracy. Despite the wide national consensus on the problem, there is much less agreement on priorities. The American public wants laws changed to stem the role of money and politics but isn't in a particular hurry to do so. As a result, a tiny fraction of the population continues to give millions of dollars with only limited restraints on giving even more in the future.

Court interpretations of the Constitution have also rendered complex and often contradictory judgments on money and politics. The original authors of the Constitution worried greatly about self-interest and constructed a system of government and democratic representation to ward off the risk of corruption, both real and perceived. Virtue and public interest dominated discussion of the early days of the Republic, yet within a generation, money came to define politics and vice versa. In order to understand American political development, we must pay close attention to the close relationship between access to money and access to political power, not just in the abstract but also in very tangible ways. From the development of political party machines to Jim Crow to *Citizens United*, the nation's legal apparatus has struggled with how money has been used to leverage political power for increasingly entrenched self-interests.

These two perspectives are important but incomplete. This chapter brings a third critical perspective to the topic: business. While corporations may share much in common with the elite set of big money donors described in Chapter 2, they must be treated distinctly. Despite the claims made in *Citizens United*, corporations are not people, and even if they are afforded certain rights, the ways that corporations participate in politics demonstrate different aspects of American politics. Corporations, much like individuals, come in different varieties, and in this chapter I aim to describe some of the ways that the business community (what I sometimes call Big Business, Corporate America, or business interests) has changed its political behaviors since the 1970s, how varied business interests relate to different political strategies, and how these new corporate political behaviors relate to elections and public policy. I end the chapter with several theoretical explanations for these trends, but first the chapter starts with a case study of the political activities of one company.

ONE COMPANY'S POLITICAL STRATEGY

In 1849, Charles Pfizer and Charles Ehart, cousins, opened Charles Pfizer & Company in Brooklyn, New York.[1] As the Civil War heated up, the company supplied a variety of chemical compounds (morphine, chloroform, and iodine) to the Union Army. By the end of the war, the company had 150 employees and a new headquarters in Manhattan. Over 150 years later, the company employs nearly 80,000 workers worldwide and is one of the most profitable companies on the globe, selling everything from Advil to ChapStick.[2]

In addition to being a leader in pharmaceutical sales and research, Pfizer also has had deep interests in government. The company explains that "public policy affects our ability to meet patient needs and provide shareholder value."[3] Whether the issue is counterfeit drugs, intellectual property, or illegal importation, Pfizer cares a lot about how the government, including the National Institutes of Health, the Department of Health and Human Services, and the Department of Justice, address health and pharmaceutical policy. For these reasons, the company is not an indifferent political actor; it actively participates: "We believe that public policy engagement is an important and appropriate role for companies in open societies, when conducted in a legal and transparent manner."[4]

Pfizer's political strategy has been multifaceted, comprehensive, and— from what they claim—open (see Figure 4.1). The company states that it discloses "our corporate political contributions and employee Political Action Committee contributions on our Web site" and that it has

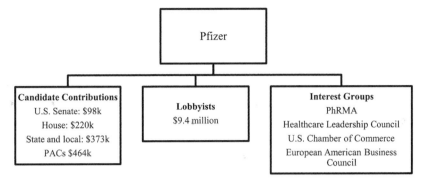

Figure 4.1   Pfizer's Multifaceted Political Strategy

"adopted a strict policy against making independent expenditures" in compliance with federal law. From this, we know, with some level of accuracy, the exact amounts the company has spent to influence electoral outcomes. Two committees oversee the political activities of the company: Political Contributions Policy Committee and Pfizer PAC Steering Committee. These committees determine how the company and its associated PACs participate in political campaigns at the national and state levels as well as the direction of its lobbying, both individually and as a part of coalitions.

In 2014, Pfizer (through its PAC) made contributions to candidates for the U.S. Senate ($98,450), U.S. House of Representatives ($220,330), state and local candidates ($373,771), and PACs ($464,250). Based on these varied campaign targets, we can gather the company's interests in the electoral politics of certain states.[5] In Texas, for example, the company backed Republican Senator John Cornyn with a contribution of $9,500, a partisan mix of House candidates (five Republicans and six Democrats), and Republican candidates for governor ($7,500), lieutenant governor ($7,500), state controller ($3,500), and state attorney general ($10,392.73). In total, Pfizer gave to 88 different candidates (nearly all up for reelection) in 2014 and only lost in eight races. In Vermont, on the contrary, Pfizer's total donations were much smaller, though the partisan mix was similar. Pfizer spent the most money backing one House Democrat, Peter Welch, with a contribution of $2,000 and supported a combination of Republican and Democratic candidates for state offices but none for more than $1,000. Pfizer supported 11 Vermont candidates; all won their races in 2014.

Pfizer also hires lobbyists to influence politics. In 2014, according to the Center for Responsive Politics, Pfizer reported spending $9.4 million on lobbying, interestingly its lowest level of lobbying in a decade.[6] The volume of the company's lobbying tracks with congressional action on health care policy. For example, in 2009, during the passage of the Affordable Care Act (or, Obamacare), Pfizer spent $25.8 million on lobbying, nearly three times its 2014 amount. During that heated debate, Pfizer was second only to the trade association, Pharmaceutical Research and Manufacturers of America (PhRMA), which spent $26.1 million on lobbying. Not surprisingly, Pfizer is also a member of that association. In 2014, Pfizer's lobbyists were actively influencing discussions of the Patent Abuse Reduction Act and the Pharmaceutical Quality, Security, and Accountability Act in the Senate and the Drug Quality and Security Act and the Patent Quality Improvement Act in the House.[7] As of 2015, neither bill had been approved by Congress. Pfizer was also involved in issues further afield such as trade policy, research policy, and education policy.

A final way that the company participates in politics is through membership in trade associations and coalitions. Trade associations, like PhRMA, pool together likeminded companies and advocate on their behalf through lobbying, giving campaign donations, and other policy activities. In addition to PhRMA, Pfizer reported being a member of other health-focused organizations such as the Council for Responsible Nutrition and the Healthcare Leadership Council. Pfizer was a part of more broad-based business groups such as the National Association of Manufacturers and the U.S. Chamber of Commerce. Pfizer also participated in international organizations, including the European American Business Council and the European Federation of Pharmaceutical Manufacturers and Associations.

There are likely numerous other ways that Pfizer influences public policy, including advising the executive branch through rule making, submitting briefs to the Supreme Court, and promoting grassroots and social media campaigns. Pfizer's political strategies stretch across all of the legal ways that companies can influence the political process. It seeks influence at the international, national, and state/local levels of the policy process. It advocates on pharmaceutical issues, health care issues, as well as dozens of other business, trade, and education issues. Pfizer seeks to influence Republicans, Democrats, and other party officials, directly through helping them get elected and then later through paid lobbyists.

Finally, Pfizer joins with others to advocate together, especially on big issues like the direction of health and economic policy.

ASSESSING THE ROLE OF BUSINESS IN POLITICS

Pfizer's high levels of political activity are clear from its own documentation. What is less clear is what to make of this wide-ranging political strategy. First, is it a unique strategy? Second, is it effective: does Pfizer get its way? Third, is it fair: do all pharmaceutical companies pursue such a comprehensive strategy and what about consumers? In order to answer these questions, it is first important to place Pfizer into a bit of historical context. By first understanding where American businesses have been on the political process, we can better assess the state of affairs today.

One aspect of the roots of corporate involvement in politics goes back to the long history of advocacy for the wealthy, a pattern that mirrors the political development of the country that saw the center of politics shift from statehouses to Washington, DC. Isaac William Martin's book, *Rich People's Movement*, traced this 100-year history, and the ways that activists across the country pushed for state laws that would have the immediate effect of improving the economic well-being of the rich.

Whether pushing to reduce taxes in the 1920s, 1950s, or 1970s, the country has a lengthy history of political movements with similarly upper-crust motivations. There have been repeated national movements with complex mobilization across state boundaries. For example, Martin summarized these movements in his book as "twentieth-century campaigns for tax cuts that were explicitly targeted to high-income or high-wealth households, led by special purpose associations, unaffiliated with a particular political party or administration, that attempted to get their way by mobilizing demonstrations of civic support for their demands far outside the halls of power in Washington, DC, and that had active campaign operations in multiple states."[8] Movements differed over time in terms of their center of energy, the exact details of the policy demands, and composition of the advocates. To this point, Martin continued, "The tax club activists of the 1920s were mainly country bankers in the South and Midwest; the activists for income tax repeal in the 1950s and 1960s included an unlikely coalition of California heiresses, Southern entrepreneurs, and ranchers from mountain states; and the late-twentieth century campaigns for tax limitations and estate tax repeal mobilized homeowners and small businesspeople from old and new industries all over the country."[9] So these movements had unique characteristics but shared much in common—an interest in advocating for business interests and the wealthy.

Despite the similarities of goals, how movement leaders explain their goals has shifted over time. Today, advocates for tax reductions often frame policy arguments in terms of individual and economic liberty and downplay concerns about equity. One such group, The Club for Growth, explains that it "is a national network of over 100,000 Americans, from all walks of life and from all 50 states, who believe that prosperity and opportunity come through economic freedom."[10] Quite to the contrary, Martin's work claimed that across much of this history, the motivations of anti-tax advocates were overtly self-interested and purposefully unequal. He explained, "These movements were rich people's movements because they favored those who had *either* great wealth or great income *relative to others* in their society . . . The participants in every one of these movements defined their constituency explicitly on the basis of riches."[11] He continued, "The spokes people for these movements spoke up frankly and unabashedly in favor of more economic inequality. They typically claimed that a policy of unequal rewards was in the universal interests."[12]

As such, Martin's research dispels some of the recent rhetoric of anti-tax advocates, often voiced on behalf of business owners, that has tied reductions in property, income, and inheritance taxes to the principles of individual liberty, freedom, and the common good. Irrespective of the issue framing, for the first half of the 20th century, anti-tax advocates had a mixed record of policy success. Martin wrote of the ultimate failure of the movement to repeal the Income Tax: "progressives painted the tax club movement as a front group for the greedy rich."[13] During the 20th century, organized opposition thwarted some anti-tax movement ambitions. The labor movement's political power in states and also at the national level during the midcentury acted as a buffer against advocates for the wealthy, power that labor has largely lost at the start of this century.[14]

While I return to the significance of the labor movement later in the book, the sporadic success of anti-tax groups that Martin documented happens as certain American companies began to grow larger and a smaller number of companies controlled a larger share of the economy. There are many reasons for these changes in the American economy, including numerous mergers in the manufacturing[15] and agricultural sectors[16] as well as technological change and pro-business government policy. As Corporate America became increasingly dominated by a smaller and smaller number of larger and larger firms, collective action became much more feasible and the world of political influence increasingly attractive. As Mancur Olson would have predicted, a handful of large companies could coalesce around a common political platform much easier than could a constellation of small businesses.[17]

For the most part, these growing American companies—IBM, Ford, General Electric, and Pfizer—were absent from politics and policy making during the first half of the 20th century. Advocacy for business interests, at least according to Martin's retelling, happened in the loose style of a social movement, often lacking in effective coordination, resources, and consistent policy success. Until the 1970s, Big Business employed few lobbyists and wielded little explicit influence in Washington, which is not to say that national policy makers were deaf to the interests of business; rather, the influence of business was implicit and widely accepted on faith, thereby allowing most companies to safely claim that they stayed clear of politics.

It is hard to say exactly when American businesses woke up to their potential influence in Washington, but Jacob Hacker and Paul Pierson point to a significant memo written by a future justice of the Supreme Court.[18] Lewis Powell was appointed by President Nixon to the Court in 1971 and helped shape the Court's ruling in *Buckey v. Valeo*. Earlier that year, Powell, then a prominent tobacco industry lawyer and member of the U.S. Chamber of Commerce, addressed what he called an "Attack on American Free Enterprise System."[19] Powell's diagnosis of the problem, which he shared in memorandum form with the Chamber, focused on "the Communists, New Leftists, and other revolutionaries who would destroy the entire system," presumably the free market, capitalist system.[20] At the time, with Richard Nixon in the White House, this range of "varied and diffused" enemies was hardly a revelation. What was more surprising was what Powell recommended next. He wrote, "The painful truth is that business, including the boards of directors and the top executives of corporations great and small and business organizations at all levels have responded—if at all—by appeasement, ineptitude, and often ignoring the problem."[21] Powell found the existing "uncoordinated" corporate approach insufficient to the challenge. Instead, he called on "careful long-range planning and implementation, in consistency of action over an indefinite period of years, in the scale of financing available only through joint effort, and in political power only through united action and national organizations."[22] Powell believed the U.S. Chamber of Commerce "should consider assuming a broader and more vigorous role in the political arena" and that corporations needed to spend much more to help the Chamber do so.[23]

According to research by Lee Drutman, Powell's assessment of Corporate America, if not its foes, was essentially correct. Lobbying by corporations during the first half of the century was largely a hands-off affair. Drutman showed that prior to the 1970s, "Few companies saw the need to have their own representation in Washington," in part because of the generally favorable view held of Corporate American, but, in addition, Drutman explained that "The lack of any pressing government threat to business autonomy also meant that there was little reason for companies to spend much money on politics."[24] Rather than the type of direct lobbying and aggressive campaign work indicative of Pfizer today, a small number of Washington representatives of companies addressed legal difficulties and corporate communications and left the politicking to others, especially general business associations.[25]

Powell's advice to the U.S. Chamber apparently was met with an eager response, and the trade association initiated an aggressive move to expand corporate influence in Washington. This change occurred along two tracks—expanded association-based advocacy on the behalf of the business sector and massive growth in corporate lobbying to advance the interests of individual companies. Leading the charge on the association side was the U.S. Chamber of Commerce.

We now think about the Chamber as the loudest anti-government, pro-business voice in Washington. Indicative of this, Chamber president, Thomas Donohue, was quoted as complaining, "It's about time that our leaders in Washington start making the tough decisions that we pay them to make."[26] Surprising to most, this hostility to Washington was not always the case for the Chamber. Businesses in the early part of the 20th century asked President William Howard Taft to help them get started. They had been organized as an assortment of state and local Chambers but had no formal presence in the capital. In response to their pleas, President Taft made a call for a national business organization during his 1912 State of the Union and then later coordinated a summit to found the association. According to Alyssa Katz's *The Influence Machine*, "more than seven hundred merchants, bankers, tradesmen, and manufacturers, doing commerce in hides, cotton, dollars, wood, groceries, metals, and more, converged on Washington's new Williard Hotel" to found the new Chamber of Commerce.[27] Taft welcomed these businessmen from across the country and hoped their "disinterested advice" would aid government regulators.

By the 1970s, the U.S. Chamber operated as one of the primary voices of American business, but it had relatively few members and thus lacked the resources to intensify its lobbying efforts greatly. Again according to Katz, the Chamber soon expanded, growing its membership base from under 50,000 in 1976 to close to a quarter-million (234,000) by the early 1980s.[28] And with this growing base of member companies, the Chamber's budget tripled, permitting it to meet Powell's challenge.[29]

While the Chamber was growing its corporate membership, new, sometimes competing groups formed as well. The Business Roundtable, for one, soon joined the corporate fight in Washington but from an even more elevated perch. While the Chamber reflected its roots as the voice of companies large and small, the Business Roundtable, a 1972 merger of three other business organizations, had more exclusive goals. According to Hacker and Pierson, the Roundtable was "the first business association whose membership was restricted to top corporate CEOs."[30] Thus, the early 1970s were not notable simply for the awakening of business to politics but also the segmentation of business interests. As government had grown complex over the 20th century, businesses also grew specialized, and what might be in the interest of small businesses might not in fact meet the wishes of major corporations.

At the same time business associations ramped up advocacy efforts, individual companies began establishing new DC offices to pursue their own private goals. Just as manufacturers might not agree with financial institutions on how best to pursue fiscal policy, individual companies had particular interests, especially when it came to winning government contracts and congressional earmarks or "pork." As such, another innovation—if not invention—of this time period was the corporate lobbyist. Following the lead of men like Bryce Harlow at Proctor & Gamble, the major companies of the country created a new vocation in Washington: the DC company man.[31] Hacker and Pierson culled data that showed the number of corporations with a DC office grew five-fold between 1968 and 1978, the number of corporations with lobbyists increased by a factor of 14 between 1971 and 1982, and the number of corporate PACs increased fourfold between 1976 and 1980.[32] Hacker and Pierson concluded "On every dimension of corporate political activity, the numbers reveal a dramatic, rapid mobilization of business resources in the mid-1970s."[33]

Whereas a decade earlier, the U.S. Chamber of Commerce sat quietly in many Washington policy debates, the politics of the 1970s, 1980s, and beyond, heard the voice of business expressed much more loudly and with a greater variation of tone. Business, of course, was not alone. Other segments of the political arena found new representation in professional associations, citizen groups, and single-issue organizations.[34] But in terms of the magnitude of change, it was the explosion of business interests that so greatly changed how politics was to be done as the nation moved toward the end of the century. For example, in 1978, corporate PAC donations were on par with donations from labor PACs and trade association PACs at around $20 million. Just ten years later, in 1988, corporate PACs had doubled their contributions to $50 million, while labor PACs grew by less than 50%.[35]

Size and Characteristics of Business Spending on Politics

The expansion in the size of American business interests in national politics is hardly debated. What is contested, though, is whether growth has led to success. Has the awakening of business to politics over the last 50 years resulted in consistent victories in elections? Do powerful CEOs get to pick their elected representatives irrespective of what the rest of us want? And do those elected officials serve CEOs first?

Before we get to winning and losing, it makes sense to start with a better overview of recent corporate giving. If we compare other large corporations to Pfizer, we can see common but not identical political strategies. Some groups do not make any campaign contributions at all. Others give but do so infrequently and in minor amounts. And some give a lot, particularly relative to the overall size of the company. To demonstrate this, I collected data on 2014 campaign contributions and lobbying for all of the American companies in *Forbes* magazine list of largest companies in the world. These are massive companies with an average market value of $137 billion, including industrial giants, Exxon Mobil, Johnson & Johnson, and Boeing, as well as newer technology companies such as Apple, Google, and Microsoft. In Table 4.1 the top 15 from this list can be seen.

Table 4.1   Lobbying and PAC Campaign Contributions from Large
U.S. Corporations (ranked by Forbes)

Company	Market Value (in billions)	Total Lobbying (2014)	PAC Contributions (2014)
Berkshire Hathaway	$354.80	$7,204,000	$3,495,852
JPMorgan Chase	225.5	$6,280,000	$2,674,519
Exxon Mobil	357.1	$12,650,000	$1,931,230
General Electric	253.5	$15,170,000	$3,965,924
Wells Fargo	278.3	$6,400,000	$2,609,493
Apple	741.8	$4,110,000	$130,579
Chevron	201	$8,280,000	$2,122,682
Walmart Stores	261.3	$7,000,000	$2,366,579
Citigroup	156.7	$5,380,000	$2,577,433
Verizon Communications	202.5	$13,290,000	$3,414,629
Bank of America	163.2	$2,730,000	$2,992,884
Microsoft	340.8	$8,330,000	$2,941,683
AT&T	173	$14,200,000	$4,274,740
Johnson & Johnson	275.7	$7,667,500	$757,788
Procter & Gamble	224.3	$5,409,275	$383,516

Source: Data on company size from *Forbes*, "The World's Biggest Companies," http://www.forbes.com/global2000/list/#country:United%20States; Lobbying and PAC data from the Center for Responsive Politics, https://www.opensecrets.org/orgs/.

The way these companies participate in politics tells us a lot about the behaviors of major companies, if not companies in general. Figure 4.2 is a scatterplot of company size and campaign contributions. One of the first things we can see from this figure is that, at least for 2014, there was a positive correlation between the size of the company and the amount of campaign donations—larger companies seem to give more total contributions to support candidates. The magnitude of that relationship, though, is quite minor (correlation coefficient of .16). The same can be said for lobbying—large companies spend the most on lobbyists but the relationship between company size and lobbying is relatively small (correlation coefficient of .19).

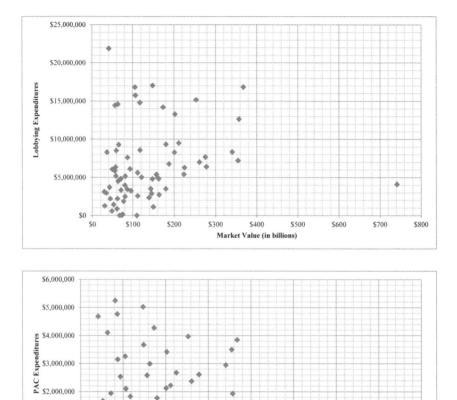

Figure 4.2   Relationship between Market Value and PAC/Lobbying Expenditures for Forbes Large Companies (Open Secrets, https://www .opensecrets.org/pacs/search.php)

One of the reasons for these weak correlations is that some companies spend almost nothing on lobbying or contributing: just 60% of Fortune 500 companies even maintain a PAC.[36] For example, Schlumberger, a multinational oil and gas services company with a headquarters in Houston, Texas, reported almost no political activity in 2014. Schlumberger's corporate philosophy prohibits direct political involvement: "Schlumberger is politically neutral, and has a long standing policy (set forth in our

Code of Conduct) against making financial or in-kind contributions to political parties or candidates, even when permitted by law. Our policy prohibits the use of Company funds or assets for political purposes, including for contributions to any political party, candidate or committee, whether Federal, state or local."[37] So the company does not maintain a PAC and prohibits the trade associations it joins, including the American Petroleum Institute and the Independent Petroleum Association of America, "from using Schlumberger funds to directly or indirectly engage in political expenditures."[38] So at least in terms of overt political involvement in American politics, Schlumberger is purposefully inactive, which is not to say that the company has no influence over energy policy making; it is just that its influence is not through the direct channels pursued by others.

Schlumberger differs greatly from other companies that engage in aggressive political action. For example, Anthem, the health care insurance company that operates Blue Cross and Blue Shield, ranks low on the list of largest companies, #167 on *Forbes* global ranking, but in 2014 was the largest on the list in terms of reported lobbying, $21,888,774.[39] Anthem also made $4.6 million in campaign contributions, ranking it the fifth largest corporate campaign donor on the list.

From these data, we can also observe that even for the largest corporate givers, contributions are tiny compared to the overall size of these companies. For instance, on average, these companies have $350,000 in market value for every $1 in campaign contribution, and somewhat less, $63,511, for every $1 in lobbying expenditure. So, while these are major campaign contributors, politics remains a miniscule percentage of company expenditures. This type of finding has pushed others in the past to ponder, not the magnitude of corporate spending, but "Why is there so little money in politics?"[40] This may be an overstatement, but even the most politically active corporation, likely spends more money on the most mundane elements of its business compared to the amount they spend on politics.

For companies that do participate in politics, lobbying and contributing to candidates often happens in a coordinated political strategy. As such, Figure 4.3 shows how contributions and lobbying are correlated for this group of large companies. We can see from these data that there is a positive relationship between contributing and lobbying, and this relationship is much stronger (correlation coefficient of .58) than for company size and lobbying or contributing. Most of these companies

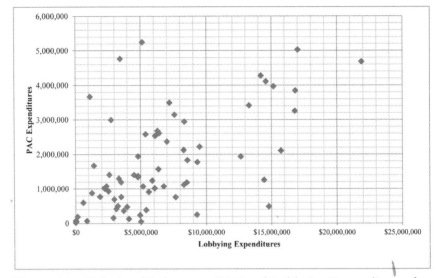

Figure 4.3   Relationship between PAC and Lobbying Expenditures for Forbes Large Companies (Open Secrets, https://www.opensecrets.org/pacs/search.php)

follow a similar pattern of lobbying and contributing, with just a handful of exceptions, such as Home Depot, which contributes ($3.6 million), much more than it lobbies ($1.1 million); and CVS Caremark, which lobbies ($14.7 million), more than it contributes ($485,325). On average, these large companies spend $3.78 in lobbying for every $1 in campaign contributions. It is important to note that this pattern may be more prevalent for large companies than for companies and interest groups in general, where previous research found a weaker connection.[41]

If we now go back to consider Pfizer's place in the assortment of major American companies, these data show that it is above average, much more politically active than others. Pfizer's 2014 lobbying of $9.4 million places it $3 million dollars above the average of $6.4 million for others in the group. Similarly, Pfizer is more active in campaigns that the typical large company. The average amount contributed is $1.7 million compared to Pfizer's $2.2 million in contributions in 2014.

Pfizer is a larger company, but it is also a company in the pharmaceutical sector. Another way to examine corporate participation in politics is to look at sectoral differences. American businesses pursue very different customers and commercial opportunities, possibly opening the need for different political strategies. For example, we might ask whether the technology sector, which has emerged over the last 20 years, uses a different approach to politics than more traditional industrial and financial companies. The evidence shows that, as the technology sector has grown in size, lobbying from that sector has also grown. The Mercatus Center found that, in the late 1990s, the information technology sector (including telecommunications, television/music/movies, telephone, and computer/Internet) spent under $200 million on lobbying.[42] Twenty-five years later, the industry doubled its lobbying, to just under $400 million. Within the sector, the computer/Internet subsector increased its lobbying the most, from less than $50 million to more than $100 million, with Google, Microsoft, and Hewlett Packard leading the way. This growth in spending from the sector makes sense because, over the same time period, the federal government has begun to address more sector issues, including regulating taxes on Internet sales, cybersecurity, and high-skilled immigration. Interest group scholar, David Truman, described such a theory of politics, called *Group Theory*, to explain how the emergence of new policy issues stimulates the growth of interest groups.[43] The increasing political engagement of technology companies follows from Truman's conception of political influence.

Nevertheless, the increases in spending from the technology sector have occurred while other sectors continue to maintain large lobbying and contribution totals. In 2014, the technology sector ranked fifth in terms of total reported lobbying ($122 million), behind lobbying for the pharmaceutical ($229 million), insurance ($151 million), and energy sectors ($141 million) and eighth in total contributions ($116 million) behind the financial industry ($507 million) (see Table 4.2). So the business sector has grown overall, adding new sectors to the range of what is considered in the interest of American business.

These various sectors may pursue some distinct political strategies, but they come together in the form of multisector trade associations. For example, as described earlier in the chapter, the U.S. Chamber of Commerce is one of the loudest supporters of American businesses and also a major campaign donor. Since the late 1990s, the Chamber has steadily increased its spending on campaigns to close to $300 million in 2014, primarily in independent expenditures.[44]

Finally, in addition to money from corporate PACs and money from business-affiliated trade associations, following the *Citizens United* decision detailed in the previous chapter, corporations can give money to

Table 4.2 Federal Lobbying Expenditures by Sector (2014)

Industry	Total Lobbying (2014)
Pharmaceuticals/Health Products	$124,832,898
Insurance	$75,304,905
Business Associations	$65,929,187
Oil & Gas	$64,252,393
Electronics Manufacturing & Equipment	$62,183,256
Electric Utilities	$61,371,043
Miscellaneous Manufacturing & Distributing	$55,044,971
Health Professionals	$52,017,259
Securities & Investment	$48,219,705
Hospitals/Nursing Homes	$46,758,462

Source: Data on lobbying drawn from Center for Responsive Politics, Open Secrets database, https://www.opensecrets.org/lobby/top.php?indexType=i&showYear=2015.

super PACs. In 2010, 19% of total super PAC revenue came from corporate PACs; two years later that had increased to 23% of the $800 million in total super PAC receipts.[45] To be sure, much of the remaining support for super PACs comes from individuals with close ties to business and not directly from corporations. For this reason, super PACs thus must be considered as a primary, and growing, source of political activity for business interests. I pick up the case of super PACs in more detail in Chapter 6.

BUSINESS AND WINNING CAMPAIGNS, CONGRESSIONAL VOTES, AND POLICY

Based on this historical evidence, it is hard to question the relative prominence of money from an assortment of business interests in politics. What remains uncertain is what results from this spending. In particular: (1) Do corporations get their way during election season?; (2) Do corporations get their way after the election during the legislative process?; (3) and do corporations get their way during the longer-term policy process? These seemingly obvious questions are actually quite difficult to answer without complex statistical calculations. Corporate donors spend money on campaigns and choose candidates to back for a variety of reasons. Business supports a mix of Democrats and Republicans, incumbents and challengers, as well as candidates that would likely win with no support and candidates with little hope of winning. The effect of an additional dollar of corporate money has only limited predictive power as to how many votes a candidates gets or how they will vote once in office. There are hundreds of interesting studies to demonstrate these complexities, but in the interest of space, I present several recent and important studies to portray the trend of the research.

First, spending more money on a campaign does not seem to lead to a larger share of the vote. Scholars have documented this with experimental and nonexperimental studies over the last several decades.[46] We also know that more money and electoral victory are not always linked: the wealthiest candidate doesn't always win. Jeffrey Milyo and Timothy Groseclose showed that congressional candidates' wealth did not predict electoral victory nor does it diminish the quality of opposition by scaring away less wealthy or well-supported competition.[47] Illustrative of this, Linda McMahon, CEO of World Wrestling Entertainment, twice lost in her quest to become the U.S. senator from Connecticut, despite spending $97 million of her own money, substantially more than her Democratic rivals.[48] Moreover, many candidates who raise a considerable amount of money from corporate PACs do win, but it is not always clear that the victory was contingent on the contributions. For example, in 2012, winning Senate candidates raised $724 million while losing candidates raised $387 million.[49] However, in close races, the two leading candidates often raised just about the same amount, as was the case in the 2012 presidential race, where President Barack Obama and Governor Mitt Romney raised similar amounts of money. In *Money Matters*, Robert Goidel, Donald Gross, and Todd Shields showed that some candidates who are outspent win congressional elections, and the authors conceded that "money provides no guarantee of electoral success," though they go on to explain that other factors, such as partisanship, strongly relate to which candidates typically have more money to spend.[50] So, corporate contributions do not guarantee electoral wins.

Second, it also seems that money and most visible aspects of legislating are not directly related. One of the seminal articles on the subject by John Wright found little evidence that PAC donations resulted in clear influence over legislative (roll call) votes.[51] One of the reasons for this is that other factors, such as partisan affiliation, have a much more consistent influence over how legislators vote. Indicative of this, Stephen Bronars and John Lott studied whether campaign donations might change how a legislator voted, what would be called "vote-buying."[52] It may be that a contribution from business acts as an exchange for that official to agree to vote in a certain way in the future, even if that exchange is not explicitly agreed upon and thus not an illegal bribe. Bronars and Lott, though, found that there was little evidence for the *vote-buying hypothesis*— member voting patterns rarely change, suggesting that a contribution given to shift a legislator's voting patterns would be wasted money, either the legislator agrees with you or they don't. Consistent with this evidence, former Congressman-turned-lobbyist Bob Walker explained in an interview for a book on lobbying, "The dirty little secret on lobbying is that nobody can persuade anybody to do something they wouldn't be in favor of doing anyhow," and continued about contributions, "the fact is, even without the money, the legislator would have made that decision anyway."[53] In the most cited meta-study of these relationships, Stephen Ansolabehere, John M. de Figueiredo, and James M. Snyder Jr. examined 40 studies and concluded "Overall, PAC contributions show relatively few effects on voting behavior."[54]

Third, in the aggregate, there is some agreement that corporate PAC contributions do not directly lead to control over legislative voting. Upon closer examination, however, contributions do seem to relate to certain types of legislative activity. Christopher Witko argued that if we take into account issue salience and partisanship, PAC contributions were correlated with the efforts committees put into legislative issues and legislative voting.[55] He looked at 20 congressional issues and found that campaign money increased the effort a committee put into partisan/ideological issues and influenced voting on nonideological/nonvisible issues. What this suggests is that money can increase the attention paid by committees to issues that are hotly contested along party or ideological lines. At the same time, on ideological issues, members of Congress can look to their party for guidance on how to vote, whereas on non-ideological issues, the party will provide less guidance, thus contributions can be more influential. While Witko conceded the larger point about PAC contributions and vote-buying, he raised this significant caution that certain forms of monetary influence may exist and may simply be a bit harder to observe.

Fourth, another reason for the unclear relationship between PAC donations and legislative voting is that while corporate PACs have increased candidate contributions over the last several decades, from under $50 million in 1990 to over $365 million in 2012, they seem to pursue risk-averse strategies and often reflect moderate ideologies. Business interests—corporate PACs and trade associations—tend to support those already in power rather than outsiders seeking power. Lobbyist Bob Walker explained, "Most of the money goes to your friends—to people who have supported you in the past and who have a record of being supportive of your issues."[56] So corporate PACs are not using money to win new friends; they are usually maintaining a relationship with the friends they already have. Political scientists refer to this as buying *access*, rather than buying legislative *votes*, and experimental evidence suggests that it works. Joshua Kalla and David Broockman designed an experiment where they sought to schedule a meeting with congressional offices but randomly assigned information about whether or not those attending the meeting were campaign donors.[57] Offices that received a meeting request indicating campaign donors would be attending were three to four times more likely to grant the meeting.

Corporate PACs use this logic when they develop campaign strategies. Those *friends* to whom Walker contributes often sit on the committees a corporation cares most about, meaning friendships can be short lived. For example, Eleanor Neff Powell and Justin Grimmer compared PAC donations to members of Congress who had lost versus gained key seats on policy committees following elections where majority control changed. They wanted to observe whether PACs, hoping to maintain access to those policy committees, rewarded those who gained a seat and punished those who lost a seat. Unlike the behavior of other types of PACs, they found that "business PAC contributions are consistent with a spot-market for short-term policy influence" by shifting donations to newcomers on key committees and away from those recently pulled off those committees.[58] This evidence suggests that corporate PACs are particularly attuned to using money to protect access, even ahead of partisan considerations or loyalty to old friends.

Further evidence of this can be found in the research of Suzanne Robbins on the medical industry. She found major trade medical associations almost always backed those in office: between 70% and 90% of the donations from the leading associations went to incumbents.[59] And when these groups do back open seat races, they spend the most on winners. Similarly, Jake Haselswerdt and Christopher Deering documented the preference for incumbents within the defense industry in 2010 and 2012.[60] As with the health care industry, defense companies targeted funding to incumbents with key positions on defense committees, suggesting again that access motivates corporate spending in the defense industry, not legislative vote-buying.

Not all research backs this impression that businesses make strategic donations to well-positioned members of Congress. Amy McKay examined campaign contributions by health care lobbyists to senators during the 2009 health care debate. McKay concluded, "Contrary to the access-buying hypothesis, we find that lobbyists do not take full advantage of their right to donate to the politicians who are writing legislation of great importance to the lobbying organization."[61]

Fifth, whether businesses do or do not target the right members of Congress, the preference to support friends and incumbent candidates is both a means to maintain legislative access and also a less risky proposition. Adam Bonica et al. showed that Fortune 400 companies split campaign contributions along partisan lines—some companies strongly favoring one party, while other companies favoring the opposite, but these corporate contributors tended to be ideological moderates, not partisan extremists.[62] One might, then, wrongly assume that a company that only gave to Republicans was solely interested in strongly conservative policies. Instead, for many companies, ideology is much more in the middle. This moderate sentiment fits with other findings on how corporate PACs contribute. Michael Franz found that corporations "hope to avoid a public airing of their political preferences," so they leave independent expenditures to trade associations.[63] Recall that independent expenditures typically pay for campaign advertisements. Using independent expenditures on advertisements would force the company to be quite public in their political views and partisan stance (i.e., "Company XYZ paid for this advertisement"), potentially risking offending customers who do not share the corporations views on politics. Instead, even though campaign contributions must be disclosed to the FEC, those disclosures are not usually aired on television and, thus, are somewhat more discrete for the company. This division of work, corporate PACs contributing to candidates while trade groups spending on independent expenditures, advances business interests while at the same time keeping company hands clean.

Sixth, it seems that money does not usually buy election wins or votes in Congress for business, but how does corporate money relate to broader policy outcomes? Policy making occurs across many institutions and venues of government, not just Congress, so it may be that when we expand our view, the prominence of business may grow. In *Lobbying and Policy Change*, Frank Baumgartner et al. provided one of the more comprehensive examinations of who influences federal government decisions.[64] We learn from that book that business is very well-represented in policy debates. More than a third (35%) of groups mentioned by those in their study advocated for business interests: trade and business associations (21%) or corporations (14%).[65] These findings align with research by Gilens and Page that found business interest groups possess numerical advantages in most policy disputes.[66] These advantages are magnified when we look at the volume of lobbying: Lee Drutman calculated that businesses spend $34 on lobbying for every $1 spent by nonbusiness interests, and 95 of the top 100 organizations that lobby represent business.[67] Businesses, though, were not alone in the Baumgartner et al. study: a quarter (26%) of the groups mentioned were citizen groups, 11% professional associations, and 6% unions. Business interests play a major part in policy making, much as they do during elections, but other nonbusiness interests do get a say.

In this public policy process with a mix of interests, businesses still maintain a large role, thus may extract the most positive outcomes. Much like the other unsupported hypotheses about business and politics, the evidence on this claim is also shaky. More corporate lobbying does seem to lead to somewhat better financial returns to shareholders, even holding constant the quality of the company.[68] A study by Frank Yu and Xiaoyun Yu found that companies that lobby more are less likely to be caught committing fraud.[69] Another study by Brian Richter, Krislert Samphantharak, and Jeffrey F. Timmons examined the amount corporations spent on lobbying versus their tax rate, expecting that lobbying could secure friendly tax arrangements. The authors found, "on average firms with higher lobbying expenditures in one year pay lower effective tax rates in the following year," but they did not "find that all firms that lobby obtain tax benefits."[70] Furthermore, while corporations clearly benefited from this lobbying, the authors concluded that the net public impact was likely to be relatively small: "If all of these firms increased their lobbying expenditures by 1%, the government would reduce the tax rate on these firms by 1.07%. The revenue loss the government would incur in this scenario would be approximately $12B."[71] So businesses may be able to extract particular benefits from government, but in doing so they may not greatly alter the direction of government.

Other research finds somewhat less convincing evidence for the strong link between corporate lobbying and public policy outcomes. Baumgartner et al. found that businesses with more resources—defined as a large amount of lobbying, contributions, and financial resources—"are slightly more likely to achieve their preferred policy position."[72] Another study by Marie Hojnacki et al. examined the role of business interests in a sample of 89 policy decisions in the 2000s to see which side typically wins and loses.[73] They found remarkable parity between business interests and nonbusiness interests. Business won many of the policy debates, but they also lost out just about as often as citizen groups and unions. Business interests do have certain advantages that relate to its largesse and cohesion.[74] Since businesses employ so many lobbyists, they are able to lobby on more issues and usually do it with a common policy view.[75] This means on some issues, businesses are nearly the only interest represented, and when this happens, they are much more likely to get their way than when other interests lobby alone.

So, businesses have policy clear advantages, but the system of advocacy does not always work in direct or obvious ways. In fact, there is evidence that lobbying, in general, irrespective of who is lobbying, has little impact on congressional action. Paul Burstein studied the resilience and eventual enactment of 60 policy proposals.[76] He showed that almost no measure of the size of advocacy related to how far a proposal got in Congress nor in whether it was enacted. So it may be that businesses are no different than any other organized interests; all similarly are perplexed by how best to influence policy outcomes.

Reconciling the Uncertain Influence of Business in Politics

The research evidence from political scientists, economists, and others is a mixed bag of support for the hypothesis that American business has grown all-powerful in American politics. While some important research, including the work of Gilens and Page, suggests that business interests get their way in general, when we look at the actual influence of specific corporate lobbying or contributing, the findings are less clear. What explains this lack of consistent social science evidence? There are at least three compelling theoretical explanations to reconcile this situation. One explanation rests on the resilience of the public policy status quo and strength of electoral incumbency, what we may call the *Family Dinner Thesis.* In many families, as most would attest, the weekly dinner tradition is a predictable affair, be it Sunday supper or taco Tuesday. Like it or not, food will be served at 5 p.m. on Sunday and tacos are *not* going to be served on Wednesday. Someone in the family, a favorite daughter or a grumpy uncle, often gets to choose their favorite meal and is always served first. The rest of the family still gets to eat but is usually served later. Much the same characterizes the role of business in Washington. At the federal level of government, at least, public policy choices are durable and designed to avoid frequent change. Change is not unheard of, but policy debates often result in negotiated compromises and only minor changes to the status quo. For business, often the favored child in the family, most government decisions already have strongly reflected their dominant voice in designing public policies. Businesses get to choose the meal and always eat first.

However, other competing interests, waiting patiently to be served later, can still help shape policy outcomes, and once a decision is reached, those interests are likely to fight as fiercely to maintain their concessions as business is to push for additional change. The last scraps of dinner can still be a meal. To this point, among the country's largest campaign contributors are labor unions, often opposed to business interests. The Service Employees International Union (SEIU) gave $222 million in contributions in 2014 and approximately $93 million came from both the American Federation of State/County/Municipal Employees and the National Education Association (NEA).[77] Unions, though they are declining in membership and influence, still remain a voice of opposition to corporate lobbying, and are often joined by citizen, ideological, and single-issue groups. So while business interests may give more money overall, they are not the only ones giving or participating in politics.

A policy process that has businesses overrepresented, but not alone, will tend over time to make repeated business-friendly decisions, although often the result of compromise. It is, then, hard to find an existing federal policy in which business interests lost outright, meaning businesses rarely lobby on issues that they have not already been successful in the past. Baumgartner et al. argued, "whatever bias in the mobilization of various social, business, and corporate interests may exist in Washington, this bias should already be reflected in the status quo . . . existing public policy is already the fruit of policy discussions, debates, and accumulated wisdom . . . if the wealthy are better mobilized and more prone to get what they want in Washington, they should already have gotten what they wanted in previous rounds of the policy process."[78] To belabor the dinner metaphor: years ago, businesses got to choose taco Tuesday; they cannot later change the menu, just because they want tacos on Monday.

So, if the business sector already dominates most public policy domains but cannot greatly alter that status quo, what explains such active lobbying and campaign activity? One way that scholars have reconciled this unpredictable tangle of relationships between business, contributions, and lobbying is to reinterpret the underlying assumptions and mechanism of the legislative process. Instead of vote-buying, as noted earlier, many scholars accept Richard Hall and Alan Deardorff's theory of *legislative subsidy*.[79] Rather than buying votes or using money to convince a legislator to change her mind, a corporate lobbyist—or any lobbyist for that matter—uses contributions to support already allied members of Congress. These members of Congress, short on time and staff, not only rely upon lobbyists to support reelection, but also, as importantly, to aid their legislative work. A corporate lobbyist can provide free information, analysis, and even bill writing to a member of Congress. Influence, then, will be seen in less obvious ways than voting, such as shaping which questions a legislator might ask in committee hearings. In these ways, money may buy a corporation a certain type of influence, but that influence cannot be easily observed in some of the visible ways we might expect. Business influence on policy making and legislating is much more implicit and subtle.

There is a corollary to this policy status quo argument in how to explain the imprecise relationship between corporate contributions and elections. As noted earlier, corporate PACs do not choose candidates at random; rather, they use electoral viability to rationalize campaign spending. Incumbent candidates begin a campaign from an advantageous electoral viability position because of institutional benefits such as franking privileges and numerous free opportunities to maintain high name recognition. These privileges are associated with fundraising advantages that lead to corporate PAC support. Incumbent candidates then tend to have more campaign money to spend and can raise money with less effort than challengers.[80] So incumbents start with financial advantages and seem to end with financial advantages as well, often in the form of an electoral victory.

Additionally, the political system is highly resistant to change. Changes in federal law and landmark court cases do not always have the major effects we would expect. For example, when the Court ruled in *Citizens United*, there were great expectations that business associations, such as the U.S. Chamber of Commerce, would change campaign strategies, possibly taking on a much more aggressive tone in communications. In 2010, following the ruling, the Chamber increased its overall political contributions, but the composition of that spending did not change markedly. Robert Boatright found that "the Chamber did not obviously change its strategy in response to *Citizens United*."[81] And in terms of the substance of the advertisements it paid for, Boatright claimed, "the Chamber did not do anything radically different from what it had done in the past." So before and after *Citizen United*, the Chamber and other business groups spent a lot of money on campaigns, but the new rules did not alter the underlying strategy. Interestingly, financial markets seemed similarly ambivalent to the ruling. Rather than anticipating that corporations could extract riches from new opportunities to support and oppose candidates, investors seemed to pay little attention. Timothy Werner found that after the *Citizens United* ruling, the stock prices of politically active companies did not change significantly compared to nonpolitically active companies. Werner concluded, "The result is that financial markets anticipated effectively zero future net effect on to firms' profits as a result of their new ability to independently spend unlimited amounts of money to engage in express advocacy at any time."[82] Thus, if corporations did not react to *Citizens United* as expected and financial markets did not react as expected, then maybe corporate political activity does not lead to exactly what we think it does.

In all of these cases, the power of the status quo and incumbency does not render money meaningless; rather, it suggests that other considerations precede decisions about money, thus the straightforward linear hypothesis about the relationship cannot be substantiated. A second argument to explain the role of business in politics suggests that the weak relationship between more political activity and consistently positive policy outcomes for business may be the mismatched incentives faced by corporate lobbyists and the companies that hire them, what we might call the *Self-Perpetuating Thesis*. The simple version of Lee Drutman's theory of the growth of lobbying, touched on earlier in this chapter, argues that lobbying begets more lobbying. Once a company establishes a lobbying presence in Washington to address a specific problem, the company's lobbyists will inevitably find new problems, regardless of whether the original problem was solved. So a technology company will invest in one DC lobbyist to fix a regulatory issue with the Federal Trade Commission (FTC) but soon finds a new federal grant from the National Science Foundation (NSF) or agency loan program from the Small Business Administration (SBA) that will require a second and third lobbyist. And once those lobbyists are in place, outfitted with a sleek K Street office, and senior company executives have been educated on how Washington politics works, the company will be unlikely to ever shut down the DC office. Drutman's argument suggests that the growth in lobbying expenditures and corporate lobbying may be occurring independently of whether or not those lobbyists are effective, rendering the relationship between lobbying and policy outcomes weak and unpredictable. Just as watering a garden twice as much will not necessarily yield a better crop, more and more lobbyists do not necessarily lead to more wins for business. Businesses may have grown in stature in Washington and wield great power, but the inefficiency of their lobbying expenditures make their influence unclear.

Mark Mizruchi puts forward a third explanation to evaluate the role played by American businesses over the last 40 years, what we might call the *Unconscientious CEO Thesis*.[83] For Mizruchi, today's business community wields little influence over federal policy making, because business leaders have become fragmented and obsessed with annual company profits rather than the longer-term interests of the business sector. Much like Lee Drutman, Mizruchi draws a stark difference between the period before and after the 1970s, not just in how businesses hired more and more lobbyists, but also in how willing business leaders have been to help solve national problems. According to Mizruchi, "there is a significant difference between the postwar era, which dates from 1945 to roughly 1973, and the period since then, in the willingness of American business leaders to mount a systemic effort to address the problems of our age." Mizruchi recognized that business has always had its parochial interests in mind, yet for the first half of the 20th century, business leaders could balance those with larger public interests and compromise with competing interests in a system of pluralism.[84] He wrote, "In earlier decades, the United States had a corporate elite that, however imperfect, was willing to see beyond the short-term interests of the firms that its members directed," which Mizruchi credited to "a relatively active and highly legitimate state, a well-organized and relatively powerful labor movement, and the financial community, which served as a source of interfirm consensus."[85] Mizruchi contrasted that period to our current predicament: "The corporate elite that exists today is a disorganized, largely ineffectual group . . . As a group, they are fragmented, however. Unlike their predecessors in earlier decades, they are either unwilling or unable to mount any systemic approach to addressing even the problems of their own community, let alone those of the larger society."[86]

For these reasons, addressing some of the most pressing issues of the day—health care reform, educational achievement, and management of the nation's finances—has been prone to gridlock and held hostage to the political extremes of two parties. Business leaders of the past would have been a force of consensus on these issues instead of a force of division.

Rather than share in a national conversation to reach consensus on the common good, Mizruchi sees the current Washington business community perfectly willing to go along with political voices that are unconcerned with government shutdowns or defaults on federal debts, both unambiguously bad policy outcome for business.

INDIRECT INFLUENCE OF BUSINESS

These three theses—*Dinner Table, Self-Perpetuating*, and *Unconscientious CEO*—each reconcile aspects of the mismatch between what many assume about the influence of businesses and the social science evidence. A fourth possibility is that we are simply looking in the wrong place for corporate influence over politics and policy. All three of the extant theories may be generally correct, and still the real influence of corporations may be found outside of the formal politics of legislating, what we might call the *Hidden Dragon, Crouching Tiger* theory. Corporations have several alternative, indirect routes to influence policy—Gilens and Page called this the *second face* of power—that may precede and be hidden from the first face of power that happens during the legislative process.[87] John Kingdon famously portrayed the agenda setting aspects of the policy-making process as occurring in three streams: politics, policy, and problem.[88] Much of the existing research on the relationship between money and politics has been firmly situated in that politics stream, where congressional committees consider final decisions and later vote on legislation and presidents issue executive orders and execute national policy. Less attention has focused on corporate influence in the other two streams of Kingdon's model, and it is in those parts of the policy-making process that corporations also are playing a growing role.

Policy Stream

Rather than elected officials, think tanks and research institutions make up the policy stream. Since World War II, think tanks, such as the Brookings Institution, were purposefully independent, both from partisan politics and also outside influence.[89] Think tanks were to function as miniature universities and produce scientific evidence on government. Over time, though, think tanks have grown much more politicized and ideological. At the same time, corporations and corporate money have played more prominent roles in funding think tank operations. Take the Center for American Progress (CAP), one of the leading progressive think tanks in the country. While companies provide only 6% of total revenues, many of the leading corporate contributors to political campaigns are also donors to CAP. Apple, Google, Citigroup, and Walmart all gave between $100,000 and $499,000 in 2014.[90] These donations—often channeled through a foundation associated with the company—do not count as lobbying, but they clearly help CAP advance policy positions and shape policy outcomes. And because CAP is registered as a 501(c)(3) nonprofit organization (it also maintains a separate but related 501(c)(4)), it is not required to disclose the sources of its funding, and the donations are tax deductible. CAP released information on its funders only after there was increasing media attention to its political activities.[91] CAP is not alone; corporate foundations have also funded other think tanks of different ideological orientations with growing enthusiasm.

What a company gets from its corporate foundation's grant-making activities is not always clear. In some instances, it appears that grants lead to support in policy debates that are important to the corporation. For example, the *New York Times* investigated the relationship between Comcast's corporate philanthropy and the work of its grantees.[92] At issue was Comcast's disputed merger with Time Warner. The Federal Communications Commission (FCC) was considering whether to approve the merger or whether it would violate antitrust laws. The FCC received thousands of comments supporting and opposing the deal, many from those with close financial ties to Comcast. Important think tanks, including Americans for Tax Reform, the American Enterprise Institute, the Institute for Policy Innovation, Competitive Enterprise Institute, the Free State Foundation, and the Center for Individual Freedom, all publicly endorsed the merger and had received grant support from Comcast.

This does not prove that the Comcast grants resulted in the think tank endorsements, but the intermingling of charity with policy is hard to deny. Because of limited disclosure regulations, it is hard to fully appreciate the influence of corporations on the policy work of think tanks and research organizations. As they do for candidates and elected officials, corporations are likely to donate to think tanks that already share an ideological perspective or view on policy. Nevertheless, the same questions about the appearance of undue influence from corporate PAC contributions can also be raised about corporate support for think tanks. For instance, will a donation shift the research agenda of a think tank from one issue to another? Will corporate donors have a say over the final policy recommendations made by think tank researchers? It is hard to answer these questions, but companies do seem to care about supporting think tank operations, and this suggests that these questions should be answered.

Problem Stream

In addition to indirect influence over policy through the policy stream, in Kingdon's problem stream—where researchers and nonprofit practitioners collect and analyze data to measure and address policy problems—business leaders have also become much more directly involved. Foundations, including corporate foundations, often provide the funding to support nonprofit organizations engaged in this type of policy work. Recall, corporations can also support the issue advocacy and election work of politically oriented 501(c)(4) nonprofit organizations. In addition, 501(c)(3) nonprofits participate in advancing policy agendas outside of the electoral realm, opening another avenue for corporate policy influence without having to disclose anything to the government or the public. Corporations can then indirectly influence policy by funding certain nonprofit organizations that pursue a common view of policy and not funding others.

To be sure, all types of foundation grant funding have grown of late, but corporate philanthropy alone grew nearly $2 billion over the last decade from $3.4 billion in 2002 to $5.3 billion in 2013, as the total number of corporate foundations remained stable (2,357 in 2002, 2,577 in 2013).[93] Most large companies now maintain a corporate foundation to do charitable philanthropy—80% of the group of large companies studied at the start of this chapter—and some of that money goes to influencing public policy.[94] Interestingly, as there was a positive correlation between company size and direct forms of political influence, lobbying, and campaign contributions, there also is a positive correlation for this indirect form of political influence. Figure 4.4 shows this positive relationship with data on total corporate foundation spending.

Other changes in philanthropy have brought an even closer connection between those with money and the public policy work of nonprofit organizations. Historically, private foundations were established in the name of a wealthy and recently deceased individual. The staff and board of a foundation would then carry out the last wishes of the departed philanthropist into the future. In more recent decades, there has been an increase in living philanthropists who want to spend their earned riches on changing the world while they are still alive. Rather

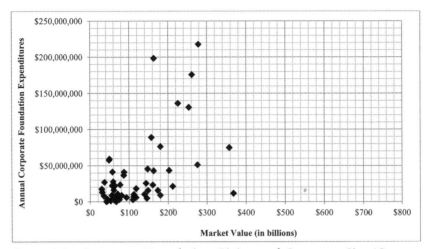

Figure 4.4   Corporate Foundation Giving and Company Size (Open Secrets, https://www.opensecrets.org/pacs/search.php)

than neutral donors, newer trends in giving have created hands-on foundations with strong policy preferences. For example, Sarah Reckhow showed in her book, *Follow the Money: How Foundation Dollars Change Public School Politics*, that living philanthropists have helped funnel money through their foundations to pursue a particular agenda on school reform.[95] She wrote, "Newly wealthy individuals have taken charge of giving away their own money, and they are actively seeking to change public policy."[96] The Bill and Melinda Gates Foundation, though not directly affiliated with Microsoft, relies on an enormous reserve of money to support nonprofit organizations that align with the foundation's view of education, which emphasizes choice and testing, diminished teacher union control, and small schools. Reckhow showed, "Most of the grants from the Gates Foundation to grantees in New York City—around $20 million in 2005—were devoted to nonprofits to support the creation of small schools."[97] Without this large amount of foundation support, it seems much less likely that this dimension of education policy reform would be as successful.

Whether money comes from corporate foundations or from the private foundations set up by business leaders, none of this supposedly philanthropic money is counted as a form of lobbying. Despite its profound influence on the direction of public policy, few concerned about money and politics connect philanthropy to the advancement of corporate interests. This much more hidden type of influence thus must be accounted for when we consider the deeper questions about how the business sector can shape politics and public policy.

CONCLUSION

Business has always had a role in politics, Chapter 3 confirmed that truism. The nature of that role has shifted from scattered social movements pushing for tax relief for the wealthy to much better organized and well-funded national lobbying and electioneering. While businesses have increasingly mobilized together, individual businesses have sought out their own private stake through teams of corporate lobbyists. What was once a fight for the broad interests of the rich and general well-being of big business has been transformed by the self-interest of individual corporate lobbying, such as Pfizer. In some cases, this leads to clear benefits for individual firms, such as lower taxes and government earmarks; in other cases, the evidence is much less clear.

In the process of this transformation of Washington politics, the age-old questions about corruption must be revisited. While the U.S. Chamber of Commerce may not fight for all Americans, at least when it contributes to a candidate or lobby a member of Congress, it can claim to represent thousands of companies and be acting out of the collective interest of a major sector or the economy. When Pfizer, Anthem, or Google does the same, can we be so sure? If corruption relates to extracting private benefits from public actors, this age of corporate political activism may just be the age of legalized corruption or the emergence of what some have dubbed plutocracy in America.[98]

While unquestionably prominent, social science research suggests that corporate and business leaders do not always get their way. If the massively larger spending on lobbying and campaign contributions does not systematically lead to predictable outcomes, we also must sharpen our thesis about the relationship between money and politics. Since corporations regularly walk the line between influence and bribery with uncertain rewards, then other factors must also be considered.

The next two chapters add new perspectives to this inquiry. The next chapter moves members of Congress to the center in order to address the question: how have elected officials participated in the evolution of money and politics? Rather than passive players, legislators bear the brunt of a system of increasing amounts of political money, while at the same time creating the mechanisms that facilitate that process. Have they done their jobs to promote political participation while curbing various forms of corruption? The next chapter offers an answer.

Overall, though, the evidence from this chapter continues the paradoxical story of money and politics in American politics. Once passive participants in politics, in every measurable way, corporations have increased the money they use to influence politics. It remains puzzling why these increases have not been linked to consistently measurable policy outcomes. Perhaps the three theoretical perspectives offered at the end of the chapter offer explanations, but the real answer may be found in more precise and fine-grained analysis of new data. The transparency measures created by various acts of Congress result in considerable new information, though it may not be the right kind of data to discover the real ways that money influences politics. For this reason, novel transparency measures may offer a greater hope to researchers and those interested in public corruption. For example, we may need to know more about corporate philanthropy and donations to 501(c)(3) nonprofit organizations to dig deeper into the influence of corporations on public policy. More research on the changing role of think tanks, research organizations, and nonprofit organizations may also fill important gaps in the literature. In the final chapter, I examine these proposals and their feasibility and what they might offer future researchers.

Chapter 5

Money at the Capitol

Each year, Citizens for Responsibility and Ethics in Washington (CREW) announces its list of the "Most Corrupt Members of Congress."[1] This rogues' gallery of misconduct and dishonor highlights the most egregious violators of the public trust and the law.

In 2013, CREW began the report detailing the misdeeds of Democratic Congressman Rob Andrews of New Jersey. Andrews had the bad habit of using campaign contributions on his family and friends. He spent $13,000 in campaign funds to fly his family to Edinburgh, Scotland, to attend a wedding. While Andrews explained that this was acceptable because the wedding was of a campaign donor, he reimbursed his campaign committee after an investigation by the Office of Congressional Ethics. Later in the year, Andrews hosted a campaign event that doubled as a graduation party for his daughter. His campaign committee paid $10,000 for the festivities. At other times, CREW reported, the Andrews campaign committee spent $100,000 on trips to California for Andrews and his daughter and made tens of thousands of dollars in donations to various theatrical performances in which his daughter was a featured performer. Andrews also helped to direct $1.5 million in congressional earmarks to Rutgers University School of Law, at which his wife was employed as a dean.

These acts committed by an elected official border on the farcical. Most would demand: how did you think you could get away with it? Andrews offended most principles of public trust and possibly violated ethics rules of the House of Representatives and aspects of FECA. Misdeeds like these also likely explain the fact that confidence in Congress has remained below 30% for the last decade.[2] Nevertheless, amid congressional investigations, Congressman Andrews resigned from

Congress and joined a private law firm to run its government affairs group.[3] Andrews's reward for violating public trust, if not the law, was probably a significant bump in salary and the opportunity to lobby his former House colleagues for the firm's clients.

This is the type of public corruption that generates headlines and public attention, and money is often the trigger. Public officials who use their authority to redirect money from the general good to their private benefit are corrupt, even if a successful prosecution of such violations is exceedingly difficult. And Andrews's apparent temptations did not make him unusual: members of Congress are routinely investigated. Ask most people what they know about Congress and many will mention the type of pay-to-play relationships at the center of the "Casino" Jack Abramoff scandal of the mid-2000s that led to the conviction of Congressman Bob Ney of Ohio.[4] Or when the FBI found $90,000 in bribes wrapped in tinfoil in the refrigerator of Louisiana Congressman William Jefferson.[5] Perhaps most infamously, in 2005, Congressman Randall "Duke" Cunningham, also from Louisiana, was sentenced to an eight years for bribery and tax evasion. Cunningham pleaded guilty to charges that he accepted $2.4 million in bribes from defense industry executives for helping them win $240 million in military contracts.[6] At the time of the writing of this book, ten members of Congress were under ethics investigation, four Republicans and six Democrats.

Earlier in the book, I tracked concerns about these types of corruption back to the founding of the country. Overt forms of corruption remain a public problem, particularly for Congress, and illegal. However, as Chapter 4 showed, covert or indirect forms of influence and corruption must also be better understood. For every Rob Andrews, there are hundreds of members of Congress who will never be investigated for violating campaign finance laws and ethics rules, yet each must raise hundreds of thousands of dollars to win reelection. How does this change the way Congress functions and legislative power is distributed? Thus far, we have looked at the phenomenon of money and politics from the outside, from the perspective of the public-at-large, mega campaign donors and Corporate America. This chapter shifts focus to the elected officials who sit at the center of the nexus of money and politics. How has the increase in corporate money changed how members of Congress do their jobs while in Congress and after? And, if the public-at-large is so uncomfortable with the outsized role of money and politics, how do elected officials represent these concerns in an era of increasing inequality and polarization?

MONEY AND RUNNING FOR CONGRESS

The last chapter went far in describing the magnitude of change in money and politics. American business interests greatly expanded participation in Washington politics and did so by spending enormous amounts on lobbying elected officials and contributing to candidates. On the other side of those contributions are incumbent members of Congress—or campaign challengers—eager to win elections. From the perspective of congressional candidates, the enormity of the change in money and politics is just as dramatic as the change for business.

Without recounting the long history of the institution, recall that the Constitution established Congress as the bicameral home of lawmaking. Intended to be the center of the new federal system of government, the Framers of the Constitution conferred numerous powers to the House and Senate, including the power to set taxes, spend money, and regulate interstate commerce. Frequent elections, particularly in the House of Representatives, would tie elected officials to their constituents and promote a benign representative orientation to the work of Congress. Corruption, vice, and self-service would be limited by compelling members of the House to seek out votes from those in their district every two years. It would then be in the best interest of an ambitious member of Congress to serve the interests of constituents first and with great devotion, knowing that an opponent could be lurking in the wings, waiting to pounce on any indiscretion. In *Federalist* No. 57, James Madison wrote, "Such will be the relation between the House of Representatives and their constituents. Duty, gratitude, interest, ambition itself, are the chords by which they will be bound to fidelity and sympathy with the great mass of the people."[7]

Though the Founders were opposed to public campaigning for office as an unseemly aspect of democracy, political parties soon formed and competition for elective office grew to become a national pastime. For most of American history, political parties operated the machine of political campaigning. The power of parties, according to David C. W. Parker, meant "the need to gather electoral resources outside the party apparatus was low."[8] Candidates for a seat in Congress could rely upon a robust and well-funded partisan operation of communication, staffing, and voter turnout.

As parties waned in influence in the 20th century, the fundraising burden has shifted to candidates. Indicative of this, at the time of the passage of FECA, and before the *Buckey v. Valeo* decision, spending in all House races totaled $211 million (adjusted for inflation).[9] According to the Campaign Finance Institute, 40 years later, in 2014, that figure had quadrupled to $821 million, despite no increase in the size of Congress or a major change in the number of contested races. A major difference between then and now is the ability of incumbent candidates to raise and spend money. In 1974, incumbents and challengers spent about the same: on average, $271,497 for incumbents and $192,150 for challengers. Incumbents had a spending advantage but a limited one. Today, incumbents in the House spend, on average, $1.44 million, nearly triple the amount compared to the $498,941 for challengers.

Incumbents have always had advantages in reelections, but the differential access to money has deepened the advantage, increasing the percentage of incumbent wins in Congress from around 85% in the 1960s to around 95% in the 2000s.[10] For example, in 1986, winning candidates in the House of Representatives spent on average $359,577 ($776,687 in 2014 dollars) and $3.06 million ($6.6 million in 2014 dollars) in the Senate. In 2014, House winners spent on average $1.46 million and Senate winners spent $9.65 million. For the 22 successful challengers in 2012, the cost to beat an incumbent, a rare occurrence, was $2.4 million, on average.[11] These are substantial increases in the amount of money a candidate, be it an incumbent or challenger, must raise in order to win.

Much of this money, as the previous chapter showed, comes from corporate PAC contributions, but that has not been the only change in the way money has shaped congressional campaigns. Another major change has been in which ways congressional campaigns spend money. Campaigns pay for all sorts of ways to promote the candidate, including purchasing many classic campaign items such as $3,100 spent by Jim Graves for Congress on buttons, $18,000 worth of lawn signs bought by Recchia for Congress, and $5,300 from Mia Love's congressional campaign to pay for bumper stickers.[12] From the 1960s onward, campaigns increasingly relied upon television advertising to sell candidates to voters.[13] A televised ad can promote the legislative accomplishments of an incumbent candidate or the new vision and promise of a challenger. Whether positive or negative, personal or policy oriented, the time for a televised advertisement must be bought from a television station. Unlike previous campaign tactics, such as yard signs, posters, and bumper stickers, advertising on television is expensive. While the price per advertisement on local television ranges considerably from market to market, the *Washington Post* reported one typical 30-second advertisement purchased by Bruce Braley in the 2014 Iowa Senate race cost $2,290.[14] In 2014, approximately 28% of the $952 million spent on congressional races went to advertising (around 12% went for fundraising and 42% for salaries and administration), much of that for television advertising.[15] With public data, it is difficult to know exactly how much the televised advertising cost, but the Wesleyan Media Project estimated that television advertisements cost $154 million for House races in 2014.[16]

We can understand this better by looking at how two specific candidates in the House, one a Democratic challenger, another a Republican incumbent, spent on their campaigns (See Table 5.1). Cathy McMorris Rodgers ran as a four-term incumbent from Washington State in 2014. She was a Republican on the rise, having recently been elected chair of the House Republican Conference. On the other side of the country, Clay Aiken, one of the singing stars of "American Idol," challenged Renee Ellmers, the first-term Republican member of Congress from North Carolina, who had initially won her seat as a Tea Party favorite in 2010.[17]

McMorris Rodgers ran against a Democratic challenger, Joe Pakootas, who spent just $188,062 on his campaign—44% on advertising. McMorris, though a near lock from the start of the campaign, dedicated merely a quarter (25%) of her $3 million in campaign expenditures on advertising. One of McMorris's ads was titled "Liberty" and featured her speaking directly to the camera about fighting the Obama administration on

Table 5.1 2014 Campaign Spending of Select Congressional Candidates (percentages are based on reported and categorized expenditures)

	Total Spent	Advertising	Fundraising	Salaries and Administration
Cathy McMorris Rodgers	$2.9 million	25%	32%	23%
Jay Pakootas	$188,062	44%	3%	42%
Clay Aiken	$1.1 million	29%	12%	43%
Renee Ellmers	$1.8 million	44%	2.5%	41%
All House Candidates	$1.0 billion	27%	12%	42%

Source: Data drawn from Center for Responsive Politics, Open Secrets database and the FEC database of campaign finance, http://www.opensecrets.org/politicians/.

regulations, health care reform, and the Internal Revenue Service (IRS).[18] In "Gratitude and Respect," McMorris Rodgers addressed veterans' issues.[19] Another ad, "What Drives Me," featured McMorris talking about her constituents and several bipartisan bills she passed in Congress.[20] Interestingly, compared to others, a larger percentage of her spending went to fundraising, a third (32%) of all of her campaign's spending. As a rising member of her party, McMorris Rodgers was counted on to help bring in the money to maintain the party's majority in Congress (an issue I pick up later in this chapter). McMorris Rodgers easily won the race but later faced an investigation from the Office of Congressional Ethics for improper use of campaign contributions.[21]

In North Carolina, Clay Aiken, a political novice, spent his money in a similar way to McMorris Rodgers but with less of a focus on fundraising. Aiken spent approximately $1.17 million on his campaign. Compared to McMorris Rodgers, though, Aiken faced much stiffer competition. Aiken's opponent, the incumbent Republican candidate, Congresswoman Renee Ellmers, spent $1.8 million, approximately 44% on advertising.[22] Aiken's ads, including "Open Door," focused on his personal story as a survivor of family abuse and his strong relationship with his mother.[23] Another Aiken ad, "Send a Message," attacked Ellmer's congressional voting record and statements she made during a government shutdown.[24] While Aiken and Ellmers spent about the same amount of money, the power of incumbency and a largely Republican district won out. Aiken ultimately lost to Ellmers, who was also backed by outside money, including $102,035 from Americans for a Conservative Direction.[25]

Was McMorris Rodgers's large edge in money over her opponent the reason she won? And why did Aiken lose if he could draw on a million-dollar campaign war chest? Research presented in the previous chapters showed some of the reasons why it is difficult to definitively answer these questions and why money and electoral victories are not neatly tied together in a causal chain. Nonetheless, how much it costs to win a congressional election has clearly grown. In the race to win, congressional candidates now spend enormous amounts of time raising money to run, and even once elected, fundraising for the reelection campaign begins on Day 1 in Congress. How much time members of Congress spend is difficult to know precisely. One member of Congress, speaking with anonymity, claimed than the figure is between 50% and 75% of a member's schedule.[26] A 2013 survey suggested something much lower, that members of Congress spend between 17% and 18% of their time on campaigning, much less than the time devoted to legislative work or constituent services.[27] Other evidence suggests this estimate is much too low, particularly for new members of Congress. A presentation that was delivered to incoming Democratic members by the Democratic Congressional Campaign Committee recommended spending four hours a day on "call time," a reference to when the member of Congress makes phone call after phone call to potential campaign contributors.[28] It is likely the amount of time varies by member, but there are many reasons to believe that the changing financial character of Congress has greatly increased the pressure to raise money on all members.

The importance of raising money to win a seat in Congress has also changed who serves. National office has always been dominated by elites, but overtime, those elites have come to resemble a smaller and smaller stratum of the population. Between 2004 and 2013, the median wealth of those in Congress increased from approximately $630,000 to $843,000 in the House of Representatives and $1.7 million to $2.7 in the Senate.[29] Nicholas Carnes investigated the backgrounds of members of Congress in his book *White-Collar Government*. He showed that, measured in terms of education, profession, and wealth, members of Congress are unusually well off. The average member of Congress has a median net worth 19 times the typical family living in the United States, and, in 2013, there were seven members of Congress worth more than $100 million.[30] Measured in terms of professional background, the differences are just as stark. Carnes found that half of the members of Congress were either the owner of a private business or a lawyer, compared to just a tenth of the larger American population. And of the nearly 800 members of Congress that served between 1999 and 2008, less than 1% had worked for any considerable period of time in a blue-collar job.

Money—and what is often associated with access to money—has exacerbated an already elite institution. Without money, it is nearly impossible to launch a congressional campaign. Money acts as a barrier to entry into campaigns, leaving the pool of candidates an assortment of bankers, lawyers, and minor celebrities. Money may not win an election, but it does set the parameters for who is and is not a viable candidate. Consequently, those who win a seat in Congress look like their new colleagues much more so than they do the constituents they serve.

MONEY AND THE WORK OF CONGRESS

The need to fundraise has clearly altered the work of members of Congress, even if every member does not devote the same amount of time to soliciting campaign funds. That change, though, has not happened in isolation. It occurs alongside major changes in the way Congress is run and the core motivations of the two political parties. The growing importance of maintaining majority control has reoriented power in Congress away from historic centers of power—committee chairs—toward party leaders and those members who can raise money. Whereas fragmentation of power had dominated Congress in the 1970s and 1980s, power has been centralized and institutionalized ever since. Writing about this change, Jacob Hacker and Paul Pierson surmised, "The Congressional leadership now enjoys extensive authority to decide which issues get debated and which alternatives get considered. It now eagerly uses so-called closed rules to limit debate and quell minority input. It now regularly yanks committee chairs and other perks away from wayward members."[31] These changes have been made possible through new sources and uses of money.

There was a time when campaigning was relatively inexpensive and the seniority system ruled Congress. Those days are largely over. With increasing ideological polarization across the parties and decreasing bipartisanship in Congress, according to Eric Heberlig and Bruce Larson, control of the majority has become the central motivation of Republicans and Democrats. Since the 1990s, party leaders from both parties, especially Speakers Newt Gingrich and Nancy Pelosi, have demanded growing levels of loyalty to help maintain or regain power, what David Rohde called Conditional Party Government.[32] And congressional leaders have done so by controlling money.

One of the ways that the two parties leverage money to concentrate power and seek out the majority is through dues payments charged to each member of the caucus. Staring in the 1991–1992 campaign, Vic Fazio, a leading Democrat from California, introduced a "suggested" payment of $5,000 for each Democrat in the House to the party's congressional campaign committee.[33] Under Bill Paxon of New York, the Republicans soon followed suit and began to use payment of these dues as a basis for advancement in the party.[34] By the end of the decade, both parties had fully adopted the practice, and dues rose to tens of thousands. In 2006, dues skyrocketed into the hundreds of thousands, and more—up to $600,000—if the member of Congress hoped to gain a position in the leadership.[35]

As one might expect, newly mandatory dues payments did not sit well with all members of Congress. The *New York Times* quoted Congresswoman Maxine Waters from California responding to pressure to pay party dues: "Nobody puts the screws on me. I don't allow that . . . I'm not trying to prove anything to anybody. Some years I've raised a lot, some years I've not raised so much, so I'll do whatever I do."[36] Other members of Congress have refused to pay certain dues because of disagreements with party leaders.[37]

A second factor accelerated the need for congressional leaders to squeeze their members for money. In 2002, when Congress passed BCRA, it banned the soft money that had been on the rise in the 1990s. As Chapter 3 showed, that money was a source of power, as national parties could distribute it to state parties to support electioneering. With this source of funds cut off, congressional leaders had to rely even more on incumbents able to raise money.[38] Donations from incumbents to the party's congressional committees increased from under $20 million in 1990, to over $100 million by 2010.[39] According to Heberlig and Larson, "Contributions from House incumbents are now also the most important source of direct contributions to candidates in the party network."[40] Even compared to support from the entertainment industry and energy sector, they concluded that "by 2006, incumbent contributions from House members to other candidates surpassed the contributions of each of these politically potent industries" and businesses in general.[41]

The shifting fundraising burden to incumbents helps to explain the intense focus on "call time" mentioned earlier in the chapter. Fundraising is not just a feature of self-preservation and reelection, but it is increasingly used as a way to preserve and advance the party. Congressional leaders use dues contributed by those in the party to support incumbents at risk of defeat and to support challengers. In doing so, congressional leaders have changed the nature of Congress itself. Unlike in the past, an ambitious new member of Congress must fundraise to excel in the party, to be given a prized seat on a key committee, and to be elected to a position in the leadership. Seniority no longer dictates who will rise; money does. And, according to Heberlig and Larson, incumbents who reject calls to contribute to the party "risk undermining their ability to achieve their individual goals."[42]

Money, then, shapes the daily work of every member of Congress, their future electoral success, and any hope they have to rise in their party. One of the great ironies of the last two decades of Congress has been while fundraising and campaign spending has grown considerably, Congress has worked to end the way money has typically functioned in Congress: earmarks. Whether they are called a pet project, district pork, or an earmark, members of Congress have always used their authority over federal spending to direct money back to their districts. Unlike most federal spending, which is distributed based on a formula, criteria, or existing program, an earmark is a specified amount of money in a spending bill dedicated to a particular project. In its most romantic form, this has been viewed as a way that members represented faraway constituents in DC and also curried their favor for reelection. Members of Congress campaigned on their ability to bring money back to the district and made sure to take credit for every federal dollar that ended up spent in the home district. Whether it was the construction of a military facility, road, or research project housed at a local university, these projects accrued to powerful members of Congress and promoted stability by ensuring senior members would be reelected. Typically, earmarks benefited those on key committees, such as the Appropriations Committee in the Senate. Christopher Berry and Anthony Fowler found that those serving on the Appropriations Committee were given twice as much in earmark expenditures than those not on the committee, though they suggested that difference was not only explained by committee membership, and the most demonstrable benefits came to committee chairs.[43]

Earmarks also frequently aligned with bipartisanship, since many states have a mix of Republican and Democratic members of Congress. Between 2008 and 2010, many of the largest earmarks were requested by a Democrat and Republican working together. Senators Thomas Harkin (D) and Charles Grassley (R) from Iowa requested a $500,000 earmark as a part of funding the Federal Highway Administration to pay for work on the "10th Avenue South Corridor Extension" in Waverly, Iowa.[44] Senators Judd Gregg (R) and Jeanne Shaheen (D) requested $1.3 million for federal support of the Appalachian National Scenic Trail in their home state of New Hampshire. To be sure, these are big money projects, but earmarks totaled a tiny fraction of total government spending, dwarfed by non-earmark spending on defense and entitlement programs, and made up even a small fraction of total discretionary spending.[45]

This type of spending, of course, also drew the ire of critics, especially budget hawks affiliated with the Tea Party, who saw it as pork, wasteful of scarce federal money, and an inefficient way to run a government.[46] Despite making up a tiny portion of overall federal spending, reforms of the late 2000s effectively ended the overt form of congressional earmarks.

In 2011, when Republicans took back control of the House, they placed a moratorium on earmarks. Jim DeMint, then a senator from South Carolina, said, "I am proud that House and Senate Republicans have united to end the earmark factory . . . It's time for Congress to stop focusing on parochial pet projects."[47] Not too surprisingly, like the clever campaign contributors able to outsmart FECA and BCRA restrictions, new avenues to support district projects emerged. *Lettermarking* and *phone-marking* are two ways that members of Congress can communicate their parochial wishes to those in the executive branch with authority over where money will be spent without legislating.[48] Sometimes called *soft earmarking,* this alternative form of pork-barrel politics shifts nominal control over spending to the bureaucrats, while maintaining the congressional goal of bringing federal money back to constituents and abiding by the ban on hard earmarks.

Nonetheless, during the era of expanding money and politics, members of Congress mustered sufficient political will to eliminate one of the most obvious ways that money and politics are related on Capitol Hill. We might ask: have members of Congress acted in other policy ways to stem corruption and represent the vast majority of their constituents? One answer is "yes." First, in the previous two chapters, I showed how Congress has passed laws, such as FECA and BCRA, each aimed to limit corruption during campaigns. And, second, following the scandals of the mid-2000s involving lobbyist Jack Abramoff, who had formed a partnership with leading Republicans on Capitol Hill based primarily around money, Congress acted to create the Office of Congressional Ethics with the passage of the Open Government Act of 2007.[49] Third, recall, it was the Supreme Court, ultimately, that rolled back some of the strongest elements of those two laws, not Congress. In the last chapter, I also presented the complex evidence on the particular influence of business on policy making. Businesses are major players in politics today, but their large spending does not always win them policy successes. From this evidence, we might conclude that, despite the increasing size of money in politics, Congress has been doing its best to fulfill its role as the even-handed voice of the people and as a bulwark against corruption. We would only be partially right. New research has cast even this conclusion in doubt. While social science research may not be able to show that Congress responds to every beck and call from Corporate America, other research suggests that Congress is listening most intently to a small set of the public-at-large, potentially undermining campaign finance and lobbying reform.

If Congress truly represented its constituents, we would expect that the average voter's views would resemble the voting patterns of the average member of Congress.[50] Martin Gilens and Benjamin Page found something quite the opposite.[51] They used a rich set of surveys (1,779 in total) on public opinion on policy issues. Importantly, the surveys they studied could be broken down by income level, meaning they could compare the public opinion of those with incomes at the 50th percentile (middle class) with those at the 90th percentile (fairly affluent) to see which group favored the eventual policy decision. They found that the views of the middle class are rarely reflected in policy decisions. The probability of any policy being adopted does not relate at all to whether a small or large portion of the middle class supports the change. In short, decision makers, principally those in Congress, rarely make policy decisions that reflect what the middle class favors. Instead, the evidence suggested that the preferences of the fairly affluent do relate to the probability of policy change. When a *small* portion of affluent citizens support a policy, the policy is adopted 18% of the time. When a *large* portion of affluent citizens support a policy, the policy is adopted 45% of the time.[52] Gilens and Page concluded, "In the United States, . . . the majority does *not* rule—at least not in the causal sense of actually determining policy outcomes."[53] To be sure, this does not mean that Congress always passes laws that are hostile to the middle class or that the middle class opposes every law made by Congress. On some issues, those living at the middle of the income distribution view policy in remarkably similar ways to those at the upper end of the distribution, a finding that other researchers have interpreted to mean that the democracy is working to represent rich and poor.[54] What the evidence does suggest is that over numerous decisions, it is the views of the affluent that are most consistently—and statistically—related to the direction of policy.

One of the reasons for this unrepresentative tendency in Congress is related to the backgrounds of members of Congress, which we know are more similar to the fairly affluent than to the middle class. While we hope that members of Congress can represent all the diversity of their constituents, perhaps they cannot detach themselves from their own backgrounds. To test this, Nicholas Carnes compared members of Congress who had previously worked in blue-collar jobs to those who had spent little or no time in blue-collar jobs. He found that professional backgrounds made a difference in ideology. Using DW-NOMINATE scores—a summative 100-point measure of congressional voting ranging from very liberal to very conservative—Carnes showed that those with blue-collar backgrounds had a ten-point more liberal score than those without a blue-collar background.[55] He found the same thing using measures from the U.S. Chamber of Commerce and the AFL-CIO: social class was significantly related to a member's ideology. These differences extended beyond just ideology to voting. Members of Congress with a background in business tended to introduce and vote for more conservative bills.[56]

The variation in congressional voting that Carnes found do not neatly align with partisan boundaries and increasing polarization. Whereas there had been a time when Democrats pursued liberal policies that addressed wealth inequality—famously championing the policies of the New Deal—the Democratic Party has changed greatly since then. Adam Bonica et al. showed that, while the parties have become increasingly polarized over the last several decades, Democrats have not become more liberal on issues related to money and inequality.[57] Much like the Republicans, Democrats have demonstrated little enthusiasm for the types of large-scale policy making that would address increasing levels of inequality; instead they have pursued a liberal agenda on opposing the war in Iraq, favoring marriage equality, and championing environmental protections. Congressional ignorance of those living below the poverty line has become a bipartisan endeavor.

Another explanation for this finding about the apathetic direction of congressional voting on income inequality issues is the upper-class bias of the population of interest groups that EE Schattschneider noted several generations ago.[58] Rather than an equal form of pluralism with groups representing various professions, identities, and interests, Congress has always heard little from those with the least. Members of Congress simply do not hear from representatives of less affluent citizens. Kay Lehman Schlozman and Philip Jones found that less than 1% of organizations in Washington politics represented the poor.[59] And even when organizations that represent those marginalized by race, ethnicity, gender, or sexual orientation lobby policy makers, they typically promote the interests of their most affluent members, not those in greatest need.[60] So even when Congress hears from nonbusiness groups, the underlying values of these groups reflect those with more money than less.

If there were equal numbers of blue-collar and white-collar members of Congress, these findings would be less alarming.[61] And if there were equal numbers of affluent and middle-class constituents, we might not care as much.[62] Instead, because most members of Congress represent large numbers of working-class voters, and most members of Congress have a background in white-collar work, this evidence suggests that the biased class background of Congress and biased system of pluralism leads to profoundly unequal legislating and representation. And that unequal relationship is likely not restricted to Congress; the presidency, the courts, and lower levels of government are just as prone to differences in money and class as Congress. I pick this point back up in the next chapter of the book.

MONEY AND LEAVING CONGRESS

Because of the power of incumbency and growing importance of money, many members of Congress have long and distinguished careers in office. Once they leave, though, even greater riches await. Some former members of Congress, such as Rob Andrews in New Jersey, move from Capitol Hill but do not leave politics behind. Lobbying has become a prominent vocation for former members of Congress—what is called the *Revolving Door* between public office and private influence. A former member of Congress offers a lot of advantages to a lobbying firm or interest group, including a deep knowledge of legislative issues, close friendships with other elected officials, and, potentially, a list of political favors to be repaid. For these reasons, there have been deep concerns about the potential of the Revolving Door to foment corruption and exacerbate political inequities. Some wonder whether a former member of Congress-turned-lobbyist is simply converting the authority invested in the old public office into personal gains. For critics, this is a type of legal corruption that harms government. Also concerning is whether the Revolving Door lobbyist transfers some portion of the authority of the public office to the lobbying client. Corporations—which have the most to spend on lobbying—might be the highest bidder for the services of Revolving Door lobbyists. This would then capture the influence of former senators and members of Congress for a limited assortment of corporate policy interests, thereby intensifying political inequities.

As a result of these concerns, federal laws (passed initially in 1989, and then amended in 2007) restrict certain professional activities after service in Congress (post-Watergate reforms in the 1970s imposed similar restrictions on high-ranking executive branch officials). There is a one-year prohibition (two years for senators) on lobbying for former members of Congress and senior staff, and for representing foreign governments in trade negotiations.[63] These so-called *cooling-off periods* aim to reduce the opportunity for members of Congress to quickly trade on their old elected offices. More recently, Congress also addressed a particular concern about members of Congress using sensitive business information to make money. In the course of serving in public office, members of Congress are privy to extensive information about financial markets and business opportunities. Many feared that some were profiting off of this privileged access. The Stop Trading on Congressional Knowledge (or STOCK) Act prohibited federal officials from insider trading, though a later modification to the law weakened certain transparency provisions that were included in the original bill.[64]

Notwithstanding these prohibitions, the Center for Responsive Politics tracked where members sought new work after the 2010, 2012, and 2014 elections (See Figure 5.1). Prior to 2010, little had been tracked about the post-Congress work of members in the past, though one estimate suggested that just 3% of those leaving Congress in 1974 became lobbyists.[65] Things have clearly changed since then. In 2014, nearly half of those former elected officials who had found work ended up at lobbying firms and another 19% began work at a political organization that employed lobbyists (Lobbying Client). Congressional staff also follow congressional leaders through the Revolving Door. Research of over a decade's worth of lobbying data found that 5,400 former congressional staffers had moved from Capitol Hill to lobby.[66] Tim LaPira and Herschel

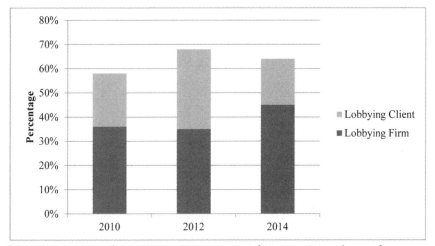

Figure 5.1 Revolving Door: Percentage of Former Members of Congress Accepting Jobs at Lobbying Firms and Lobbying Clients (Center for Responsive Politics, https://www.opensecrets.org/revolving/departing.php?cong=113)

Thomas discovered that half of a random sample of registered lobbyists had worked for Congress at some point in the past, three-quarters of the total group of Revolving Door lobbyists (the remainder had previously worked for other branches of government).[67]

These figures show that relatively few former members leave office for a life in private business, teaching, or medicine; many remain in politics, influencing policy from the outside in. But these estimates may even underestimate the full extent of the Revolving Door between Congress and lobbying. Many former members of Congress begin work for lobbying firms during the cooling-off period and never engage in legally defined lobbying (described in more detail in Chapter 2), thus remain in compliance with the law because they are not yet required to register as a lobbyist. As long as they adhere to the letter of the lobbying disclosure law, these government relations professionals or public affairs advisors may wield enormous power influencing their former colleagues in Congress through the work of other lobbyists, and never show up in official estimates.

In whichever way they are counted, the move from elected office comes with clear benefits. The previous chapter showed the enormous increase in the money spent on lobbyists. Still, it is hard to measure the full extent to which the move from Capitol Hill to lobbying results in financial payoffs. Salaries of public officials are widely shared, so we know that members of Congress earn $174,000 a year. Private salaries, though, are not routinely disclosed. Consequently, scholars have sought to estimate pay using what is shared about lobbying: revenues included on required quarterly disclosure forms. These revenue figures reflect what a lobbying firm charges a client for a lobbyist's time, so they can be used as a proxy for the amount lobbyists are paid.

Lee Drutman and Alexander Furnas used this method to generate an estimate of the median revenues generated by lobbyists.[68] They then disaggregated those estimates by the background of the lobbyists to compare former members of Congress with other lobbyists. Using this method, they found that in 2000, former members of Congress generated about the same amount in lobbying revenue as they were paid in Congress. This suggests that, at that time, whatever bump in salary they received after leaving Capitol Hill was limited in magnitude. By 2012, Revolving Door lobbyists greatly increased their revenues by nearly $100,000 above the 2000 levels, suggesting a related jump in salaries. Importantly, this finding did not seem to be driven simply by more lobbying revenue overall. Revenues generated by lobbyists with no government experience remained essentially constant at around $100,000 a year. Thus, it seems that former members of Congress generate more lobbying revenues than other lobbyists; this advantage seems to have grown over time and likely translates to a large salary premium.

These private salary returns are not restricted to individual members of Congress. The congressional staffers who follow a member from Capitol Hill to a lobbying firm also generate larger amounts of revenue. Drutman and Furnas found that the most active former members of Congress who lobby are joined by dozens of former staffers.[69] As a group, they generate tens of millions of dollars of total revenues for lobbying firms. Skeptics suggest that these returns are simply a reflection of the expertise a congressional staffers accrues while on Capitol Hill and thus not a concern. It may not be that these lobbyists are trading on their access to public officials, but rather they are trading on years of experience and other skills that lobbying firms value. Evidence, though, suggests this is not a complete explanation. In order to test this, Jordi Blanes i Vidal, Mirko Draca, and Christian Fons-Rosen examined a set of congressional staffers that later became lobbyists.[70] Their study was built on the premise that after leaving Capitol Hill, a new lobbyist has a relationship with a former boss who is still a member of the Senate or House, but at some point that former boss will lose an election or retire from office, often unexpectantly. If the lobbyist's fortunes remain unchanged, then perhaps it is the case that they were not simply trading on access. If, however, their fortunes go down, then it is likely the case that they were generating lobbying revenue mainly because of their ties to an elected official. The researchers found that when you compare the revenue generated by a Senate staffer-turned-lobbyist before and after their boss leaves Capitol Hill, the lobbying revenue they generate drops considerably. Vidal et al. concluded, "we find that lobbyists with past working experience in the office of a US Senator suffer a 24% drop in revenue—around $177,000—when their ex-employers leaves office."[71] They did not find a similar relationship for the House of Representatives.

Overall, these various social science methods try to estimate the monetary value associated with public office. Leaving aside blatant forms of corruption and bribery, these other forms of private financial benefits to service in Congress, whether it is as an elected official or high ranking staffer, are likely where the real money is to be made. It is entirely legal to lobby a former colleague, as long as it is done in compliance with disclosure laws and sufficiently long after leaving office. It may not, however, be right. Just as corporations that make campaign contributions in exchange for access to public officials are not violating the law, they may be violating what the public expects of those serving in government. For that reason, more reforms may be called for to promote the type of behaviors that would satisfy the public's desire for good government and not even the hint of corruption or self-service.

CONCLUSION

Members of Congress have caused and also addressed many of the country's concerns about the relationship between money and politics. From corruption scandals to pork project spending, what many Americans negatively associate with Washington often has its home on Capitol Hill. At the same time, members of Congress have passed FECA, BCRA, and lobbying reforms. Congress has banned earmarks and opened the Office of Congressional Ethics. The role of money in congressional politics is, thus, as prone to conflict and complexity as those presented in the rest of the book.

What seems clear is that undergirding the more comical aspects of Congress lays a deep foundation of money. Access to money distinguishes those who do and do not run for Congress, and between those who win and lose, even if those relationships are not causal. Members of Congress are richer, better educated, and have worked in a narrow set of high-profile jobs compared to most Americans. Despite how different most are from voters, once in office, money continues to provide the basis for them to remain in office. Members of Congress, who can effectively fundraise, are able to mount competitive campaigns, pay for televised advertisements, and win reelection year after year. Political parties, though, have adjusted to the new moneycentric character of congressional politics by demanding financial fealty from party incumbents. Money has been the lever for Republicans and Democrats alike to reward and punish those in and out of their respective caucuses. Money has empowered new congressional leaders who stand out from their colleagues, not for their policy acumen or knowledge of congressional rules, but for their ability to fundraise for the party.

If this story was simply about campaigns, it would be less interesting and less disturbing. Instead, the growing importance of money in Congress affects how Congress represents voters. The average voter shares little in common with the typical member of Congress, including common views on policy. The upper-class accent of Congress seems to result in routine policy making that is severely disconnected from voters. As Congress was to be the branch of government most directly connected to constituents, members tied to those they represent by frequent elections and small size of the electorate, the current state of affairs raises serious concerns. Are these concerns, however, reserved to just the legislative branch? The next chapter addresses this question by considering how the presidency fits into this story.

Chapter 6

The Moneyed Presidency

Thus far, this book has addressed an assortment of perspectives on the relationship between money and politics. There are paradoxes inherent to each of these perspectives: the Constitution was written to prevent corruption, yet has been used to protect the rights of corporations to spend unlimited amounts of money to influence politics; Congress has passed laws to tighten campaign finance, while members of Congress work day and night to raise money; and the public deplores the importance of money in politics, but most Americans do not push hard for change.

One perspective has sat in the background of the book: the presidency. This is itself a paradox, since the 2016 presidential election may ultimately be judged as transformative when it comes to money and politics. There has been a lot of money used in the past to influence Congress and the election of presidents. In 2016, though, the level of money reached unthinkable heights. The full realization of super PACs, a relatively minor player in previous elections, has rendered the race for the presidency perhaps forever changed. Money also has shaped the institution of the presidency in other ways. Far from the stoic center of government and representative of national interests, the presidency has grown increasingly politicized, partisan, and shaped by money. This chapter adds this perspective to the debate about money and politics.

PRESIDENTIAL CAMPAIGNS OF THE PAST

Mark Hanna has gone down in political lore as the first presidential campaign manager, introducing many of the same strategies that dominate presidential races today. Hanna was one of the first to institutionalize the financing of presidential campaigns by business, earning him the nickname from cartoonists of the time, "Dollar Mark."[1] He also incorporated innovative organizational, communication, and advertising strategies from the business world into politics. It is hard to appreciate the nature of contemporary campaigns without first considering the historical role played by Dollar Mark.

Hanna, a Cleveland, Ohio, banker and businessman, was a long-time associate of future-President William McKinley. In 1896, Hanna departed from the traditional party-centered campaign by personally managing McKinley's campaign separately from the Republican Party.[2] During that campaign, Hanna relied on Republican allies in the railroad industry to provide interested voters with passes to travel by train to Canton, Ohio, to directly engage with the candidate on his front porch.[3] Hanna leveraged his background in business to raise enormous amounts of campaign money for the time—$3.5 million. He spent that money on the type of mass advertising that had been growing in popularity in the commercial world but had not yet entered into politics.[4] Hanna used much of this money—approximately $500,000—to publish 200 million campaign documents printed in 13 different languages and to circulate them to likely voters.[5]

Also a harbinger of today's politics, Hanna focused his fundraising efforts in major cities. The majority, $3 million of the money raised for McKinley, was raised in New York, and much of the rest in Chicago, Illinois.[6] Hanna raised this money by systematically assessing the amount large businesses could contribute to the campaign and calling on them to pay up.[7] According to political historian, Stephen Hess, Standard Oil owed $250,000, New York Life, $50,000, and Illinois Central, $35,000.[8] In the end, Hanna's campaign strategy worked, the businesses contributed their share, and McKinley won the election, beating his challenger, William Jennings Bryan.

By today's standards, $3.5 million seems an inconsequential haul. Even minor contenders for the presidency today can muster the support of a half-hearted super PAC to spend several times that amount. But recent campaigns take from Hanna's legacy the importance of convincing wealthy contributors, often drawn from major corporations, to pony up for the candidate. Campaign managers of the 21st century also widely use Hanna's savvy adoption of the latest business marketing strategies, today a combination of technological voter outreach, digital messaging, and multimedia advertising.

Prior to the 2008 and 2012 presidential elections, campaigns had grown increasingly expensive, but public financing was a prominent part of paying the bills. Since the 1970s, and continuing in 2016, the federal government has provided matching funding for eligible presidential candidates. The funding for the program comes from voluntary contributions made by taxpayers when they pay annual income taxes.[9] During the primary phase of the campaign, the government matches as much as $250 of an individual's total contributions. In order to be eligible for the matching program, the candidate must show viability by raising more than $5,000 in at least 20 states, limit overall spending during the primary to $10 million (and $200,000 in any particular state), and limit the use of personal funds to $50,000. During the general election campaign, the two party nominees are eligible for $20 million in public funding, as long as they do not accept private contributions. Candidates receiving general election public funding can spend as much as $50,000 of their own money on the campaign and receive a set amount from the national party based on the population of each state.

From the adoption of public financing in the 1970s through the early 2000s, nearly all candidates accepted public funds. In 2000, candidate George W. Bush opted out of public financing during the primaries, though later accepted public funds during the general election campaign. By 2008, candidate Barack Obama turned down general election public financing. In 2012, neither candidate accepted public funding. What had seemed an effective way to level the financial playing field, limit the need to fundraise, and moderate total campaign expenditures, has largely been left in the past, at least on the national level. As candidates have moved away from public funding, total presidential campaign spending has grown from under $1.5 billion in 2000 to over $2.5 billion in 2012, while outside spending has soared (see Figure 6.1).

In 2012, the entirely private money supporting and opposing the two main candidates, Barack Obama and Mitt Romney, was evenly split: $985 million for Obama and $992 for Romney. Also remarkably similar was the way that money was spent. Each divided their spending between advertising—52% for Obama and 51% for Romney—and other expenditures such as direct mail (e.g., when a campaign sends material by postal mail to the homes of individual voters), which Romney's side utilized more than President Obama's. When the money was spent was also remarkably similar. Each side spent the largest portion of money in the three months leading up to the November general election. Approximately $466 million went to back Obama's campaign in September, October, and November, compared to around $458 million that backed Romney during that same time period.[10]

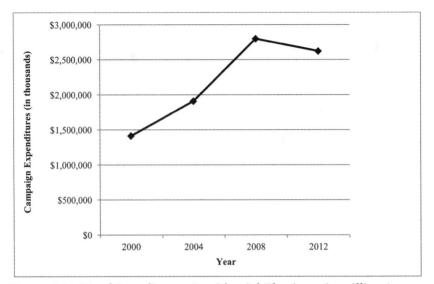

Figure 6.1 Total Spending on Presidential Elections (in millions)

Conversely, the two campaigns differed in terms of who raised and spent the money. According to the Campaign Finance Institute, the Obama campaign organization itself raised most of the money to support his campaign (62%), mainly from small-money donors: 28% of total contributions from those giving under $999.[11] The *New York Times* reported that 24% of the money raised to back the president came from the Democratic Party and 7% came from the main super PAC backing his campaign, Priorities USA.[12] Priorities USA spent $78.8 million backing Obama, most of it ($64.8 million) to pay for advertisements against Governor Romney. Conversely, the Romney campaign raised less than half (45%) of the total money backing his candidacy, split between medium (18% of contributors gave between $1,000 and $2,499) and large contributors (49% of contributors gave more than $2,500). The Republican National Committee (RNC) raised another third (37%) and the main super PAC, Restore Our Future, raised $153 million or 16% of the total for Romney. Much like Priorities USA, Restore Our Future dedicated most of its expenditures ($88.6 million) to buying television advertisements opposing President Obama.

President Obama ultimately won the 2012 election and a second term in the White House. His campaign's extensive use of digital strategies has been credited for some of his victory, as it had in 2008. Between those two electoral victories, digital media became an even more important part of the campaign, fitting into a 20-year political trend.[13] The first use of Internet-based digital technologies during presidential campaigns can be traced back to 1996. Senator Robert Dole implored viewers of the first debate with President Bill Clinton to "tap into my home page, www.dolekemp.org," an admirable foray into cutting-edge political communication, though Jennifer Stromer-Galley noted that the actual address was www.dolekemp96.org.[14] Four years later, in 2000, digital media made up fewer than $200,000 of George W. Bush's expenditures. Ever since that election, technology has become a more central aspect of presidential campaign politics, helping candidates raise and spend money in new ways.[15] In 2008, according to the *National Journal*, the Obama campaign spent $21.1 million on digital media; four years later that figure had increased threefold to $74.5 million.[16] These massive expenditures on digital media have created lucrative opportunities for new political companies. In 2012, two such companies, GMMB and Bully Pulpit Interaction, were paid millions of dollars to help get the president reelected: $389 million to GMMB and $72.6 million to Bully Pulpit. GMMB describes itself as "We are societal problem solvers. Engineers of social change. Activists. And realists. We have a point of view that keeps our compass pointed in the direction of progress. If we're working with you, it's because we're passionate about what you believe—we believe it too. It's what drives us in everything we do."[17] As much as anything, GMMB was a company that made a lot of money on the 2012 election.

Recall also that the 2012 election was the first post–*Citizens United* decision presidential election. *Citizens United* opened the door to the formation of super PACs, which could raise and spend nearly unlimited amounts of money as long as they disclose contributors to the FEC and do not contribute to, or coordinate expenditures with, the candidate's campaign team. Unlike the electoral activities of traditional PACs, which are permitted to contribute limited amounts directly to candidates, super PACs are understood to operate separately from the candidate, thus, according to the Supreme Court, pose many fewer concerns about corruption.

As has been noted throughout the book, the expectations of super PAC impact on the 2012 election were not completely met. Super PACs did not spend as much as many anticipated, and the way they spent money did not greatly change from previous elections.[18] With that noted, super PACs did participate in the 2012 election in some notable ways. First, super PACs backed Governor Mitt Romney much more so than President Obama. According to the *New York Times*, super PACs spent approximately $2.50 backing Romney (or opposed to Obama) for every $1 spent by super PACs backing Obama (or opposed Romney).[19]

Second, as we learned earlier in the book, some of the largest political contributors used super PACs to contribute huge sums of money. Sheldon and Miriam Adelson contributed $30 million, Bob Perry contributed $17.5 million, and Robert Rowling contributed $6.1 million to support super PACs backing Romney. On the other side, James Simons contributed $5 million, Fred Eychaner contributed $4.5 million, and Jeffrey Katzenberg contributed $3 million to back super PACs supporting Obama. Super PACs provide a new way for mega-donors who have hit the candidate and party contribution limit to continue to support a preferred candidate or issues.

Third, super PACs provided a way to support long-shot candidates to enter the presidential primaries but not to succeed. For example, according to the Center for Responsive Politics, super PACs spent $16.6 million to support former Speaker of the House Newt Gingrich and $4.1 million to support Texas Governor Rick Perry.[20] The advertising paid for by supportive super PACs bought each candidate some visibility in key primary states, but in the end Gingrich and Perry dropped out of the Republican primary race without winning the nomination.

Fourth, super PACs—as they did for Gingrich and Perry—focused spending on negative advertisements opposing presidential candidates more so than supporting. During the Republican primaries, Restore Our Future—the super PAC backing Governor Romney—spent most of its $20 million on advertisements opposing other Republican candidates and spent just a small fraction supporting Governor Romney.[21] During the general election campaign, super PACs continued this trend. Priorities USA paid for 13,443 advertisements in 28 media markets costing an estimated $9.5 million to back President Obama.[22] Restore Our Future spent approximately $7.9 million to buy 6,653 advertisements in 32 media markets. This uncoordinated division of labor allowed for candidate-sponsored advertisements to maintain a positive tone and for the candidates to denounce the negative campaigning of opponents.

Super PAC money played these direct roles in the 2012 election. Money also played additional roles as an unexpected meme of the Romney campaign and as a powerful macro-environmental factor of this electoral cycle. Much of the advertising against Mitt Romney used money to frame him as an out-of-touch fat cat, unsympathetic to those less well off, with a record of business dealings that harmed American workers. These advertisements built on Romney's own statements about money, including his infamous "47%" statement, as well as his professional background as a corporate leader of Bain Capital. During the campaign, the magazine, *Mother Jones*, released a secret video from a fundraiser at which Romney said:

> There are 47% of the people who will vote for the president no matter what. All right, there are 47% who are with him, who are dependent upon government, who believe they are victims, who believe that government has a responsibility to care for them . . . Forty-seven percent of Americans pay no income tax . . . And so my job is not to worry about those people— I'll never convince them that they should take personal responsibility and care for their lives.[23]

Romney claimed that the comment was simply about the Democrats already holding 47% of the electorate and that he was going to focus on convincing the other 53% of voters to support him. Many, though, took the comments as a broad assault on the working class and all voters who received government assistance of any sort. For critics, Romney's comment was not a reflection of his sense of partisan strategy; rather it was deeply ideological and represented his personal views on the middle class.

In July of 2012, allies of President Obama, especially the super PAC Priorities USA, jumped on the opportunity to paint Romney as insensitive and unsympathetic. One advertisement ("Doors") juxtaposed Romney's statement about the 47% with assertions about how Romney would harm middle-class Americans. In another, a speaker explained how, as a senior executive of Bain Capital, Romney was responsible for the closing of a paper manufacturing plant in Ohio.[24] In "Romney's Gold," Priorities USA showed footage from the Salt Lake City Olympics—which he had overseen—with an announcer explaining how various countries had benefited from the outsourcing of jobs, off-shore bank accounts, and "secretive corporations" all tied to Romney.[25]

Looking back, many voters probably recall little about the campaign other than the "47%" statement and the perception of Romney as the worst illustration of money and politics. Romney had a lot of money, disparaged those without money, and was seeking to win the most important political job in the country. For many voters, this was just too much to stomach.

The evidence that either the "47%" gaffe, the work at Bain Capital, or perceptions of Romney's lack of empathy greatly altered the outcome of the election, though, has been less convincing. John Sides and Lynn Vavreck dismissed these money-related problems and negative advertising directed at the Romney campaign as nothing more than a blip on the radar of public opinion and fodder for punditry.[26] They pointed out that the anti-Romney/Bain Capital advertisements did not air for that many weeks and that Romney supporters responded with some equally stinging advertisements about the president. As a result, Sides and Vavreck found that there was little change in Romney's standing among voters: before and after these ads Romney's favorability was around 40%. Similarly, they concluded that after the release of the "47%" video, few voters seemed to change their mind about Romney or about his views on the poor and on the wealthy. In the end, then, the issue of money and wealth drew much negative attention to Romney, but it did little to determine the outcome of the election.

In *The Gamble*, the seminal social science account of the campaign, Sides and Vavreck instead credited another role for money—the positive state of the economy—as the single most important factor that decided the race for President Obama.[27] As the incumbent, much like the advantages accrued to those in Congress described in the last chapter, President Obama was in the enviable position of claiming credit for an array of positive economic indicators. It wasn't Romney's religion or conservatism, the effective campaign tactics of the Obama campaign, or Romney's gaffes; it was simply the case that the economy grew in the first six months of the election year, and many credited the sitting president. Based on the 1.1% growth in GDP in those months, Sides and Vavreck's statistical models predicted an additional 2.4-point gain in share of the votes.[28] In fact, this analysis of presidential election voting suggested that GDP growth has almost always had this relationship with the incumbent's share of the vote. Money matters to presidential elections, not always in the obvious ways we might think, but in other deeper ways. When voters feel confident about the economy, secure in their employment, and satisfied with the amount of money they have in their pockets, they credit the incumbent candidate for the White House. When money is scarce, the incumbent pays the electoral price. To be sure, this finding does not suggest large cross-party voting: a strong economy does not lead Democrats to vote for incumbent Republicans in larger numbers or vice versa. But, in a closely divided partisan country, economic fundamentals and money go a long way to explaining who turns out to vote and who ultimately wins in a presidential election.

2016 PRESIDENTIAL CANDIDATE SELECTION: PRELUDE TO THE BIG EVENT

Since—based on what we know from Chapter 2—so few Americans contribute to candidates, the public has been largely left out of the recent growth of money in presidential elections. The public, though, has not been ignorant of the trend. Even if all the money in 2012 did not exactly swing the election, the public was not entertained by all those expensive advertisements or lucrative deals with political consultants. At the start of the 2016 presidential campaign, a third of likely voters listed the influence of the wealthy and corporations as their number-one concern about the upcoming election.[29] Another 12% said that "too many candidates are wealthy and don't understand the economic problems of average Americans."[30] Despite these concerns, the upward trajectory of money grew even steeper as the early stages of the 2016 presidential race commenced. And the role of super PACs in 2016 made 2012 look like a hesitant dip of the toe into the pool of presidential politics.

Several important features emerged early in the 2016 race. For one, the large number of contenders for the Republican nomination meant that there were many more individuals in need of money. At one point, there were 17 total officially announced candidates, each with a remarkable record of accomplishments, some with distinguished careers in government. The assortment of candidates meant that potential campaign contributors had many visions of the Republican Party from which to choose. From sitting governors, such as John Kasich from Ohio, Chris Christie from New Jersey, Bobby Jindal from Louisiana, Scott Walker from Wisconsin, to a former CEO, Carly Fiorina, to a retired neurosurgeon, Ben Carson, the candidates varied in professional background. Senators Ted Cruz (TX), Marco Rubio (FL), Rand Paul (KY), and Lindsay Graham (SC) presented four different views from Congress on the proper role of government. And former governors, Rick Perry (TX), Jeb Bush (FL), Jim Gilmore (VA), Mike Huckabee (AR), and George Pataki (NY) joined the race as well as a former senator, Rick Santorum (PA), and, of course, Donald Trump.

In the early days of the campaign, when all 17 candidates were fighting for survival, Ted Cruz had raised the most, $14 million, split between small ($6.7 million) and large ($6.0 million) contributors. Jeb Bush, who had declared his candidacy much later than Cruz, was next with $10.9 million, nearly all (89%) from large contributors. Carson ($10.6 million), Rubio ($8.0 million), and Paul ($6.9 million) followed the leaders, with the rest of the pack barely keeping up.

On the Democratic side, just three prominent candidates entered the race early: the front-runner, former senator and secretary of state, Hillary Clinton; former governor of Maryland, Martin O'Malley; as well as incumbent senator from Vermont, Bernie Sanders. At the onset of the Democratic primary race, Clinton had a significant advantage in money raised. In the summer of 2015, according to data from the FEC, Clinton had raised $46.4 million from individuals, two-third (67%) from relatively large contributors giving more than $2,000.[31] Senator Sanders had raised $13.6 million, two-thirds of it from small contributors giving fewer than $200. O'Malley trailed both other Democrats by a wide margin, totaling under $2 million.

These figures were astronomical for that early point in the presidential election. Early spending in 2015 was twice the level as at the same point in the calendar four years earlier, a point that itself had been historic.[32] Interestingly, the overall split in early money between Republican and Democratic candidates was nearly even, with Democrats raising slightly more ($64.2 million) compared to Republicans ($61.2 million). The real differences in money during the primaries was not in money raised by candidates directly, but in the money raised by associated—but not coordinated—super PACs. During the summer of 2015, there was the first official public disclosure of who was supporting each candidate through super PACs. That disclosure gave a glimpse as to why 2016 was unlike any presidential election of the past, including the remarkable 2012 election. In total, just halfway through the 2015 calendar year, various super PACs had raised $400 million.

Most of the super PAC action in the early primary contest was on the Republican side. Though Jeb Bush trailed Ted Cruz in fundraising, the super PACs that supported Bush dwarfed fundraising by Cruz and any other candidate. According to the *Washington Post*, two super PACs, Right to Rise ($103.2 million) and Right to Rise PAC ($5.4 million), raised more than $100 million before the summer was over.[33]

Bush-related super PACs were far in the fundraising lead but were not alone. Keep the Promise raised $37.8 million to support Cruz, Unintimidated PAC and Our American Revival together raised $26.2 million for Walker, and Conservative Solutions PAC and Reclaim America raised $17.3 million to back Rubio. In comparison, super PACs supporting Hillary Clinton (Priorities USA Action and Correct the Record) mustered just $17.1 million, a considerable amount in any previous election, but just fifthmost in the summer of 2015.

The contributions received by super PACs were from small numbers of contributors. The super PACs backing Bush raised millions from a couple dozen contributors, while other Republican candidates gathered large checks from a handful of supporters. Overall, *Politico* estimated that as a group merely 67 $1 million-or-more super PAC contributors had given three times the amount as the 500,000 small contributors combined.[34] For example, nearly all of the money raised to back Ted Cruz came from three contributors: members of the Wilks family ($15 million), Robert McNair ($11 million), and Toby Neugebauer ($10 million). Two large contributors, Diane Hendricks ($5 million) and Joe and Marlene Rickets ($5.1 million), made up much of the money for Walker's super PACs. The super PACs supporting Hillary Clinton had only a single mega-donor, Haim and Cheryl Saban, who gave $2 million to back her campaign. Conversely, the other prominent Democrat in the race, Bernie Sanders, had refused outside money, and no super PACs were raising money to back his campaign.

The concentration of super PAC contributors was a defining feature of the 2016 election. Another of the slipperiest issues confronting campaigns and super PACs was over *coordination*. Recall, the Supreme Court argued that unlimited super PAC contributions and spending would not lead to corruption, because super PACs would operate entirely apart from the candidate. As such, FEC rules made it illegal for super PACs to coordinate campaign strategy with candidates, especially the candidate that the super PAC was formed to support. The key question, though, was: what is coordination? On paper, the FEC used a three-prong test to determine coordination: (1) payment, (2) content, and (3) conduct.[35] First, the expenditure in question had to be paid for by anyone other than the candidate, traditional PAC, or party. Second, the content of the communication that had been paid for had to either: expressly advocate for the election or defeat of a candidate; relate to an election and occur 30 days before a primary or 60 days before the general election; refer to a House or Senate candidate within 90 days of an election or refer to a presidential/vice presidential candidate within 120 days of the primary election through the general election. Third, coordination occurred if the communication has been requested/suggested by the candidate; if the candidates has been "materially involved" in the design of the content or the content is based on a "substantial discussion" with the candidate; if the super PAC uses a vendor in common with the candidate to produce the communication; or if a former campaign staffer (or independent contractor) of the candidate relays information to the super PAC that leads to the communication. If a public communication meets these criteria, then it has been coordinated and is against the law.

The FEC has rarely charged anyone with violating the three-prong coordination test, yet in the 2016 cycle, super PACs seemed to routinely push the regulatory boundaries. In one case, a group called the American Democracy Legal Fund filed a petition with the FEC challenging what they viewed as a violation of these coordination rules by two Republican organizations: GOP Data Trust and i360. Both companies managed voter databases to which mainly Republican candidates supplied updated personal information. Super PACs then paid to use the database to target political communications. The two companies were, American Democracy Legal Fund alleged, a "common vendor" for many Republican candidates and super PACs that support them, a potential violation of FEC coordination rules, specifically the third conduct prong. American Democracy Legal Fund concluded, "both the Data Trust and i360 are in blatant violation of the Commission regulations and have made tens of millions of dollars in illegal in-kind contributions to Republican candidates."[36]

In other cases, super PACs devised ways to get around the FEC rules. Super PAC officials went on broadcast news programs and announced when and where they had made advertising buys, thus signaling to the campaign where to focus advertising without illegal coordination.[37] Other super PACs used social media platforms, such as Twitter, to distribute new polling data in semiencrypted forms for those on the campaign to gather, also not a violation of the coordination rules. And, Right to Rise PAC, a backer of Jeb Bush, recorded video of the not-yet-a-candidate before he announced his run so that they could later use the footage for advertising after the noncoordination rules set in.[38] All of these seemingly legal ways to comply with the FEC regulations raised serious questions about whether the current rules could effectively regulate the rise of super PACs.

Another interesting development in the growth of super PAC fundraising was the differential costs associated with operating these nonparty and noncandidate entities. Television stations, which are paid to air political advertisements, are required by federal law to charge a particularly low rate to candidates. The law aims to encourage a more informed electorate through the mass communication benefits of television. Super PACs, though, are not protected by the law, thereby permitting stations to charge as much as they please for advertisements. The *National Journal* reported on these differential prices during the run-up to the Republican primaries and caucuses.[39] Then-candidate Marco Rubio paid $225 per 30-second advertisement on local Iowa television.

In advance of the Iowa caucus in January 2016, Rubio's campaign team used that low rate to buy 218 spots, totaling $48,000. Conversely, the super PAC backing candidate Scott Walker paid $1,775 per ad during the same time period, possibly explaining why they reserved only 83 total ads. (Walker dropped out of the race before these ads were aired.) Similar patterns emerged in other early primary states as well, possibly signaling a great inefficiency of a campaign strategy based on funneling money through super PACs as opposed to through candidates directly.

As other candidates, and their associated super PACs, were scouring the country in search of money, media, and votes, one candidate stood out for his own personal fortune. Donald Trump was the outlier in the Republican race, a billionaire housing developer, who bragged of his previous mega-contributions but decried his opponents' reliance on super PACs. In one of the more candid moments of the first Republican debate in August 2015, a debate moderator questioned Trump, then ahead in the polls, about his campaign contributions. After claiming he gave widely, including contributions to all of his opponents on the debate stage, Trump said, "I will tell you that our system is broken. I give to many people. I give to everybody, when they call I give, and you know what? When I need something from them, two years, three years later, I call, they are there for me."[40] Trump did not indicate specifically to whom he donated or when he later called on them, but the admission struck at the heart of the deeper question of corruption in American politics at the center of this book. Trump admitted to the type of corruption that is perfectly legal in American politics. Since he did not claim that a specific campaign donation was connected to a specific promise of support, he was not admitting to the type of *quid pro quo* exchange that is against the law. Instead, he described how money can be used to buy access and that those with ample means do not use this to buy access with a single elected official; instead the money is shared widely to hedge against electoral losses. Not surprisingly, none of the other candidates on the stage or the debate moderators followed up on the exchange with a sound criticism of how Trump had used his money in the past, perhaps all too aware of how perfectly normal his comments were.

The federal office charged with overseeing this very expensive election was similarly quiet on the rising cost of the election. Though the FEC had the authority to investigate violations of election regulations, the commissioners pursued few claims. The unusually low level of activity led the FEC chair at the time, Ann Ravel, to explain to the *New York Times*, "there is not going to be any real enforcement" of FEC rules in

the 2016 election.[41] She continued, "People think the F.E.C. is dysfunctional. It's worse than dysfunctional."[42] The evenly split FEC commissioners, three Democrats and three Republicans, resulted in an inability
of the Commission to render decisions or reach any agreement on how
to enforce the laws. As a consequence, the primary institutional mechanism established in the 1970s to check money and politics became a
spectator in the most expensive presidential race in American history.

DOES MONEY MATTER TO THE PRESIDENCY?

Presidential campaigns have become big money affairs, to be sure. If
current trends persist, the money may grow even larger in the future possibly topping $8 billion in 2016. A persistent question asked throughout
this book is the degree to which this trend matters. Earlier, I showed
that some campaign contributors are later given federal appointments,
including foreign ambassadorships. For a country with a government
the size of the United States, awarding a certain number of political jobs
to contributors would hardly seem to sway national interests. And, in
fact, presidents have long held to the notion that they, more than any
other elected official, serve the country as a whole. Unlike members of
Congress, who serve particular constituencies, the president is chosen by
the country at-large. As such, presidents have historically claimed that
they represent the broad national interest, favoring no particular district,
state, or special interest. Presidential scholar Clinton Rossiter wrote of
the expectations of the presidency in the *New York Times* in 1956: "In
a constitutional system compounded of diversity and antagonism, the
presidency looms up as the countervailing force of unity and harmony.
In a society ridden by centrifugal forces, it is the only point of reference
we all have in common."[43] Rossiter also noted, somewhat paradoxically,
that the president is also head of the party. How presidents have fulfilled
their role as a force of national unity and a party leader often comes
down to money.

For the last 100 years, the institution of the presidency has grown
in size, scope, and significance. Whereas early presidents were deemed
"weak and ineffectual," by the 20th century, the public and Congress
came to expect many more things from the president, including a clear
policy vision and position on the allocation of the federal budget.[44]
The amount of money overseen by the president and senior administration officials across the government and in the White House grew as
Congress authorized the creation of new agencies funded by growing

revenues from federal income taxes. President Franklin Roosevelt oversaw a White House staff of 14 and a $4.5 billion federal budget. Less than a century later, Barack Obama began his time in office with a staff of 468 and a $3.5 trillion budget.[45] The scope and scale of the presidencies of George Washington or Thomas Jefferson appear nearly quaint compared to the institution that grew and grew over the 20th century.

As the size and expectations of the presidency has grown, the White House has become a deeply political and partisan institution. Presidents boast of electoral mandates to pursue ambitious policy agendas, often commencing before they have even been inaugurated.[46] Presidents now oversee a White House with complex communications, outreach, and policy apparatus to advance policy goals.[47] They rely upon the power to appoint loyal officials across the federal government to ensure that the bureaucracy does not interfere with implementation of their agenda.[48]

In pursuing these far-reaching policy goals, much political science scholarship has approached presidents as nonpartisan centrists, intent on fulfilling the broad representative functions of the office. On the contrary, B. Dan Wood argued in *The Myth of Presidential Representation* that, far from being Washingtonian centrists, presidents in recent times have been strong partisans. While Wood's finding is hardly surprising to even the novice watcher of recent presidential politics, his evidence confirms that the myth of the nonpartisan statesmen in the White House is anecdotally *and* empirically wrong.

Moreover, recent evidence suggests that in pursuing these partisan policy ambitions, presidents listen and respond to a narrow segment of the populace. For a representative democracy of three million people, how a president and White House staff can know what the public desires is a logistical problem. Relying on extensive archival data on presidential polling, James Druckman and Lawrence Jacobs investigated exactly how presidents have sought to reflect American public opinion. What they discovered was that certain recent presidents, especially President Ronald Reagan, used frequent polls to identify the opinions of important subgroups, what they called *segmented representation* or *segmentation*. Reagan increased the number of polls and also how extensive the pollsters probed public sentiment. For example, Kennedy fielded just 15 polls and asked 674 questions; by Reagan's time in the White House, the number of polls had increased to 204 and the total questions asked to 10,153.[49]

In addition to investigating public opinion more frequently, Reagan had a particular objective for his polling. Rather than pursue a polling strategy to understand broad national, Republican, or conservative sentiments, Reagan and other presidents sought out small portions of the electorate, often the wealthy. Druckman and Jacobs found that "One component of [Reagan's] segmentation was his disproportionate attention to the preferences of the highest-income earners."[50] Further, once these presidents understood the preferences of the rich, they then pursued policy strategies focused on advancing these interests and convincing others of the merits. Druckman and Jacobs concluded that these findings "question the self-serving proclamations of presidents that they are 'stewards of the people' who serve the entire country and its greater good."[51]

That presidents do not listen equally to all Americans is hardly a surprise. That they listen to the wealthy in particular might also be expected given what Nicholas Carnes showed about the elite backgrounds of most presidents.[52] Scholars of the presidency also have documented the increasing politicization of the presidency. President are now seen as the head of their party, charged with carrying out policy mandates as well as helping members of Congress get elected.[53] Presidents use their authority over federal spending to meet these partisan electoral demands, what and Douglas Kriner and Andrew Reeves described as the *particularistic presidency*.[54] We can observe this in the ways that presidents have used authority over federal grants. John Hudak studied the distribution of federal discretionary funds—what he called *presidential pork*—to measure whether electoral factors related to patterns of spending. To be sure, Congress makes many of the decisions about where federal money will go, but there are numerous federal grant programs over which federal agencies have been given authority. Might that authority lead to skewed federal spending patterns? Hudak found that electoral swing states—those states that are competitive in presidential elections—get around 7% more total grants and 5.7% more dollars of grant funding than other states.[55] This translates to a difference of millions of dollars based on whether the state is viewed as an electoral ambition for the president. Kriner and Reeves found a similar positive relationship for grants awarded to parts of the country aligned with the core constituencies of the president.[56] And in another study, researchers found that presidents use an analogous partisan electoral strategy to adjust tariff agreements to benefit industries focused in competitive electoral states.[57] Hudak concluded, "What is clear is that the Office of the President is now more politically and electorally motivated than in previous periods."[58]

The evidence underscores the political dimension of governing for the president and how money can leverage electoral advantages. Money also drives how the federal bureaucracy makes decisions, quite separately from the president. Chapter 3 showed how interest groups and businesses expend much of their time and money focusing on Congress, but there is also considerable lobbying of the executive branch. With the passage of Administrative Procedure Act of 1946 and the Federal Advisory Committee Act of 1972, interest groups of all sorts have been given a formal role in federal decision making.[59] As with lobbying of Congress, business interests, in particular, are heavily represented during the process of federal rule making and regulating. Thorough lobbying of federal agencies by business groups and the active revolving door between the regulators and the regulated leads to concerns about *agency capture*. Rather than regulating in a rational, unbiased fashion, a captured agency might systematically favor one side of an issue because regulators maintain mixed loyalties and ongoing conflicts of interest. Many fear that money, in the form of future employment opportunities or enormous lobbying expenditures, will then distort federal policy making and bias the behavior federal policy makers.

Though theoretically substantial, concerns about agency capture by business have been hard to substantiate with empirical evidence. Much as with participation in congressional lobbying, business groups are the most active in federal rule making. Scott Furlong and Cornelius Kerwin found that during the open comment period on federal rules, business groups and trade associations participate in the most rules (business groups participated in on average 19 rules, trade associations 11, public interest groups 7.8), offer the most number of comments (on average 21 for business groups and 8 for trade associations, compared to fewer than 1 for unions and 2 for public interest groups), and represent the largest percentage of comments submitted (on average 30% of comments are from business groups, followed by 20% from trade associations, .45% from unions, and 5% from public interest groups).[60] Further, this comparative advantage in rule-making participation translates to somewhat stronger influence. Robert Lowry and Matthew Potoski found that interest groups, in general, do influence aggregate federal spending, and Susan Yackee showed that interest groups that participate can influence the outcome of rule making.[61] Since many of those participating groups represent businesses, it reasons that business interests often get their way. On this *macro*-level of federal policy making, there does seem to be evidence that interest groups shape how rules and regulations are written. On the more *micro*-level, however, the picture is much less clear. As with the mixed evidence on business interests' record of policy success demonstrated in Chapter 3, businesses and groups pushing for particular policy outcomes with enormous sums of money do not succeed all the time. For example, Beth Leech discovered a weak link between organizations that lobby and the likelihood of winning a federal grant.[62] And Baumgartner et al. concluded that, though business groups do seem to win many policy fights, money and resources do not always lead to positive outcomes for those lobbying.[63] The business sector is the biggest outside player in federal policy making, as it is in congressional legislating, though the sector is far from invincible.

CONCLUSION

As with other perspective of money and politics, presidents have been defined by paradox. The presidency has stood as a symbol of national unity and the common interest. Over time, though, we have come to expect presidents to pursue ambitious policy agendas, which almost by definition have to be shaped by a distinct ideology and pursued along partisan lines. Presidents claim to represent the nation, though as they seek to learn what the nation wants, they listen more intently to some sectors than others. Finally, money has become such a defining part of the race for the presidency that the massive increases in campaign spending in 2012 and then again in the 2016 race must make everyone rethink the durability of the institution.

Can a president remain true to the oath of office when the path to the White House requires raising hundreds of millions of dollars from a tiny fraction of the population? Can the increasing politicization of the White House, which has been abetted by a larger and larger pool of money to disperse, permit future presidents to claim a national mandate and rally the country together in unity during difficult times?

Reformers worry that the answer to these questions are deeply troubling. Instead, they argue that change is needed to reorient the relationship between money and politics in the presidency, Congress, and the policy process. The next chapter examines an assortment of reform proposals to judge the feasibility of future change.

Chapter 7

Reforming the Political System

From whichever perspective you look, money and politics are linked together today more so than ever before. This book has catalogued several important linkages. First, the Constitution is now used to protect the very political activities that the Founders of the country probably believed it was established to prevent. Second, there is more money coming from mega-donors than was imaginable when FECA was passed 40 years ago. Third, there is more money coming from corporations than even the most cynical good government reformers of the 1970s could have predicted. Fourth, there is more money sloshing around Congress than congressional leaders of a generation ago would have anticipated. And, fifth, the presidency, once the center of national interests, has become inundated with huge volumes of money from a tiny fraction of the population. Money defines the democracy in the United States.

The extent of this acceleration of the role that money plays in politics demands a comprehensive examination of what can and should be done. Has money become so important to choosing the next president that ideas, issues, and experience do not matter at all? Do campaign contributors capture the White House long before a single vote is cast? Or are these trends really mere political posturing, drowned out by more powerful forces of government gridlock, the policy status quo, and the power of incumbency? In the end, should we encourage more or less money to enter politics in the future?

To be sure, money has changed power and influence in Washington in ways that the public deplores. The public believes the wealthy have too much power over politicians, lobbyists are untrustworthy, and recent Supreme Court decisions have improperly opened politics to excessive

Table 7.1 Money and Politics Reforms

Lower the Ceiling	Raise the Roof	Open the Windows	Close the Blinds
Adopt constitutional amendment to overturn *Citizens United*	Introduce $25 "My Voice" tax credit	Clarify IRS nonprofit political regulations	Bring back earmarks
Raise at least half the campaign money in the candidate's district	Subsidize lobbying for underrepresented groups and issues	Mandate additional political spending disclosure for government contractors	Permit more back-channel legislating
Expand public financing and small-donor matching program	Raise campaign contribution limits to parties	Broaden definition of lobbying	

amounts of money. If ever there was a time to consider reform, it would seem to be now. Because of the complexity of the political system, reforms come in different varieties, each seeking to address a slightly different type of problem, using different policy tools. While there may be wide agreement that there is a problem with the relationship between money and politics, there is little consensus as to the nature of that problem or the solution.

In this chapter, I argue that reforms fit generally into four categories, which I call Lowering the Ceiling, Raising the Roof, Opening the Windows, and Closing the Blinds. Table 7.1 shows how several prominent proposals fit into these broad categories, understanding that this is a careful sampling, not an exhaustive list. I discuss each below as well as their potential effectiveness and political feasibility.

LOWERING THE CEILING

The most conventional approach to campaign finance reform follows from previous efforts in FECA and BCRA to limit, cap, or contain spending on elections, overall or by certain entities. I call this *lowering the ceiling*. After the two seminal Supreme Court decisions in the last decade, advocates of this approach have had to comply with the parameters established by the Court that the Constitution protects nearly unlimited spending by corporations (*Citizens United*) and protects contributions, including by corporations, as a type of political speech (*McCutcheon*). These court rulings have made proposals (such as the Anti-Corruption Act) that would require super PACs to follow the same contribution limits as other political committees and also toughen the rules preventing coordination between super PACs and political campaigns, constitutionally tenuous.[1]

Consequently, reformers—including several members of Congress—have backed an amendment to the Constitution that would largely invalidate previous court rulings and give Congress explicit authority to regulate campaign spending. The amendment would also give Congress the power to treat corporations as distinct from individuals when legislating on campaign finance. In the "Democracy for All" amendment, sponsors included two main provisions:

> Section 1. To advance democratic self-government and political equality, and to protect the integrity of government and the electoral process, Congress and the States may regulate and set reasonable limits on the raising and spending of money by candidates and others to influence elections.
>
> Section 2. Congress and the States shall have power to implement and enforce this article by appropriate legislation, and may distinguish between natural persons and corporations or other artificial entities created by law, including by prohibiting such entities from spending money to influence elections.

If Congress acted on this new constitutional authority, it could lower the ceiling on campaign contributions and spending with fewer fears that the Court would later rule those actions unconstitutional. This amendment would likely result in changes to FECA and BCRA that would reduce the maximum amount individuals, corporations, and PACs were permitted to contribute to candidates, PACs, or other political organizations. As a consequence, certain types of money would surely be reduced.

The political feasibility of such an approach is much more dubious. As I show later in this chapter, there is almost no support for this approach within Republican circles, meaning the Democrats would have to win back control of the House and Senate by wide margins to even begin debating the proposal. Moreover, passing a constitutional amendment, either through Congress or through the states, is an arduous affair. There has not been a successful amendment to the Constitution in a quarter century, and that amendment—the Twenty-seventh Amendment regarding congressional compensation—took over two centuries to pass. Perhaps aware of these political barriers, and in order to stimulate support for passage of the amendment, two organizations, Say No to Big Money and People for the American Way, launched a video contest in the summer of 2015—offering $64,000 to the winner—to get people interested. It may be that money in making videos could incentivize citizens to get rid of money in politics.

Another approach to lowering the ceiling has been to shift the funding of campaigns from private to public sources. Public financing has been a long-preferred approach to disentangling the relationship between money and politics. For those who back national public financing plans, the primary problem of the current system is twofold: the amount of money needed to run discourages a wider spectrum of candidates from entering politics; and for those who do decide to run, too much of their time is spent raising money from a select group of wealthy and special interest donors.

Public financing could equalize opportunities to enter politics and shift the ways campaigns operate away from a single-minded focus on fundraising. As noted in Chapter 6, public financing at the presidential level has been all but abandoned by major candidates. Public funding at the state level, though, remains an option in certain parts of the country. And the evidence from these state-level public funding plans in Hawaii, Minnesota, Wisconsin, Arizona, Connecticut, and Maine suggest that they can actually work. Michael Miller studied several of these plans in his book, *Subsidizing Democracy*.[2] Miller compared states with partial and fully funded systems expecting to observe whether there was a difference in the amount of time devoted to fundraising, meeting voters, and possibly even voter turnout. He found that candidates in fully funded public finance systems devoted "a significantly lower percentage of their campaign time to fundraising"—less than 2%—compared to other financing systems, both partially funded and traditional.[3] Moreover, candidates in fully funded public finance systems spent more time—11.5 percentage points more—meeting voters and on other field activities. Miller did not discover a similarly positive difference in voter turnout associated to public funding, but his results suggest that additional experiments in public funding, possibly for congressional races, could alter several of the negative consequences of the current campaign system.

The most prominent public funding proposal is the Fair Elections Now Act (FENA). Sponsored in the House by Democrats John Larson (CT) and John Sarbarnes (MD), the policy would match small-dollar contributions for congressional candidates who spurn PAC donations. Funding would come from what the sponsors call the Freedom from Influence Fund, which would match—at a $5- or $6-to-$1 ratio—small-dollar contributions to candidates who opt in to the financing plan. This plan could increase the number of small-dollar contributors and orient candidates away from mega-donors.

Another approach to campaign finance reform that might have the effect of lowering the total cost of campaigns, or at least shifting where money is raised, was backed by former Republican Speaker of the House, Dennis Hastert. From Hastert's point of view, the primary problem in the current system is the centralization of political contributions in a handful of cities. As a result of the concentration of wealth in New York, Chicago, and Los Angeles, candidates for office raise most of the money to run far from their constituents, potentially disconnecting the viability of their campaigns from the voters they will be representing if elected. Hastert argued that the political system would greatly improve if candidates had to "Raise at least half the money in your campaign in your district" and then make that fundraising available to the public within a day.[4] Hastert opined, "It's complete transparency so the press and voters know where the money is coming from. If they raise money in their own district, they're not running off to Wall Street or Hollywood. Let them raise their money where the voters are." For candidates running outside of the financial centers of the country, the effect would likely be to greatly lower the total cost of campaigning and tie them more closely to constituents.

RAISING THE ROOF

Cognizant of the constitutional rulings made by the Supreme Court and how difficult it would be to lower the ceiling on spending, another set of reformers seeks to increase, rather than decrease, political money, what I call *raising the roof*. The logic of this approach is that political money is dominated by a small and unrepresentative segment of the population. As I showed in Chapter 2, very few voters ever contribute to a candidate for office, and those who do tend to be more affluent or act on behalf of large corporations. For this reason, the aim of these reformers is to target the people and groups that have been out spent or under-represented in the recent past. By broadening the base of contributors, perhaps candidates would listen to a much wider array of constituents and be less beholden to mega-donors.

Consistent with this strategy, John Sarbanes from Maryland has backed the "Government by the People Act," which would give interested voters a contribution voucher, worth a $25 tax credit (or more in other iterations).[5] Voters could then use that money to contribute to one or more eligible candidates. This approach was also a component of anti-big-money presidential candidate Lawrence Lessig's "Citizens Equality Act." Knowing that all constituents eligible for the tax credit become viable contributors, candidates might be more prone to seek out their support. Rather than devoting nearly all fundraising time to wealthy and big money donors, Sarbanes's tax credit might democratize campaign contributions and broaden the pool of candidate financial supporters.

The advantage of *raising the roof* campaign reforms is that they would not alter the contributions of other individuals or corporations, thus would likely be deemed constitutional. However, they would require new federal expenditures or, at least, a potential loss of federal revenue from reduced tax returns. For decades, there has been a weak appetite on Capitol Hill for any new federal programs that are not offset with spending cuts, casting doubt on the political feasibility of the tax credit reforms. Moreover, even if the plan was politically viable, it may not be effective if voters are uninformed about how it works. Understanding that the aim of the policy is to engage those voters who are presently disengaged from politics, it would be difficult to convince them to use the campaign contribution tax credit. Researchers have tested this proposition using experimental methods. Robert Boatright, Donald P. Green, and Michael J. Malbin designed an experiment to see if direct mail to voters could increase participation in Ohio's state-level tax credit plan.[6] They found that those in the treatment group, the ones who received the mailing with information on the tax credit, had "a modest and marginally significant increase" in participation in the program compared to those in the control group. These are less than overwhelming findings but suggest the possibility of this approach increasing small-dollar contributions and political equality if there is a prominent public outreach and information component of the policy. As such, in order to increase participation and fulfill policy goals, it would likely require additional funding to market the plan, further diminishing the chances for adoption of this type of proposal.

Others have approached political reform of lobbying in a similar fashion, seeking targeted expansion rather than reductions. Lee Drutman of New America has called for a program to better balance the unequal lobbying advantages of business interests. As Chapter 4 showed, businesses out spend most opponents by huge margins. Under Drutman's plan, competing interests—citizen groups, single-issue organizations, or unions—could petition to receive a federal subsidy to support their lobbying.[7] To become eligible, underrepresented groups and issues organizations would have to pass some threshold of broad-based appeal to their issue in order to qualify for the lobbying subsidy from the federal government.

As with the campaign contribution tax credit, Drutman's plan would not infringe on the freedom of any other lobbyists, be they from business or otherwise. Rather, the subsidy would increase total lobbying on issues, broadening the interests represented in many policy debates. Also similar to the campaign contribution plan, Drutman's plan would require a new federal spending program, a likely nonstarter for many members of Congress.

Another approach to addressing the role of money and politics comes from a group that might best be called anti-reform reformers, or what Jonathan Rauch has called *realists*.[8] From this realist perspective, the recent proliferation of super PACs is the unintended and predictable consequence of campaign finance reforms over the last 40 years. The summative effect, Rauch and others argue, has been a weakening of parties and scattering of financial influence to the margins of politics. Rauch surmised, "The result [of campaign finance reform of the 1970s] was not to reduce the amount of money in politics or to reduce the influence of special interests but to drive money to unrestricted channels, such as party committees."[9] So the caps that were put in place on how much individuals could give directly to candidates and to political parties, the backbone of campaign finance reform, simply shifted where money entered into politics. After BCRA further limited how parties could coordinate spending with candidates, Rauch claimed, "the result was to push money into so-called 'independent' spending by super PACs, nonprofit organizations, billionaires, and other actors who are less accountable, less pragmatic, and less transparent than Tammany ever was."[10] Rather than empowering voters and marginalized groups, this has harmed politics in Washington because it destabilized political leadership and undermined the moderating role played by parties. As a result, the current regulatory system "has created a gray market in coordination; driven resources, professional talent, and influence to accountable outside groups; hindered candidates' and parties' ability to control and transmit their message; and underwritten the growth of a burgeoning independent political infrastructure which is difficult (at best) for leaders to organize and influence."[11] Another scholar in this tradition, Ray La Raja, concurred that "the campaign finance rules constrain coherent, party-based organizing to such an extent that partisans have sidestepped the rules to create organizations such as super PACs." La Raja continued, "Super PACs exist primarily because partisans have the motive and means to create party-like structures to offset constraints on party committees."[12] In short, regulations have done much more harm than good.

For these reasons, Richard Pildes wrote in the *Washington Post*, "I suggest, we might, for example, change campaign-finance law to encourage more money to flow to the parties—rather than to outside groups or individual candidates—and to play a bigger role in their candidate's campaigns."[13] In more specific terms, Rauch called for raising the FECA limits on contributions to candidates and parties and eliminating the BCRA ban on coordination between parties, candidates, and outside groups. Another variant of this approach was La Raja's call to increase the level of campaign contribution limits to the original value set by FECA in 1974. La Raja's argument was that limits need to keep up with changing political times and inflation. This would have a similar effect as Rauch's call for increasing contribution limits. By shifting money back to parties and possibly away from outside groups and super PACs, Rauch claimed that the power of peripheral candidates and extreme influences would also be moderated. Rauch wrote, "extremists might still get the nod in extreme districts, but allowing professionals to do more gatekeeping could give candidates and officeholders second thoughts about going rogue after the election."[14]

The feasibility of this approach rests on whether the proverbial horses can be forced back into the barn. Super PACs emerged as shadow parties in 2016, paying millions for staff, office space, advertising, and consultants. Super PACs have created new political winners, not just in the ballot box, but also in the establishment of new commitments, loyalty, and affiliation. Even if the realists' proposals were adopted by Congress, would the vast money contributed to super PACs in 2016 simply shift to political parties in 2018, 2020, and beyond? Would contributors to 501(c)(4) nonprofits, whose identities have been largely protected from public viewing, welcome the chance to disclose contributions to candidates in the future? It seems reasonable to think that they may not, rendering these types of reforms unpredictable in reorienting politics in the way they are intended.

OPENING THE WINDOWS

Raising the roof and lowering the ceiling are two approaches that will both require considerable political and legislative work. Other reforms approach the problem of money and politics with more limited but potentially effective strategies. For some of these reformers, an important dimension of the political problem is a lack of clarity and transparency about how and where money enters into the political system. This problem calls for more transparency, what I call *opening the windows*.

There are numerous transparency measures in existing laws, including mandatory disclosure for lobbyists, campaign contributors, and during federal rule making. Candidate Jimmy Carter went so far as to campaign on opening government in a 1976 political advertisement: "We need a sunshine law in Washington to open up the deliberations of the executive and legislative branches of government to the public, so that we can understand what decisions are made about our own lives, what went on behind those locked doors. There's no doubt in my mind that every lobbyist in Washington knows what goes on behind those locked doors, when the Congress is passing a tax measure or spending our tax money. But I was a governor of 5 million people, and I didn't know, so we need a sunshine law to open up government so the people can understand it."[15] As a result of sunshine laws, politics today may not be fully transparent to the public, but it is far from the closed-door, smoked-filled rooms of the past.

Reformers, though, see additional ways to shed light on important political processes. Darrell West, in his book, *Billionaires*, focused on one way that so-called *dark money* has entered into political campaigns. As noted earlier in the book, 501(c)(4) nonprofit organizations can participate in elections in certain ways, particularly through issue advertising. Current rules, though, do not require the corporations—or others individuals or organizations—to disclose donations to these nonprofits nor do they require the nonprofits to disclose donors. As a result, Naila Awan and Liz Kennedy of Demos estimated that 80% of large corporations do not voluntarily disclose how much they contribute to 501(c)(4) nonprofits.[16] This type of secret or dark money then can be used to frame policy issues and advance certain candidates with little knowledge of whose interests are at stake. As I showed in the last chapter, since these corporations also bid for government contracts and grants, transparency advocates, including the Brennan Center for Justice, have called for an executive order that requires companies applying for government contracts to disclose donations to 501(c)(4) nonprofits.[17] This type of policy change would make much clearer whether those contractor donations are linked to winning future government contracts and lead to the type of cronyism many criticize.

Similar uncertainty relates to how much lobbying is permitted by non-profit organizations, leading to a great confusion as to what is and is not permitted. Darrell West called for regulators to "clarify the regulations that govern each type of advocacy" pursued by nonprofit organizations in order to address this hidden source of influence on campaigns.[18] The Bright Lines Project associated with Public Citizen, too, has called for the IRS to make it much clearer what nonprofit organizations are and are not allowed to do in regard to politics. In a letter to one Senate committee, the Project authors stated, "We believe that so long as Congress has chosen to treat partisan and nonpartisan activities differently under the Internal Revenue Code (IRC), it is essential for the IRS to provide clear, predictable guidance so that people can engage in the civic affairs of their towns, cities, counties, states, and nation with confidence that the IRS will be fair in the enforcement of federal tax law."[19] Such clarity, though, could come at the cost of the participation of other types of non-profits, especially 501(c)(3) nonprofits, which are established for nonpolitical reasons but often represent those in the greatest need. As such, a bolder distinction issued by the IRS on nonprofit political activity could discourage 501(c)(3)s from any form advocacy, possibly undermining the already limited political voice of the truly disadvantaged.

A related area of confusion that reformers believe more clarity will help is the legal distinction between lobbying and advocacy. As noted throughout the book, lobbying has a particular legal definition, and those whose work qualifies for this definition must follow congressional disclosure rules. The specificity of the rule, though, means many of the most influential individuals outside of government do not qualify and thus are not forced to report their work as lobbying. I explained in Chapter 5 that this loophole has frustrated rules on the revolving door between government and lobbying, because many former members of Congress can pursue lucrative nonlobbying government influence during the mandatory cooling-off period.

One surprising reformer with this concern was candidate for president and former governor, Jeb Bush. During the 2016 campaign, he called for extending the cooling-off period for members of Congress to six years but also argued, "The definition of the word lobbyist should be expanded to address the cadre of government relations and government affairs specialists now populating the Capitol, as well."[20] Bush did not specify exactly what the new definition would entail but believed that this would contribute to a more transparent form of policy making in Washington. Moreover, Bush also called for disclosure of the meetings lobbyists hold with lawmakers. Bush said, "Here is what I propose: every time a lobbyist meets with any member of Congress, that should be reported online—every week, and on the member's official website."[21] New, micro-level reporting would greatly expand what we know about influence. These data might help overcome the difficulty researchers, especially those highlighted in Chapter 4, have had in proving a causal link between money and policy outcomes. Campaign promises about reform, though delivered loudly and with great vitriol, rarely amount to much when they are made months before the first primary votes are cast. If candidate are serious about extending disclosure rules and expanding lobbying prohibitions, they likely would impose those rules on their own campaign teams. Candidates, including Jeb Bush, have historically been loathed to do so.

CLOSING THE BLINDS

Others see the dysfunction of government as a result of the unintended consequences of sunshine laws and other efforts to open government. Much as the political realists described above push for more money in politics; another approach to addressing the problems of today's political and policy-making process is to let a little less light in, what I call *closing the blinds*. This approach might also be called sausage-making reform, an allusion to the oft-used phrase to describe the unpleasant way that laws are usually made and meat processed. Politics, from this vantage point, is inherently messy and necessarily ugly. The most honorable members of Congress must twist their colleagues' arms and cajole unwilling allies with offers of support—sometimes monetary. Far from a negative feature of American government, perhaps this is a strong point; allowing for difficult compromises to be reached in an expedient fashion.

As described earlier, reforms to Congress, including the banning of earmarks and lobbing disclosure, inhibit this type of legislative system from functioning. Congressional leaders have little to give intransigent colleagues in exchange for their support, often resulting in gridlock. And when most legislative meetings are held in public with the press listening, candor and friendly negotiation are sacrificed in favor of stolid partisan showmanship. Thus, Jonathan Rauch claimed that "Congress should do more business through back channels, off camera."[22] While this is a provocative idea, how it would work in practice is much less clear. In a 24-hour news environment, with a growing array of digital politics bloggers in need of content to drive clicks, it is hard to imagine how Congress would limit media access to its proceedings.

Rauch and others have a more practical solution drawn from the same spirit but focused on earmarks. Jason Grumet, the president of the Bipartisan Policy Center, called on Congress to "Bring back earmarks." He argued that "Targeted appropriations for local interests have enabled almost every major legislative accomplishment of the past century, and they do not increase overall government spending . . . Earmarks are part of the essential balance between local and national imperatives that lies at the crux of our Constitution. They should be restored with reasonable expectations of public notice and legislative deliberation."[23] Repealing the congressional ban on earmarks might head off future budget show-downs and disempower small cadres of members of Congress, such as those affiliated with the Tea Party, from bringing the government to the edge of debt default.[24] Moreover, earmark repeal might also return to Congress budgetary control that it had ceded to the executive branch over the last generation. According to Republican Senator James Inhofe (OK), "With no congressional earmarks, the stimulus bill still resulted in hundreds of outrageous expenditures that were doled out through presidential earmarks by unelected government officials."[25] Since, as I described earlier in the book, *de facto* earmarks persisted in practice even after the *de jure* ban, repealing the ban might be possible in a future Congress but only if congressional leaders could stomach the negative public repercussions of the change, something they have been unwilling to, thus far.

CONCLUDING THOUGHTS

The preceding is just a partial list of policy proposals; there are dozens of others. Yet if history is any basis on which to predict the future, many of these proposals will languish in Congress and remain in the primordial soup of policy making in Washington. Much as more money does not always move policy forward, even a widely agreed-upon policy problem, does not always lead to satisfactory resolution. The policy process is much stickier and intractable than even the most ambitious corporate PAC, trade lobbyist, or citizen activist ever anticipates.

Another reason for the strong likelihood of another generation of the status quo approach to money and politics is our contemporary conception of corruption. It seems that our current focus on the most egregious examples of corruption, those that end up with a public official being lead off in handcuffs, have distorted a clearer idea of the public good. Public attitudes toward politics have grown so cynical and detached that few are aware of the deeper political processes where legal corruption runs rampant and the influence of wealth prevails but can barely be observed. This may be why there is such a wide consensus on money and politics being a problem but little enthusiasm to push forward change. The courts have reinforced this narrow view of corruption by ruling against most restrictions on campaign finance that are not focused on *quid pro quo* corruption. Anything short of delivering a briefcase full of cash on the floor of Congress has come to be protected by the Constitution and cynically accepted as how government operates. For change to occur, a collective reflection on what is and is not corruption, possibly not in a purely legal sense but using a broader ethical framework may be needed.

For some, such reflection would serve to recapture the past. Zephyr Teachout has called for the reemergence of the anti-corruption principle—a standard essential to the nation's founding according to Teachout—to ground discussions about these issues, in and out of the courts.[26] For Teachout, returning to a view of the public interest as a virtuous aspiration to be comprehensively protected—including from even the appearance of impropriety—would advance our common hopes for an equal, open, and democratic system of government. In order to meet this lofty aspiration, perhaps Teachout can form common cause with those Tea Party protesters of 2009, so fond of a return to the high-minded spirit of the American Revolution and reclamation of the original intent of the Constitution.

Such a change and cross-cutting coalition is unlikely if the concern for corruption remains a largely partisan affair. At the start of the book, I recounted the assortment of Democratic and Republican presidential candidates who criticized the current system of money and politics. This would suggest some level of support on Capitol Hill for reform. In fact, quite the opposite is true. Members of Congress have sponsored legislation, including many of the reforms described earlier in this chapter, but few ever mention campaign finance or lobbying reform (see Figure 7.1).[27] Less than half (41%) of a sample of congressional websites included any mention of either, and less than a fifth of Republicans did so (63% of Democrats did). As noted earlier, over 80% of the country believes that money and politics is a problem and the *Citizens United* decision should be reconsidered, yet many in Congress, especially those in the Republican Party, remain silent on the issue.

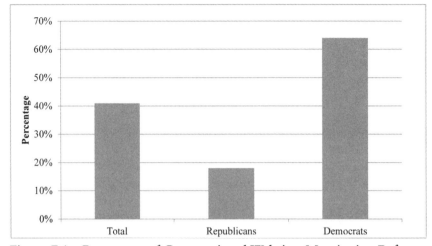

Figure 7.1   Percentage of Congressional Websites Mentioning Reforms to Money and Politics

Writing for the conservative *Weekly Standard*, Jay Cost lamented just this issue. He questioned, "Where is the anti-corruption agenda of the right?"[28] For Cost, Democrats have put forward an array of reforms, with which Republicans have largely disagreed, but they have offered no response. When BCRA was signed by President Bush in the early 2000s, it reflected few conservative ideas or proposals. Cost recently wrote, "Conservatives have spent enormous intellectual capital on issues like education, health care, and taxes—but what about corruption? When Democratic pols rail against Citizens United, what reforms can Republicans counter with?"

Cost's assessment was probably true of the conservative intellectual class in Washington, but it suggests a more general political passivity on the Right that may be less true. Our current campaign finance system and approach to corruption is not the result simply of neglect. There has been a concerted fight against campaign finance reform, and it has been overseen by conservative organizations for decades. Common Cause found that for 20 years the National Right to Life Committee, the Christian Coalition, the National Organization for Marriage, and Focus on the Family have spearheaded a legal movement to weaken campaign finance laws, both at the federal and state levels of government.[29] These organizations—many with a mission to promote conservative social policy issues—were not established to fight against restrictions on money and politics, but they have received enormous amounts of money from foundations, including the DeVos Family Foundation, the Bradley Foundation, and the Susan B. Anthony List Education Foundation, to pursue this cause.

Perhaps, then, an equally spirited social movement of opposition is needed to combat this heavy lobbying against campaign and political reform; one like the campus-based program, Democracy Matters.[30] Jacob Hacker and Paul Pierson called for something like this in their book, *Winner-Takes-All Politics*: "the politics of renewal cannot become deeply grounded without mass engagement as well as elite leadership . . . Political reformers will need to mobilize for the long haul, appreciating that it is not electoral competitions alone that are decisive, but also the creation of organized capacity to cement a meaningful middle-class democracy by turning electoral victories into substantive and sustainable triumphs."[31] Recent mass movements, though, have proven fleeting and ambivalent about these types of specific policy achievements. The Occupy Movement, for one, mustered a certain level of support and symbolic victories but showed little interest in institutionalizing these successes in slates of electoral candidates, a particular policy agenda, or a lasting organizational structure.[32] It may not be reasonable to expect a future version of Occupy to address these money and politics issues.

Moreover, there are additional reasons to be pessimistic. Other recent populist efforts to promote public engagement in government, including participatory budgeting and local consultations, have been successfully turned into business opportunities and sometimes co-opted by business interests. Caroline Lee found that once-well-meaning exercises in expanding civic participation, such as holding open town hall meetings and soliciting community feedback, have spawned an industry of experts, consultants, and new businesses.[33] In professionalizing how communities come together to engage government and other institutions, the independence and critical voice of public dissent may be set aside in favor of order and expediency. Even the idea of grassroots movements has taken on increasingly corporate tones. Edward Walker showed that the business community has seen the profit-potential of grassroots organizing.[34] Businesses stimulate grassroots support to grow profits and now can hire private companies to do the organizing. Social media is just one realm where the promise for a truly open and democratic space for citizen engagement shows signs of being crowded out by sponsored corporate content. In an environment where money has crept into mass mobilization, citizen engagement, and public participation, is there any hope for truly major reform movements to emerge? Is it plausible to expect businesses to support an agenda aimed to diminish corporate political power?

Short of a controversy the magnitude of Watergate, it is reasonable to expect most of our current system to remain intact. If, in the end, we are stuck with our current arrangement—a system of campaigns with laughably large amount of money spent on television commercials that everyone deplores; a system of policy making with lobbyists massively outnumbering those with the authority to make government decisions; a system of public service where the greatest rewards accrue to those savvy enough to retire with a golden parachute of private influence; a system that holds thousands of open elections but rarely listens to the vast majority of voters who are not millionaires—what are we to do? If this system of money and politics, in fact, defines the democracy in the United States, at least we can marvel at Donald Trump's tumultuous rise and fall and eagerly anticipate another election in 2020.

Notes

CHAPTER 1: INTRODUCTION

1. Phillip Rucker, "Hillary Clinton Says She Would Support a Constitutional Amendment on Campaign Finance Reform," *Washington Post*, April 14, 2015, http://www.washingtonpost.com/blogs/post-politics/wp/2015/04/14/hillary-clinton-says-she-would-support-a-constitutional-amendment-on-campaign-finance-reform/.

2. *Hillary: The Movie*, http://www.hillarythemovie.com/; Stephen Labaton, "The 1992 Campaign: Campaign Finances; Despite Economy, Clinton Sets Record for Funds," *The New York Times*, October 24, 1992, http://www.nytimes.com/1992/10/24/us/1992-campaign-campaign-finances-despite-economy-clinton-sets-record-for-funds.html.

3. Bernie Sanders, https://web.archive.org/web/20150702015955/https://berniesanders.com/issues/money-in-politics/.

4. Martin O'Malley, https://martinomalley.com/vision/.

5. Matea Gold, "Big Money in Politics Emerges as a Rising Issue in 2016 Campaign," *Washington Post*, April 19, 2015, http://www.washingtonpost.com/politics/big-money-in-politics-emerges-as-a-rising-issue-in-2016-campaign/2015/04/19/c695cbb8-e51c-11e4-905f-cc896d379a32_story.html?hpid=z1.

6. Ibid.

7. David Graham, "GOP Candidates Discover the Problems with Money in Politics," *The Atlantic*, April 2015, http://www.theatlantic.com/politics/archive/2015/04/not-all-republicans/390912/.

8. Jake Miller, "Is Martin O'Malley's New Super PAC a Jab at Hillary Clinton?," CBS News, May 28, 2015, http://www.cbsnews.com/news/election-2016-is-martin-omalleys-new-super-pac-a-jab-at-hillary-clinton/.

9. Mark Halperin, "Exclusive: New Ted Cruz Super-PACs Take in Record Haul," *Bloomberg*, April 8, 2015, http://www.bloomberg.com/politics/articles/2015-04-08/exclusive-new-ted-cruz-super-pacs-take-in-record-haul.

10. New York Times/CBS News, "A New York Times/CBS News Poll on Money and Politics," *New York Times*, June 2, 2015, http://www.nytimes.com/interactive/2015/06/01/us/politics/document-poll-may-28-31.html.

11. Ibid.

12. Government Procurement Office, "U.S.C. Title 18," http://www.gpo.gov/fdsys/pkg/USCODE-2012-title18/html/USCODE-2012-title18-partI-chap11-sec201.htm: "§201. Bribery of public officials and witnesses: . . . directly or indirectly, corruptly gives, offers or promises anything of value . . . to influence any official act; or . . . to influence such public official or person who has been selected to be a public official to commit or aid in committing, or collude in, or allow, any fraud, or make opportunity for the commission of any fraud, on the United States; or . . . to induce such public official or such person who has been selected to be a public official to do or omit to do any act in violation of the lawful duty of such official or person;" "being a public official or person selected to be a public official, directly or indirectly, corruptly demands, seeks, receives, accepts, or agrees to receive or accept anything of value personally or for any other person or entity, in return for: (A) being influenced in the performance of any official act; (B) being influenced to commit or aid in committing, or to collude in, or allow, any fraud, or make opportunity for the commission of any fraud, on the United States; or (C) being induced to do or omit to do any act in violation of the official duty of such official or person."

13. Lee Drutman, "Bring Back Corruption!," *Democracy Journal* 35 (Winter 2015), http://www.democracyjournal.org/35/bring-back-corruption.php?page=all.

14. Matt Smith and Deanna Hackney, "Ex-New Orleans Mayor Ray Nagin Guilty after Courtroom 'Belly Flop,'" CNN, February 14, 2014, http://www.cnn.com/2014/02/12/justice/louisiana-nagin-convicted/.

15. Ben Kasimar, "Court Tosses Ex-Gov. Blagojevich Conviction Over Obama's Senate Seat," *The Hill*, July 21, 2015, http://thehill.com/blogs/blog-briefing-room/248707-ex-gov-blagojevich-gets-some-corruption-convictions-over turned.

16. Nicholas Carnes, *White Collar Government: The Hidden Role of Class in Economic Policy Making* (Chicago: University of Chicago Press, 2014), 16.

17. West cites research from Benjamin Page, Larry Bartels, and Jason Seawright, "Democracy and the Policy Preferences of Wealthy Americans," *Perspectives on Politics* 11 (March 2013).

18. Ibid.

19. Kay Schlozman, Sidney Verba, and Henry Brady, *The Unheavenly Chorus: Unequal Political Voice and the Broken Promise of American Democracy* (Princeton, NJ: Princeton University Press, 2013), 6.

20. Martin Gilens and Benjamin Page, "Testing Theories of American Politics: Elites, Interest Groups, and Average Citizens," *Perspectives on Politics* 12, no. 3 (2014): 572.

21. Ibid.

22. Jennifer Lawless and Richard Fox, *Running from Office: Why Young Americans Are Turned Off to Politics* (New York: Oxford University Press, 2015), 12.

23. Mark Hetherington and Thomas Rudolph, *Why Washington Won't Work* (Chicago: University of Chicago Press, 2015).

24. Nicholas Carnes, *White Collar Government: The Hidden Role of Class in Economic Policy Making* (Chicago: University of Chicago Press, 2014), 12–18.

25. Calculation based on 2014 inflation adjusted data from the Campaign Finance Institute, http://www.cfinst.org/pdf/vital/VitalStats_t1.pdf.

26. Open Secrets, https://www.opensecrets.org/lobby/.

27. Ford Foundation http://www.fordfoundation.org/grants/grantdetails?grantid=120961.

28. Larry Bartels, *Unequal Democracy: The Political Economy of the New Gilded Age* (Princeton, NJ: Princeton University Press, 2008), 2.

29. "Who Exactly Are the 1%?," *The Economist*, January 21, 2012, http://www.economist.com/node/21543178.

30. Bartels, *Unequal Democracy*, 11.

31. Gilens and Page, Testing Theories."

32. Open Secrets, https://www.opensecrets.org/parties/softsource.php.

33. Paul Herrnson, "A New Era of Interest Group Participation in Federal Elections," in *Interest Groups Unleashed*, ed. Paul S. Herrnson, Christopher J. Deering, and Clyde Wilcox (Thousand Oaks, CA: CQ Press, 2013), 13.

34. Ibid., 17.

35. Tim Harford, "There's Not Enough Money in Politics," *Slate*, February 2006, http://www.slate.com/articles/arts/the_undercover_economist/2006/04/theres_not_enough_money_in_politics.html.

36. "20 Ways Americans Are Blowing Their Money," *USA Today*, March 24, 2014, http://www.usatoday.com/story/money/personalfinance/2014/03/24/20-ways-we-blow-our-money/6826633/; Lucas Reilly, "By the Numbers: How Americans Spend Their Money," Mental Floss, July 17, 2012, http://mentalfloss.com/article/31222/numbers-how-americans-spend-their-money.

37. Jonathan Rauch, *Political Realism: How Hacks, Machines, and Big Money and Back-Room Deals Can Strengthen American Democracy* (Washington, DC: Brookings Institution Press, 2015), 161.

38. "Congressional Pig Book," CAGW, http://cagw.org/reporting/pig-book; "Wastebook 2014," Federalist Society, November 22, 2014, http://thefederalist.com/2014/10/22/wastebook-2014-eight-absurd-government-projects-funded-with-your-money/.

39. Raymond J. La Raja and Brian F. Schaffner, *Campaign Finance and Political Polarization: When Purists Prevail* (Ann Arbor: University of Michigan Press, 2015).

CHAPTER 2: THE PUBLIC AND POLITICAL MONEY

1. John Myers, "The Cheap Date That Was California's 2014 Race for Governor," KQED, January 31, 2015, http://ww2.kqed.org/news/2015/01/31/2014-race-for-california-governor-cheapest-in-decades/.

2. Sherry Bebitch Jeffe and Douglas Jeffe, "The Most Expensive Political Contest in California Is for an Office Nobody's Heard of," *Reuters*, November 3, 2014, http://blogs.reuters.com/great-debate/2014/11/03/the-most-expensive-political-contest-in-california-is-for-an-office-nobodys-heard-of/.

3. California budget summary, http://www.dof.ca.gov/budgeting/budget_faqs/documents/CHART-E.pdf; California education personnel summary, http://www.cde.ca.gov/ds/sd/cb/ceffingertipfacts.asp.

4. Ron Chernow, *The House of Morgan: An American Banking Dynasty and the Rise of Modern Finance* (New York: Grove Press, 2001).

5. FEC, http://www.fec.gov/info/contriblimitschart1516.pdf.

6. Open Secrets, https://www.opensecrets.org/overview/donordemographics.php.

7. Open Secrets, https://www.opensecrets.org/overview/mccutcheon.php.

8. Kurt Walters, "Country Club Politics," Public Campaign, 2012, http://www.publicampaign.org/files/CountryClubPolitics.pdf.

9. Open Secrets, https://www.opensecrets.org/outsidespending/summ.php?cycle=2014&disp=D&type=V.

10. Katia Savchuk, "Billionaire Tom Steyer on Money in Politics, Spending $74 M on the Election," *Forbes,* November 3, 2014, http://www.forbes.com/sites/katiasavchuk/2014/11/03/billionaire-tom-steyer-on-money-in-politics-spending-74-m-on-the-election/.

11. Ibid.

12. Ibid.

13. "In Conversation: Michael Bloomberg," *New York Magazine*, September 2013, http://nymag.com/news/politics/bloomberg/in-conversation-2013-9/index3.html.

14. Kevin McDermott, "At $37 Million and Counting, Mega-Donor Sinquefield Says He's Not Going Anywhere," *St. Louis Today,* January 19, 2015, http://www.stltoday.com/news/local/govt-and-politics/at-million-and-counting-mega-donor-sinquefield-says-he-s/article_9f75ba07-618d-56ff-bd47-2a35ee2a2e5e.html.

15. Ibid.

16. Sean Sullivan, "Meet the Billionaire Hedge Fund Manager Quietly Shaping the GOP Gay Marriage Debate," *Washington Post,* May 3, 2013, http://www.washingtonpost.com/blogs/the-fix/wp/2013/05/03/meet-the-billionaire-hedge-fund-manager-quietly-shaping-the-gop-gay-marriage-debate/.

17. Open Secrets, http://www.opensecrets.org/outsidespending/recips.php?cmte=American+Unity+PAC&cycle=2014.

18. Monica Langley, "Texas Billionaire Doles Out Election's Biggest Checks," *Wall Street Journal*, January 22, 2013, http://www.wsj.com/articles/SB10001424052702303812904577291450562940874.

19. Melissa Harris, "Ken Griffin Interview: Billionaire Talks Politics and Money," *Chicago Tribune*, March 11, 2012, http://articles.chicagotribune.com/2012-03-11/business/ct-biz-0311-confidential-griffin-web-version-20120311_1_american-crossroads-politics-republicans-and-democrats/2.

20. Ibid.

21. Daniel McCoy, "Charles Koch: Business Giant, Bogeyman, Benefactor and Elusive (Until Now)—Exclusive Interview," *Wichita Business Journal*, February 28, 2014, http://www.bizjournals.com/wichita/blog/2014/02/40-minutes-with-charles-koch.html.

22. Ibid.

23. Open Secrets, https://www.opensecrets.org/orgs/summary.php?id=D000024046&cycle=2012.

24. Wyatt Andrews and Phil Hirschkorn, "Jeffrey Katzenberg Explains Super PAC Donation," CBS News, April 6, 2012, http://www.cbsnews.com/news/jeffrey-katzenberg-explains-super-pac-donation/.

25. Ibid.

26. Mike Allen, "Sheldon Adelson: Inside the Mind of the Mega-Donor," *Politico*, September 23, 2012, http://www.politico.com/story/2012/09/sheldon-adelson-inside-the-mind-of-the-mega-donor-081588.

27. Ibid.

28. Langley, "Texas Billionaire."

29. Savchuk, "Billionaire Tom Steyer."

30. Annie Linskey, "Seth Klarman Opens Up about His Financial Support of GOP," *Boston Globe*, May 29, 2015, https://www.bostonglobe.com/news/politics/2015/05/29/boston-fund-manager-seth-klarman-opens-about-his-financial-support-gop/AOfozraNcbBsV8HH90ugoO/story.html.

31. Andrews, "Jeffrey Katzenberg."

32. Savchuk, "Billionaire Tom Steyer."

33. Andrews, "Jeffrey Katzenberg."

34. Savchuk, "Billionaire Tom Steyer."

35. Langley, "Texas Billionaire."

36. Savchuk, "Billionaire Tom Steyer."

37. Langley, "Texas Billionaire."

38. Allen, "Sheldon Adelson."

39. Wyatt Andrews and Phil Hirschkorn, "Billionaire Super PAC Donor Julian Robertson Speaks Out," CBS News, April 7, 2012, http://www.cbsnews.com/news/billionaire-super-pac-donor-julian-robertson-speaks-out/.

40. Ibid.

41. AFSA, http://www.afsa.org/list-ambassadorial-appointments.

42. Dave Weigel, "Nominee for Ambassador to Argentina Hasn't Been There, but Has Raised Lots of Money for Obama," *Slate,* February 7, 2014, http://www.slate.com/blogs/weigel/2014/02/07/nominee_for_ambassador_to_argentina_hasn_t_been_there_but_has_raised_lots.html.

43. Evan Halper, "Koch Brothers, Big Utilities Attack Solar, Green Energy Policies," *LA Times*, April 19, 2014, http://www.latimes.com/nation/la-na-solar-kochs-20140420-story.html#page=1; Editorial Board, "The Koch Cycle of Endless Cash," *New York Times*, June 14, 2014, http://www.nytimes.com/2014/06/14/opinion/the-koch-cycle-of-endless-cash.html?module=Search&mabRewward=relbias%3Ar%2C%7B.

44. Nicholas Confessore and Eric Lipton, "Seeking to Ban Online Betting, G.O.P. Donor Tests Influence," *New York Times,* March 27, 2014, http://www.nytimes.com/2014/03/28/us/politics/major-gop-donor-tests-his-influence-in-push-to-ban-online-gambling.html?hpw&rref=us&_r=0.

45. Coalition to Stop Internet Gambling, http://stopinternetgambling.com/about-coalition-to-stop-internet-gambling/.

46. Confessore and Lipton, "Seeking to Ban."

47. Carrie Kahn, "Head of Shrek's Studio Puts Millions behind Obama," *NPR*, May 11, 2012, http://www.npr.org/2012/05/11/152349916/head-of-shreks-studio-puts-millions-behind-obama.

48. Rachel Abrams, "China's Film Quota Cracked," *Variety,* February 20, 2012, http://variety.com/2012/film/news/china-s-film-quota-cracked-1118050508/.

49. Open Secrets, https://www.opensecrets.org/overview/donordemographics.php.

50. Molly Redden, "The Wealthy Woman behind Wendy Davis," *New Republic,* July 8, 2013, http://www.newrepublic.com/article/113760/meet-amber-mostyn-wendy-daviss-most-powerful-political-patron; Open Secrets, https://www.opensecrets.org/outsidespending/summ.php?cycle=2014&disp=D&type=V&superonly=N.

51. Ellen Miller, "Who Gives?," *The American Prospect,* December 19, 2001, http://prospect.org/article/who-gives.

52. Open Secrets, https://www.opensecrets.org/overview/donordemographics.php.

53. According to the U.S. Census Bureau, the median family income in 2013 was $53,046. See http://quickfacts.census.gov/qfd/states/00000.html.

54. Jennifer Lawless and Richard Fox, *Running from Office* (New York: Oxford University Press, 2015), 20.

55. Ibid.

56. Sidney Verba, Kay Schlozman, and Henry Brady, *Voice and Equality: Civic Voluntarism in American Politics* (Cambridge, MA: Harvard University Press, 1995).

57. Pew Research Center, http://www.people-press.org/2014/06/12/political-contributions/.

58. Verba et al., *Voice and Equality.*

59. Pew Research Center.

60. Clyde Wilcox, Alexandra Cooper, Peter Francia, John Green, Paul S. Herrnson, Lynda Powell, Jason Reifler, Mark J. Rozell, and Benjamin A. Webster, "With Limits Raised, Who Will Give More? The Impact of BCRA on Individual Donors," in *Life After Reform: When the Bipartisan Campaign Reform Act Meets Politics*, ed. Michael J. Malbin (Lanham, MD: Rowman & Littlefield, 2003), 61–79.

61. James Gimpel, Frances Lee, and Joshua Kaminski, "The Political Geography of Campaign Contributions in American Politics," *Journal of Politics* 68, no. 3 (2006): 626–39.

62. Open Secrets, https://www.opensecrets.org/overview/topzips.php.

63. "Money in Politics with a Gender Lens," National Council for Research on Women, January 2014, http://regender.org/sites/ncrw.org/files/moneyinpolitics withagenderlens_0.pdf.

64. Ibid.

65. She Should Run, "Vote with Your Purse: Lessons Learned: Women, Money, and Politics in the 2010 Election Cycle," 2010, http://d3n8a8pro7vhmx.cloud front.net/womenandpolitics/pages/50/attachments/original/1378712276/vote -with-your-purse.pdf?1378712276.

66. Peter Francia, Paul S. Herrnson, John C. Green, Linda W. Powell, and Clyde Wilcox, *The Financiers of Congressional Elections: Investors, Ideologues, and Intimates* (New York: Columbia University Press, 2003), 69–126; Henry Brady, Kay Lehman Schlozman, and Sidney Verba, "Prospecting for Participants: Rational Expectations and the Recruitment of Political Activists," *American Political Science Review* 93, no. 1 (1999): 153–68.

67. Nathanial Persily and Kelli Lammie, "Perceptions of Corruption and Campaign Finance: When Public Opinion Determines Constitutional Law," *Faculty Scholarship,* Paper 30 (2004), http://scholarship.law.upenn.edu/cgi/ viewcontent.cgi?article=1029&context=faculty_scholarship.

68. *New York Times*/CBS News 2015, https://s3.amazonaws.com/s3.document cloud.org/documents/2091162/poll-may-28-31.pdf.

69. Persily and Lammie, "Perceptions of Corruption," 147–55.

70. Clyde Wilcox et al., "With Limits Raised," 61–79.

71. Karin Kamp, "Majority of Americans Want Money Out of Politics," BillMoyers.com, November 21, 2014, http://billmoyers.com/2014/11/21/majority -americans-want-money-politics/.

72. *New York Times*/CBS News.

73. Rasmussen Reports, "54% Say Government Should Regulate Campaign Contributions," April 7, 2014, http://www.rasmussenreports.com/public_content /politics/general_politics/april_2014/54_say_government_should_regulate _campaign_contributions.

74. Lydia Saad, "Half in U.S. Support Publicly Financed Federal Campaigns," Gallup, June 24, 2013, http://www.gallup.com/poll/163208/half-support-pub licly-financed-federal-campaigns.aspx.

75. Persily and Lammie, "Perceptions of Corruption," 147–55.

76. Ibid.

77. Shaun Bowler and Todd Donovan, "Campaign Money, Congress, and Perceptions of Corruption," *American Politics Research*, July 20, 2015, doi: 10.1177/1532673X15594232.

78. Al Kamen and Colby Itkowitz, "Want to Stop Enriching People Whose Politics You Hate: There's an App for That," *Washington Post,* August 12, 2014, http://www.washingtonpost.com/politics/want-to-stop-enriching-people -whose-politics-you-hate-theres-an-app-for-that/2014/08/12/bcf68d42-2251 -11e4-86ca-6f03cbd15c1a_story.html.

79. GQRR, http://www.gqrr.com/casestudies/facebook-likes-and-contributions.

80. Aaron Smith and Maeve Duggan, "Presidential Campaign Donations in the Digital Age," Pew Research Center, October 25, 2012, http://www.pewinternet .org/2012/10/25/presidential-campaign-donations-in-the-digital-age/.

81. David Karpf, *The MoveOn Effect* (New York: Oxford University Press, 2012).

82. Stephanie Stamm, "How Do Presidential Candidates Spend $1 Billion," *National Journal,* June 8, 2015, http://www.nationaljournal.com/2016-elections/ how-do-presidential-candidates-spend-1-billion-20150608.

83. Karpf, *MoveOn Effect*, 33.

84. Daniel Kreiss, *Taking Our Country Back: The Crafting of Networked Politics* (New York: Oxford University Press, 2012).

85. David Magleby, Jay Goodliffe, and Joseph Olson, "How the Internet, BCRA, and Super PACs Have Affected Donor Attitudes, Behavior, and Campaigns" (paper presented at the annual meeting of the American Political Science Association, Washington, DC, August 28–31, 2014, http://papers.ssrn.com/sol3/ papers.cfm?abstract_id=2454301.

86. Theda Skocpol and Vanessa Williamson, *The Tea Party and the Remaking of Republican Conservatism* (New York: Oxford University Press, 2013).

87. Heath Brown, *Tea Party Divided* (Santa Barbara, CA: Praeger, 2015), 67–68.

88. Polling by Lake Research Partners cited by John Papagiannis, Public Campaign, September 28, 2010, http://www.publicampaign.org/blog/2010/09/28/ new-polling-in-battleground-congressional-districts-shows-strong-support-for -fair-elections.

89. Kristina Peterson and Janet Hook, "Eric Cantor Loses to Tea Party's David Brat in Virginia Primary," *Wall Street Journal,* June 10, 2014, http://www.wsj .com/articles/no-2-house-republican-eric-cantor-defeated-in-virginia-primary -upset-1402445714.

90. Brown, *Tea Party Divided*, 130–50.

91. Michael Gould Wartofsky, *The Occupiers: The Making of the 99 Percent Movement* (New York: Oxford University Press, 2015).

CHAPTER 3: CASH, COURTS, AND THE CONSTITUTION

1. Zephyr Teachout, *Corruption in America: From Benjamin Franklin's Snuff Box to Citizens United* (Cambridge, MA: Harvard University Press, 2014).

2. Ibid., 3.

3. Articles of Confederation, http://avalon.law.yale.edu/18th_century/artconf .asp#art6.

4. Teachout, *Corruption in America*, 17–31.

5. Ibid.

6. Ibid., 31.

7. James Madison, "The Federalist Papers: No. 57," The Constitution Society, http://www.constitution.org/fed/federa57.htm.

8. Alexander Hamilton, "The Federalist Papers: No. 68," The Avalon Project, http://avalon.law.yale.edu/18th_century/fed68.asp.

9. Ibid.

10. James Madison, "The Federalist Papers: No. 55," The Constitution Society, http://www.constitution.org/fed/federa55.htm.

11. Seth Barrett Tillman, "*Citizens United* and the Scope of Professor Teachout's Anti-Corruption Principle," *Northwestern University Law Review* 399 (2012): 1–22, http://scholarlycommons.law.northwestern.edu/cgi/viewcontent.cgi?article =1040&context=nulr_online.

12. Madison, "The Federalist Papers: No. 55."

13. Mike O'Connor, *A Commercial Republic* (Lawrence: University Press of Kansas, 2014), 16–25.

14. Ibid., 18.

15. James Roger Sharp, *American Politics in the Early Republic: The New Nation in Crisis* (New Haven, CT: Yale University Press, 1993).

16. George Washington, http://avalon.law.yale.edu/18th_century/washing .asp.

17. Brian Murphy, *Building the Empire State: Political Economy in Early America* (Philadelphia: University of Pennsylvania Press, 2015), 90–106.

18. Ibid., 90.

19. Ibid., 79.

20. Ibid., 108.

21. Ibid., 106.

22. Smithsonian Magazine, "Thomas Jefferson, Aaron Burr and the Election of 1800," http://www.smithsonianmag.com/history/thomas-jefferson-aaron-burr -and-the-election-of-1800-131082359/?no-ist=&page=4.

23. Murphy, *Building the Empire State*, 109.

24. Gil Troy, "The Campaign Triumphant," *Wilson Quarterly*, Summer 2012, http://archive.wilsonquarterly.com/essays/campaign-triumphant.

25. Terry Golway, *Machine Made* (New York: Liveright, 2013), 7.

26. Paul Finkleman, ed., *Encyclopedia of African American History: 1896 to the Present, From the Age of Segregation to the 21st Century* (New York: Oxford University Press, 2009), 57, 143.

27. Hanes Walton Jr., Sherman C. Puckett, and Donald R. Deskins Jr., *The African American Electorate: A Statistical History* (Thousand Oaks, CA: CQ Press, 2012), 333.

28. U.S. Supreme Court, http://caselaw.findlaw.com/us-supreme-court/302/277.html.

29. Glenn Feldman, *The Solid South* (Birmingham: University of Alabama Press, 2012), 214.

30. Ibid., 211.

31. House of Representatives, http://history.house.gov/HistoricalHighlight/Detail/37045.

32. Golway, *Machine Made*, 6.

33. Edward B. Foley, "Unlawful Inducements to Vote: Distinguishing Them from Lawful Activities," Election Law @ Moritz, September 7, 2004, http://moritzlaw.osu.edu/electionlaw/ebook/part3/campaign_getout02.html.

34. Fabrice Lehoucq, "When Do Parties Buy Votes: Theoretical and Empirical Perspectives on Electoral Corruption" (paper presented at the conference, "Trading Political Rights: The Comparative Politics of Vote Buying," MIT, Cambridge, MA, August 26–27, 2002), http://web.mit.edu/cis/pdf/Lehoucq.pdf.

35. Richard Hasen, "Vote Buying," *California Law Review* 88, no. 5 (2000): 1323–72.

36. Foley, "Unlawful Inducements."

37. Robert Mutch, *Buying the Vote: A History of Campaign Finance Reform* (New York: Oxford University Press, 2014).

38. Paul Herrnson, "A New Era in Interest Group Participation in Federal Elections," in *Interest Groups Unleashed*, ed. Paul Herrnson, Christopher Deering, and Clyde Wilcox (Washington, DC: CQ Press, 2013), 9–30.

39. FEC, http://www.fec.gov/info/appfour.htm.

40. John Dickerson and Louise Dufresne, "JFK Defends 'Extravagant' Campaign Spending in 1960," CBS News, June 11, 2015, http://www.cbsnews.com/news/jfk-defends-extravagant-campaign-spending-in-1960/.

41. John F. Kennedy, "Letter to the President of the Senate and to the Speaker of the House Transmitting Bills To Carry out Recommendations of the Commission on Campaign Costs," The American Presidency Project, May 29, 1962, http://www.presidency.ucsb.edu/ws/?pid=8687.

42. "The Forever Campaign," *New York Magazine,* http://nymag.com/news/politics/elections-2012/election-timeline.html.

43. Tim Weiner, *One Man Against the World: The Tragedy of Richard Nixon* (New York: Henry Holt, 2015), 53.

44. Dan Eggen, "Post-Watergate Campaign Finance Limits Undercut by Changes," *Washington Post,* June 16, 2012, http://www.washingtonpost.com/politics/post-watergate-campaign-finance-limits-undercut-by-changes/2012/06/16/gJQAinRrhV_story.html.

45. Ibid.

46. Robert L. Jackson and Ronald J. Ostrow, "$700,000 for Nixon—Patman's Report," *San Francisco Chronicle*, September 13, 1972, http://jfk.hood.edu/Collection/White%20Materials/Watergate/Watergate%20Items%2000181%20to%2000373/Watergate%2000269.pdf.

47. Richard Nixon, "Statement on Signing the Federal Election Campaign Act of 1971," The American Presidency Project, February 7, 1972, http://www.presidency.ucsb.edu/ws/?pid=3725.

48. Deborah Goldberg ed., *Writing Reform: A Guide to Drafting State and Local Campaign Finance Laws* (New York: Brennan Center for Justice, 2008), https://www.brennancenter.org/sites/default/files/legacy/Democracy/08writingref/Writing%20Reform%202008%20-%20Chapter%201.pdf.

49. L. Paige Whitaker, "The Constitutionality of Campaign Finance Regulation: *Buckley v. Valeo* and Its Supreme Court Progeny," CRS Report for Congress RL30669, 2008, https://fas.org/sgp/crs/misc/RL30669.pdf.

50. Paul Herrnson, "The Bipartisan Campaign Reform Act and Congressional Elections," in *Congress Reconsidered*, 8th ed., ed. Lawrence Dodd and Bruce Oppenheimer (Washington, DC: Congressional Quarterly Press, 2005), 109.

51. Michael Malbin, "Assessing the Bipartisan Campaign Reform Act," in *The Election After Reform: Money, Politics, and the Bipartisan Campaign Reform Act*, ed. Michael Malbin (New York: Campaign Finance Institute, 2006), 6.

52. Herrnson, "Bipartisan," 111.

53. Ibid., 118.

54. George W. Bush, "Statement on Signing the Bipartisan Campaign Reform Act of 2002," The American Presidency Project, March 27, 2002, http://www.presidency.ucsb.edu/ws/?pid=64503.

55. Ibid.

56. Robert Lowry, "Analyzing Campaign Contributions in Context: The Effects of Political Environment and Legal Regulations on Itemized Contributions to Federal Campaign Committees," *American Politics Research* 43, no. 3 (2015): 445.

57. Ibid.

58. *McConnell v. FEC*, 2003, https://www.law.cornell.edu/supct/html/02-1674.ZO.html.

59. Ibid.

60. Ibid.

61. *Nixon v. Shrink Missouri Government PAC*, https://www.law.cornell.edu/supct/html/98-963.ZC.html.

62. Ibid.

63. *Speechnow.org v. FEC*, http://www.fec.gov/law/litigation/speechnow.shtml.

64. http://www.fec.gov/law/litigation/McCutcheon.shtml.

65. Kenneth P. Vogel and Byron Tau, "Shaun McCutcheon's Victory Lap," *Politico*, April, 14, 2014, http://www.politico.com/story/2014/04/shaun-mccutcheon-supreme-court-case-105646.html.

66. FEC, http://www.fec.gov/law/litigation/mccutcheon_sc_mcc_brief.pdf, 8.

67. Ibid., 17.

68. *McCutcheon et al. v. FEC*, Legal Information Institute, https://www.law .cornell.edu/supremecourt/text/12-536#writing-12-536_OPINION_3.

69. Michael Beckel, "The 'McCutcheon' Decision Explained—More Money to Pour into Political Process," Center for Public Integrity, April 22, 2014, http://www.publicintegrity.org/2014/04/22/14611/mccutcheon-decision -explained-more-money-pour-political-process.

70. "Reactions to the Supreme Court Reversing Limits on Corporate Spending in Political Campaigns," *Washington Post*, January 21, 2010, http://voices .washingtonpost.com/44/2010/01/reactions-to-the-supreme-court.html.

71. Ibid.

72. Bill of Rights, http://www.archives.gov/exhibits/charters/bill_of_rights _transcript.html.

73. Lobbying Disclosure Act, http://lobbyingdisclosure.house.gov/amended _lda_guide.html.

74. Thomas Holyoke, *The Ethical Lobbyist: Reforming Washington's Influence Industry* (Washington, DC: Georgetown University Press, 2015).

CHAPTER 4: BUSINESS, MONEY, AND POLITICS

1. Pfizer, http://www.pfizer.com/about/history/1849-1899.

2. Ibid.

3. Pfizer, "Lobbying and Political Contributions," http://www.pfizer.com/ responsibility/grants_contributions/lobbying_and_political_contributions.

4. Ibid.

5. Pfizer, "Pfizer Political Action Committee and Political Contributions Report," https://www.pfizer.com/about/corporate_governance/political_action _committee_report.

6. Open Secrets, http://www.opensecrets.org/lobby/clientsum.php?id=D000 000138&year=2015.

7. Open Secrets, http://www.opensecrets.org/lobby/clientbills.php?id=D000 000138&year=2014.

8. Isaac Martin, *Rich People's Movement: Grassroots Campaigns to Untax the One Percent* (New York: Oxford University Press, 2013), 3.

9. Ibid., 9.

10. "FAQS," Club for Growth, http://www.clubforgrowth.org/about/faqs/.

11. Martin, *Rich People's Movement*, 5.

12. Ibid., 7.

13. Ibid., 67.

14. Daniel Schlozman, *When Movements Anchor Parties: Electoral Alignments in American History* (Princeton, NJ: Princeton University Press, 2015).

15. Naomi R. Lamoreaux, *The Great Merger Movement in American Business, 1895–1904* (New York: Cambridge University Press, 1988).

16. R. Neal Peterson and Nora L. Brooks, *The Changing Concentration of U.S. Agricultural Production During the 20th Century: 14th Annual Report to the Congress on the Status of the Family Farm* (Washington, DC: U.S. Department of Agriculture, 1993).

17. Mancur Olson, *The Logic of Collective Action: Public Goods and the Theory of Groups* (Cambridge, MA: Harvard University Press, 1965).

18. Jacob Hacker and Paul Pierson, *Winner-Take-All-Politics: How Washington Made the Rich Richer—and Turned Its Back on the Middle Class* (New York: Simon and Schuster, 2011), 119.

19. Lewis Powell, August 23, 1971, memorandum, Lewis Powell Jr. Archives, Washington and Lee University Law School Library, http://law2.wlu.edu/deptimages/Powell%20Archives/PowellMemorandumTypescript.pdf.

20. Ibid.

21. Ibid.

22. Ibid.

23. Ibid.

24. Lee Drutman, *The Business of America Is Lobbying* (New York: Oxford University Press, 2015), 50.

25. Ira Katznelson, *Fear Itself: The New Deal and the Origins of Our Time* (New York: Liveright, 2013).

26. Sheryl Gay Stolberg, "Pugnacious Builder of the Business Lobby," *New York Times,* June 1, 2013, http://www.nytimes.com/2013/06/02/business/how-tom-donohue-transformed-the-us-chamber-of-commerce.html.

27. Alyssa Katz, *The Influence Machine* (New York: Random House, 2015), 35.

28. Ibid.

29. Hacker and Pierson, *Winner-Take-All,* 119.

30. Ibid., 120.

31. Bob Burke, *Bryce Harlow: Mr. Integrity* (Oklahoma City, OK: Oklahoma Heritage Association, 2000).

32. Hacker and Pierson, *Winner-Take-All,* 118.

33. Ibid.

34. Theda Skocpol, "Building Community Top-down or Bottom-up?: America's Voluntary Groups Thrive in a National Network," The Brookings Institution, Fall 1997, http://www.brookings.edu/research/articles/1997/09/fall-community development-skocpol; Jeffrey Berry, *The Interest Group Society* (New York: Little, Brown, 1989).

35. David Magleby, *The Money Chase: Congressional Campaign Finance Reform* (Washington, DC: Brookings Institution Press, 2010), 76.

36. Stephen Ansolabehere, John M. de Figueiredo, and James M. Snyder Jr., "Why Is There So Little Money in U.S. Politics?," *Journal of Economic Perspectives* 17, no. 1 (2003): 105–30.

37. "Political Contributions," Schlumberger, http://www.slb.com/about/global
_citizenship/political_contributions.aspx.

38. Ibid.

39. "About Us," Anthem, https://www.anthem.com/health-insurance/about
-us/anthem-overview.

40. Ansolabehere et al., "Why Is There."

41. John R. Wright, "PAC Contributions, Lobbying, and Representation," *The
Journal of Politics* 51, no. 3 (1989): 713–29.

42. Adam Thierer and Brent Skorup, "A History of Cronyism and Capture
in the Information Technology Sector" (working paper, George Mason University, Mercatus Center, July 2013), http://mercatus.org/sites/default/files/
Thierer_CronyismIT_v1.pdf.

43. David Truman, *The Governmental Process: Political Interests and Public
Opinion* (New York: Knopf, 1951).

44. U.S. Chamber of Commerce, https://www.opensecrets.org/pacs/lookup
.php?strName=US+Chamber+of+Commerce.

45. T. W. Farnam, "Corporations Are Sending More Contributions to Super
PACs," *Washington Post,* February 2, 2012, http://www.washingtonpost
.com/politics/corporations-are-sending-more-contributions-to-super-pacs
/2012/02/02/gIQAL4dYlQ_story.html; Open Secrets, https://www.opensecrets
.org/pacs/superpacs.php?cycle=2012.

46. Gary Jacobson, "The Effects of Campaign Spending in Congressional
Elections," *American Political Science Review* 72, no. 2 (1978): 469–91; Alan
Gerber, Gregory Huber, and Ebonya Washington, "Does Campaign Spending
Work? Field Experiments Provide Evidence and Suggest New Theory," *American
Political Science Review* 47, no. 2 (2004): 541–74.

47. Jeffrey Milyo and Timothy Groseclose, "The Electoral Effects of Incumbent Wealth," *Journal of Law and Economics* 42, no. 2 (1999): 699–722.

48. "Linda McMahon Reflects on Her $97 Million Senate Bids," *Bloomberg,*
November 9, 2012, http://www.bloomberg.com/bw/articles/2012-11-09/linda
-mcmahon-reflects-on-her-97-million-senate-bids.

49. Open Secrets, https://www.opensecrets.org/bigpicture/stats.php?cycle=20
12&display=T&type=W.

50. Robert K. Goidel, Donald August Gross, Todd G. Shields, *Money Matters:
Consequences of Campaign Finance Reform in U.S. House Elections* (Lanham,
MD: Rowman & Littlefield, 1999), 41.

51. John R. Wright, "PACs, Contributions, and Roll Calls: An Organizational
Perspective," *The American Political Science Review* 79, no. 2 (1985): 400–14.

52. Stephen Bronars and John Lott, "Do Campaign Donations Alter How
a Politician Votes? Or, Do Donors Support Candidates Who Value the Same
Things That They Do?," *Journal of Law and Economics* XL (October 1997):
317–50.

53. Beth Leech, *Lobbyists at Work* (New York: Apress, 2013), 21–22.

54. Ansolabehere et al., "Why Is There," 114.

55. Christopher Witko, "When Does Money Buy Votes?: Campaign Contributions and Policymaking," in *New Directions in American Politics*, ed. Matt Grossmann (New York: Routledge, 2014), 165–84.

56. Beth Leech, *Lobbyists*, 21.

57. Joshua Kalla and David Broockman, "Campaign Contributions Facilitate Access to Congressional Officials: A Randomized Field Experiment," *American Journal of Political Science*, April 2, 2015, doi: 10.1111/ajps.12180.

58. Eleanor Neff Powell and Justin Grimmer, "Money in Exile: Campaign Contributions and Committee Access" (paper presented at Applied Statistical Workshop, Harvard University, April 9, 2015), 24.

59. Suzanne M. Robbins, "Drugs, Doctors, and Hospitals; Campaigning Post -Health Care Reform," in *Interest Groups Unleashed*, ed. Paul Herrnson, Christopher J. Deering, and Clyde Wilcox (Washington, DC: CQ Press, 2013), 57–76.

60. Jake Haselswerdt and Christopher J. Deering, "More Bang for the Buck? Defense Industry Contributions and 2010 Elections," in *Interest Groups Unleashed*, ed. Paul Herrnson, Christopher J. Deering, and Clyde Wilcox (Washington, DC: CQ Press, 2013), 77–100.

61. Amy McKay, "Questioning the Access Hypothesis: Healthcare Lobbyists' Contributions During the Health Reform Debate" (paper presented at the annual meeting of the American Political Science Association, New Orleans, LA, August 30–September 2, 2012), http://ssrn.com/abstract=2107266.

62. Adam Bonica, Nolan McCarty, Keith Poole, and Howard Rosenthal, "Why Hasn't Democracy Slowed Rising Inequality?," *Journal of Economic Perspectives* 27, no. 3 (2013): 103–24.

63. Michael Franz, "Past as Prologue: The Electoral Influence of Corporations," in *Interest Groups Unleashed*, ed. Paul Herrnson, Christopher J. Deering, and Clyde Wilcox (Washington, DC: CQ Press, 2013), 101–28.

64. Frank R. Baumgartner, Jeffrey M. Berry, Marie Hojnacki, Beth L. Leech, David C. Kimball, *Lobbying and Policy Change: Who Wins, Who Loses, and Why* (Chicago, IL: University of Chicago Press, 2009).

65. Ibid., 9.

66. Martin Gilens and Benjamin Page, "Testing Theories of American Politics: Elites, Interest Groups, and Average Citizens," *Perspectives on Politics* 12, no. 3 (2014): 564–81.

67. Drutman, *Business of America*, 8–15.

68. Matthew D. Hill, G. Wayne Kelly, Brandon Lockhart, and Robert A. Van Ness, "Determinants and Effects of Corporate Lobbying," *Financial Management* 43, no. 4 (2013): 931–57.

69. Frank Yu and Xiaoyun Yu, "Corporate Lobbying and Fraud Protection," *Journal of Financial and Quantitative Analysis* 46, no. 6 (2011): 1865–91.

70. Brian Kelleher Richter, Krislert Samphantharak, and Jeffrey F. Timmons, "Lobbying and Taxes" *American Journal of Political Science* 53, no. 4 (2008): 907.

71. Ibid.

72. Baumgartner et al., *Lobbying and Policy Change*, 203.

73. Marie Hojnacki, Kathleen M. Marchetti, Frank R. Baumgartner, Jeffrey M. Berry, David C. Kimball, and Beth L. Leech, "Assessing Business Advantage in Washington Lobbying," *Interest Groups & Advocacy* 4, no. 3 (2015): 205–24.

74. Gilens and Page, *Testing Theories*.

75. Ibid.

76. Paul Burste, *American Public Opinion, Advocacy, and Policy in Congress: What the Public Wants and What It Gets* (New York: Cambridge University Press, 2014), 123.

77. Open Secrets, https://www.opensecrets.org/orgs/list.php.

78. Baumgartner et al., *Lobbying and Policy Change*, 20.

79. Richard L. Hall and Alan V. Deardorff, "Lobbying as Legislative Subsidy," *American Political Science Review* 100, no. 1 (2006): 69–84.

80. Goidel et al., *Money Matters*, 41.

81. Robert Boatright, "The U.S. Chamber of Commerce and the Citizens United Decision," in *Interest Groups Unleashed*, ed. Chris Deering, Paul Herrnson, and Clyde Wilcox (Washington, DC: Congressional, 2013), 31–56.

82. Timothy Wener, "The Sound, the Fury, and the Nonevent: Business Power and the Market Reactions to the Citizens United Decision," *American Politics Research* 39, no. 1 (2015): 137.

83. Mark Mizruchi, *The Fracturing of the American Corporate Elite* (Cambridge, MA: Harvard University Press, 2013).

84. Truman, *Governmental Process*.

85. Mizruchi, *Fracturing*, 6.

86. Ibid., 4.

87. Gilens and Page, *Testing Theories*, 576.

88. John Kingdon, *Agendas, Alternatives, and Public Policies* (Boston: Little, Brown, 1984).

89. James A. Smith, *The Idea Brokers: Think Tanks and the Rise of the New Policy Elite* (New York: The Free Press, 1991).

90. Center for American Progress, http://www.cap.org/apps/docs/cap_foundation/foundation_donor_list.pdf.

91. Greg Sargent, "Center for American Progress, Poised to Wield Influence Over 2016, Reveals Its Top Donors" *Washington Post,* January 21, 2015, https://www.washingtonpost.com/blogs/plum-line/wp/2015/01/21/center-for-american-progress-poised-to-wield-influence-over-2016-reveals-its-top-donors/.

92. Eric Lipton, "Comcast Recruits Its Beneficiaries to Lobby for Time Warner Deal," *New York Times,* April 5, 2015, http://www.nytimes.com/2015/04/06/business/media/comcast-recruits-its-beneficiaries-to-lobby-for-time-warner-deal.html?_r=0.

93. Foundation Center, http://data.foundationcenter.org/#/foundations/corporate/nationwide/total/trends:giving/2012.

94. Apple, Inc. is a notable exception for not maintaining a corporate foundation. Apple's philanthropic work goes through other channels.

95. Sara Reckhow, *Follow the Money: How Foundation Dollars Change Public School Politics* (New York: Oxford University Press, 2013), 29.

96. Ibid., 29.

97. Ibid., 63.

98. Ronald P. Formisano, *Plutocracy in America: How Increasing Inequality Destroys the Middle Class and Exploits the Poor* (Baltimore, MD: Johns Hopkins University Press, 2015).

CHAPTER 5: MONEY AT THE CAPITOL

1. CREW, http://www.crewsmostcorrupt.org/mostcorrupt/entry/most-corrupt -members-of-congress-report-2013.

2. Justin McCarthy, "Confidence in U.S. Branches of Government Remains Low," Gallup, June 15, 2015, http://www.gallup.com/poll/183605/confidence -branches-government-remains-low.aspx?utm_source=position3&utm_medium= related&utm_campaign=tiles.

3. Dilworth Law, http://www.dilworthlaw.com/Lawyers/RobertEAndrews.

4. Thomas F. Schaller, *The Stronghold: How Republicans Captured Congress But Surrendered the White House* (New Haven, CT: Yale University Press, 2015).

5. Jason Berry, "Louisiana Purchase," *Washington Monthly,* August 4, 2008, http://www.washingtonmonthly.com/features/2008/0804.berry.html.

6. George E. Condon, "Disgraced Congressman Randy 'Duke' Cunningham Is a Free Man Again," *National Journal,* July 10, 2014, http://www.nationaljournal .com/s/72617/disgraced-congressman-randy-duke-cunningham-is-free-man-again.

7. James Madison, "The Federalist Papers: No. 57," The Avalon Project, http://avalon.law.yale.edu/18th_century/fed57.asp.

8. David C. W. Parker, *The Power of Money in Congressional Campaigns, 1880–2006* (Norman: University of Oklahoma Press, 2014), 41.

9. Campaign Finance Institute, http://www.cfinst.org/pdf/vital/VitalStats _t2c.pdf.

10. Open Secrets, https://www.opensecrets.org/bigpicture/reelect.php.

11. Open Secrets, https://www.opensecrets.org/bigpicture/cost.php?cycle=2012.

12. Data drawn from publicly available information at http://www.fec.gov/ pindex.shtml.

13. Brian Arbour, *Candidate-Centered Campaigns: Political Messages, Winning Personalities, and Personal Appeals* (New York: Palgrave Macmillan, 2014).

14. Cecilia Kang and Matea Gold, "With Political Ads Expected to Hit a Record, News Stations Can Hardly Keep Up," *Washington Post,* October 31, 2014, http://www.washingtonpost.com/business/technology/with-political-ads-expected -to-hit-a-record-news-stations-can-hardly-keep-up/2014/10/31/84a9e4b4-5ebc -11e4-9f3a-7e28799e0549_story.html.

15. Calculations based on original analysis by author using publicly available FEC data.

16. Wesleyan Media Project, "Ad Spending in 2014 Elections Poised to Break $1 Billion," October 14, 2014, http://mediaproject.wesleyan.edu/releases/ ad-spending-in-2014-elections-poised-to-break-1-billion/.

17. Heath Brown, *Tea Party Divided: The Complex Politics of a Maturing Movement* (Santa Barbara, CA: Praeger), 95.

18. "Liberty," https://www.youtube.com/watch?v=-TZCaAd-PuE.

19. "Gratitude and Respect," https://www.youtube.com/watch?v=lWNF2 PBls4Y.

20. "What Drives Me," https://www.youtube.com/watch?v=apJKxOf_46A.

21. Ed O'Keefe, "No Special Ethics Investigation of Cathy McMorris Rodgers, Committee Says," *Washington Post*, March 24, 2014, http://www.washingtonpost .com/news/post-politics/wp/2014/03/24/no-special-ethics-investigation-of -cathy-mcmorris-rodgers-committee-says/.

22. Because much of the reported spending by the Ellmers campaign was uncategorized, these estimates are less precise than others.

23. "Open Door," https://www.youtube.com/watch?v=EpePzRPiB30.

24. "Send a Message," https://www.youtube.com/watch?v=mFL-DtuTwAs.

25. Open Secrets, https://www.opensecrets.org/races/summary.php?id=NC02& cycle=2014.

26. A Member of Congress, "Confessions of a Congressman," *Vox*, July 12, 2015, http://www.vox.com/2015/2/5/7978823/congress-secrets.

27. *Life in Congress: The Member Perspective*, Congressional Management Foundation and the Society for Human Resource Management, Washington, DC, 2013, http://www.congressfoundation.org/projects/life-in-congress/the-member -perspective.

28. Ryan Grim and Sabrina Siddiqui, "Call Time For Congress Shows How Fundraising Dominates Bleak Work Life," *Huffington Post*, January 8, 2013, http://www.huffingtonpost.com/2013/01/08/call-time-congressional-fundraising _n_2427291.html.

29. Open Secrets, http://www.opensecrets.org/pfds/.

30. Nicholas Carnes, *White Collar Government: The Hidden Role of Class in Economic Policy Making* (Chicago: University of Chicago Press, 2014), 5.

31. Jacob Hacker and Paul Pierson, *Winner-Take-All-Politics: How Washington Made the Rich Richer—and Turned Its Back on the Middle Class* (New York: Simon and Schuster, 2011), 11.

32. David W. Rohde, *Parties and Leaders in the Postreform House* (Chicago: University of Chicago Press, 1991).

33. Eric C. Heberlig and Bruce A. Larson, *Congressional Parties, Institutional Ambition, and the Financing of Majority Control* (Ann Arbor: University of Michigan Press, 2012), 44.

34. Matthew N. Green, *Underdog Politics: The Minority Party in the U.S. House of Representatives* (New Haven, CT: Yale University Press, 2015), 38.

35. Jeff Zeleney, "Of Party Dues and Deadbeats on Capitol Hill," *New York Times,* October 1, 2006, http://www.nytimes.com/2006/10/01/us/politics/01dues .html?pagewanted=all.

36. Ibid.

37. Jakes Sherman and Anna Palmer, "GOP Lawmaker: No Cash for Campaign Arm Because It Backs Gays," *Politico,* July 16, 2015, http://www.politico .com/story/2015/07/gop-garrett-hensarling-no-cash-for-campaign-arm-because -it-backs-gays-120201.html.

38. Green, *Underdog Politics.*

39. Heberlig and Larson, *Congressional Parties,* 4.

40. Ibid., 6.

41. Ibid., 4.

42. Ibid., 6.

43. Christopher R. Berry and Anthony Fowler, "Cardinals or Clerics? Congressional Committees and the Distribution of Pork," *American Journal of Political Science,* June 22, 2015, doi: 10.1111/ajps.12192.

44. "Earmark Data," Taxpayers for Common Sense, November 7, 2013, http://www.taxpayer.net/library/article/earmark-data.

45. Federal spending is broken down into mandatory spending that is set in law by an eligibility formula, such as Medicare, and discretionary spending that is decided annually during budget negotiations by Congress.

46. Brown, *Tea Party Divided.*

47. Naftali Bendavid, "Tea Party Wins GOP Vow to Ban Earmarks," *Wall Street Journal,* November 16, 2010, http://www.wsj.com/articles/SB100014240 52748703326204575616911269710850.

48. Ron Nixon, "Lawmakers Finance Pet Projects Without Earmarks," *The New York Times,* December 27, 2010, http://www.nytimes.com/2010/12/28/us/ politics/28earmarks.html.

49. Joseph Patton, "The Cause and Impact of Congressional Ethics Reform," in *Dirty Deals,* ed. Amy Handlin (Santa Barbara, CA: ABC-CLIO, 2014), 318–36.

50. Anthony Downs, *An Economic Theory of Democracy* (New York: Harper Collins, 1956).

51. Martin Gilens and Benjamin Page, "Testing Theories of American Politics: Elites, Interest Groups, and Average Citizens," *Perspectives on Politics* 12, no. 3 (2014): 564–81.

52. Ibid., 572.

53. Ibid., 576.

54. Stuart Soroka and Christopher Wlezien, "On the Limits to Inequality in Representation," *PS: Political Science and Politics* 41, no. 2 (2008): 319–27.

55. Carnes, *White Collar Government,* 38.

56. Ibid., 72.

57. Adam Bonica, Nolan McCarty, Keith T. Poole, and Howard Rosenthal, "Why Hasn't Democracy Slowed Rising Inequality," *Journal of Economic Perspectives* 27, no. 3 (2013): 103–24.

58. E. E. Schattschneider, *The Semi-Sovereign People: A Realist's View of Democracy in America* (New York: Holt, 1960).

59. Kay Lehman Schlozman and Philip Jones, "How Membership Associations Change the Balance of Representation in Washington (and How They Don't)," in *New Directions in Interest Group Politics*, ed. Matt Grossmann (New York: Routledge, 2014), 22–41.

60. Dara Strolovich, "The Paradoxes of Inequality and Interest Group Representation," in *New Directions in Interest Group Politics*, ed. Matt Grossmann (New York: Routledge, 2014), 60–85.

61. Carnes, *White Collar Government*.

62. Larry Bartels, *Unequal Democracy: The Political Economy of the New Gilded Age* (Princeton, NJ: Princeton University Press, 2010).

63. Jack Maskell, "Post-Employment, 'Revolving Door,' Laws for Federal Personnel" (Washington, DC: Congressional Research Service, 2014).

64. Peter Schroeder, "Obama Signs STOCK Act Modification," *The Hill,* April 15, 2013, http://thehill.com/policy/finance/293919-obama-signs-stock-act -step-back.

65. Elliot Gerson, "To Make America Great Again, We Need to Leave the Country," *The Atlantic,* July 10, 2012, http://www.theatlantic.com/national/ archive/2012/07/to-make-america-great-again-we-need-to-leave-the-country/ 259653/.

66. T. W. Farnam, "Study Shows Revolving Door of Employment between Congress, Lobbying Firms," *Washington Post,* September 13, 2011, http://www .washingtonpost.com/study-shows-revolving-door-of-employment-between -congress-lobbying-firms/2011/09/12/gIQAxPYROK_story.html.

67. Tim LaPira and Herschel Thomas, "Revolving Door Lobbyists and Interest Representation," *Interest Groups & Advocacy* 3 (2014): 4–29.

68. Lee Drutman and Alexander Furnas, "K Street Pays Top Dollar for Revolving Door Talent," Sunlight Foundation, January 21, 2014, http://sunlightfounda tion.com/blog/2014/01/21/revolving-door-lobbyists-government-experience/.

69. Sunlight Foundation, http://sunlightfoundation.com/blog/2014/01/23/ lobbyists-pt3/.

70. Jordi Blanes i Vidal, Mirko Draca, and Christian Fons-Rosen, "Revolving Door Lobbyists," *American Economic Review* 102, no. 7 (2012): 3731–48.

71. Ibid., 3747.

CHAPTER 6: THE MONEYED PRESIDENCY

1. William Horner, *Ohio's Kingmaker: Mark Hanna, Man and Myth* (Columbus: Ohio University Press, 2010), 5.

2. Robert North Roberts, Scott Hammond, and Valerie Sulfaro, *Presidential Campaigns, Slogans, Issues, and Platforms* (Santa Barbara, CA: ABC-CLIO, 2012), 72.

3. Kathleen Hall Jamieson, *Packaging the Presidency: A History and Criticism of Presidential Campaign Advertising* (New York: Oxford University Press, 1996), 16.

4. Robert C. Kennedy, "Uncle Mark: 'Not Saying a Word,'" *New York Times*, December 5, 2013, https://www.nytimes.com/learning/general/onthisday/harp/1205.html.

5. Herbert David Croly, *Marcus Alonzo Hanna: His Life and Work* (New York: Macmillan Company, 1912), 217.

6. Ibid.

7. Bradley Smith, "Campaign Finance Regulation: Faulty Assumptions and Undemocratic Consequences," *Policy Analysis* No. 238, September 13, 1995, Cato Institute, http://www.cato.org/pubs/pas/pa238.html#53.

8. Stephen Hess, "The Press and the Permanent Campaign," in *The Permanent Campaign and Its Future,* ed. Norman Ornstein and Thomas Mann (Washington, DC: AEI Press, 2000), 38–53.

9. FEC, http://www.fec.gov/pages/brochures/pubfund.shtml#Party_Limit.

10. *New York Times* data, http://elections.nytimes.com/2012/campaign-finance.

11. Campaign Finance Institute, "Aggregated Individual Contributions by Donors to 2012 Presidential Candidates," http://www.cfinst.org/pdf/federal/president/2012/Pres12Tables_YE12_AggIndivDonors.pdf.

12. *New York Times* data.

13. Jesse Baldwin-Phillipi, *Using Technology, Building Democracy: Digital Campaigning and the Construction of Citizenship* (New York: Oxford University Press, 2015).

14. Jennifer Stromer-Galley, *Presidential Campaigning in the Internet Age* (New York: Oxford University Press, 2014), 32.

15. Daniel Kreiss, *Taking Our Country Back: The Crafting of Networked Politics from Howard Dean to Barack Obama* (New York: Oxford University Press, 2012).

16. Stephanie Stamm, "How Do Presidential Candidates Spend $1 Billion?," *National Journal,* June 17, 2015, http://www.nationaljournal.com/ 2016-elections /how-do-presidential-candidates-spend-1-billion-20150608.

17. "About GMMB," http://www.gmmb.com/about/.

18. Michael Franz, "Past as Prologue: The Electoral Influence of Corporations," in *Interest Groups Unleashed*, ed. Paul Herrnson, Christopher J. Deering, and Clyde Wilcox (Washington, DC: CQ Press, 2013), 101–28.

19. Campaign 2012, *Washington Post,* http://www.washingtonpost.com/wp-srv/special/politics/super-pacs-2012/.

20. Open Secrets, https://www.opensecrets.org/pacs/superpacs.php?cycle=2012.

21. Jon Bruner, "Is Sheldon Adelson Funding Newt Gingrich's Attack Ads?," *Forbes,* February 22, 2012, http://www.forbes.com/sites/jonbruner/2012/02/22/is-sheldon-adelson-funding-newt-gingrichs-attack-ads-graph/.

22. Wesleyan Media Project, "2012 Shatters 2004 and 2008 Records for Total Ads Aired," October 24, 2012, http://mediaproject.wesleyan.edu/releases/2012-shatters-2004-and-2008-records-for-total-ads-aired/.

23. Matt Berman, "Mitt Romney: 47 Percent, What 47 Percent?," *National Journal*, July 29, 2013, http://www.nationaljournal.com/politics/mitt-romney-47-percent-what-47-percent-20130729.

24. "Stage Mitt Romney," https://www.youtube.com/watch?v=QxVqi8fuPDs.

25. "Priorities USA Action Ad: 'Romney's Gold,'" *Wall Street Journal*, July 25, 2012, http://www.wsj.com/video/priorities-usa-action-ad-romney-gold/ 00915 67C-4CD4-4515-88A0-10D5E616A006.html.

26. John Sides and Lynn Vavreck, *The Gamble: Choice and Chance in the 2012 Presidential Election* (Princeton, NJ: Princeton University Press, 2013).

27. Ibid.

28. Ibid., 223.

29. Patrick O'Connor, "Influence of Money in Politics a Top Concern for Voters," *Wall Street Journal*, June 21, 2015, http://blogs.wsj.com/washwire/2015/06/21/influence-of-money-in-politics-a-top-concern-for-voters/.

30. Ibid.

31. FEC, http://www.fec.gov/disclosurep/pnational.do.

32. Kenneth Vogel and Tarini Parti, "Campaigns Shatter Spending Records," *Politico*, July 16, 2015, http://www.politico.com/story/2015/07/fundraising-and-spending-shatter-records-120211.

33. Kennedy Elliot, Anu Narayanswamy, and Matea Gold, "The 2016 Mega-donors," *Washington Post*, August 2, 2015, http://www.washingtonpost.com/graphics/politics/2016-election/large-donors/.

34. Ken Vogel, Tarini Parti, and Theodoric Meyer, "67 Donors and Gusher of Cash Change 2016 Race," *Politico*, August 1, 2015, http://www.politico.com/story/2015/08/wealthy-donors-and-gusher-of-cash-change-2016-race-120894.html.

35. FEC, http://www.fec.gov/pages/brochures/indexp.shtml.

36. FEC Filing, American Democracy, http://americandemocracy.org/wp-content/uploads/ADLF-FEC-complaint-data-trust.pdf.

37. Michael Bender, "Jeb Bush Tries to Win Without Speaking to His Favorite Strategist," *Bloomberg Politics*, June 26, 2015, http://www.bloomberg.com/politics/articles/2015-06-26/does-anyone-believe-jeb-bush-isn-t-talking-to-his-super-pac-chief-.

38. Russ Choma, "Did Jeb Bush's Campaign and Super-PAC Cross the Line on Coordination?," *Mother Jones*, July 1, 2015, http://www.motherjones.com/politics/2015/06/jeb-bush-right-to-rise-mike-murphy.

39. Scott Bland and Adam Wollner, "Why Campaigns Have the Edge Over Super PACs on TV," *National Journal*, August 19, 2015, http://www.national journal.com/2016-elections/why-campaigns-have-the-edge-over-super-pacs-on-tv-20150819.

40. Republican Debate Transcript, *Time*, August 11, 2015, http://time.com /3988276/republican-debate-primetime-transcript-full-text/.

41. Eric Lichtblau, "F.E.C. Can't Curb 2016 Election Abuse, Commission Chief Says," *The New York Times*, May 2, 2015, http://mobile.nytimes .com/2015/05/03/us/politics/fec-cant-curb-2016-election-abuse-commission -chief-says.html?referrer=&_r=0.

42. Ibid.

43. Clinton Rossiter, "The Presidency—Focus on Leadership," *The New York Times*, November 11, 1956.

44. Richard Waterman, Carol L. Silva, and Hank Jenkins-Smith, *The Presidential Expectations Gap: Public Attitudes Concerning the Presidency* (Ann Arbor: University of Michigan Press, 2014), 9.

45. Shirley Anne Warshaw, *Guide to the White House Staff* (Thousand Oaks, CA: CQ Press, 2013). Data on size of White House in 2012 drawn from https:// www.whitehouse.gov/briefing-room/disclosures/annual-records/2012.

46. Julia Azari, *Delivering the People's Message: The Changing Politics of the Presidential Mandate* (Ithaca, NY: Cornell University Press, 2014); Heath Brown, *Lobbying the New President: Interests in Transition* (New York: Routledge, 2012).

47. Martha Joynt Kumar, *Managing the President's Message: The White House Communications Operation* (Baltimore, MD: Johns Hopkins University Press, 2007); Justin Vaughn and Jose Villalobos, *Czars in the White House: The Rise of Policy Czars as Presidential Management Tools* (Ann Arbor: University of Michigan Press, 2015).

48. David E. Lewis, *The Politics of Presidential Appointments* (Princeton, NJ: Princeton University Press, 2008).

49. James Druckman and Lawrence Jacobs, *Who Governs? Presidents, Public Opinion, and Manipulation* (Chicago: University of Chicago Press, 2015), 25.

50. Ibid., 71.

51. Ibid., 125.

52. Nicholas Carnes, *White-Collar Government: The Hidden Role of Class in Economic Policy Making* (Chicago: University of Chicago Press, 2013).

53. Julia Azaria, *Delivering the People's Message: The Changing Politics of the Presidential Mandate* (Ithaca, NY: Cornell University Press, 2014). Samuel Kernell, *Going Public: New Strategies for Presidential Leadership* (Washington, DC: CQ Press, 2007).Thomas Weko, *The Politicizing Presidency: The White House Personnel Office, 1948–1994* (Lawrence: University Press of Kansas, 1995).

54. Douglas Kriner and Andrew Reeves, *The Particularistic Presidency* (New York: Cambridge University Press, 2015).

55. John Hudak, *Presidential Pork: White House Influence Over the Distribution of Federal Grants* (Washington, DC: Brookings Institution Press), 50.

56. Kriner and Reeves, *Particularistic Presidency*, 130.

57. Kenneth Lowande, Jeffery Jenkins, and Andrew Clarke, "Presidential Pork and U.S. Trade Politics" (paper presented at the annual conference of the Midwest Political Science Association, Chicago, IL, April 16–19, 2015).

58. Hudak, *Presidential Pork*, 60.

59. Suzanne Piotrowski and David Rosenbloom, "The Legal-Institutional Framework for Interest Group Participation in Federal Administrative Policy-making," in *The Interest Group Connection*, ed. Ronald Shaiko and Paul S. Herrnson (Washington, DC: CQ Press, 2005), 258–81.

60. Scott Furlong and Cornelius Kerwin, "Interest Group Participation in Rule Making: A Decade of Change," *Journal of Public Administration Research and Theory* 15, no. 3 (2005): 353–70.

61. Robert Lowry and Matthew Potsky, "Organized Interests and the Politics of Federal Discretionary Grants," *Journal of Politics* 66, no. 2 (2004): 513–33. Susan Yackee, "Sweet-talking the Fourth Branch: The Influence of Interest Group Comments on Federal Agency Rulemaking," *Journal of Public Administration Research and Theory* 16, no. 1 (2006): 103–24.

62. Beth Leech, "Funding Faction or Buying Silence? Grants, Contracts, and Interest Group Lobbing," *Policy Studies Journal* 34, no. 1 (2006): 17–35.

63. Baumgartner et al., *Lobbying and Policy Change: Who Wins, Who Loses, and Why* (Chicago, University of Chicago Press, 2009), 208.

CHAPTER 7: REFORMING THE POLITICAL SYSTEM

1. Anti-Corruption Act, http://anticorruptionact.org/full-text/.

2. Michael Miller, *Subsidizing Democracy: How Public Funding Changes Elections and How it Can Work in the Future* (Ithaca, NY: Cornell University Press).

3. Ibid., 54.

4. Gail Russell Chaddock, "How to Fix Congress: A Former House Speaker Calls for Fewer Ethical 'Mousetraps,'" *The Christian Science Monitor,* November 2, 2014, http://www.csmonitor.com/USA/Politics/2014/1102/How-to-fix-Congress -A-former-House-speaker-calls-for-fewer-ethical-mousetraps.

5. By The People, https://sarbanes.house.gov/bythepeople.

6. Robert G. Boatright, Donald P. Green, and Michael J. Malbin, "Does Publicizing a Tax Credit for Political Contributions Increase Its Use? Results From a Randomized Field Experiment," *American Politics Research* 34, no. 5 (2006): 563–82.

7. Lee Drutman, "The Solution to Lobbying Is More Lobbying," *Washington Post*, April 29, 2015, https://www.washingtonpost.com/blogs/monkey-cage/wp/2015/04/29/the-solution-to-lobbying-is-more-lobbying/.

8. Jonathan Rauch, *Political Realism: How Hacks, Machines, and Big Money and Back-Room Deals Can Strengthen American Democracy* (Washington, DC: Brookings Institution Press, 2015).

9. Ibid., 530.

10. Ibid.

11. Ibid., 558.

12. Ray La Raja, "Why Super PACs: How the American Party System Outgrew the Campaign Finance System," *The Forum* 10, no. 4 (2012): 98.

13. Richard Pildes, "How to Fix Our Polarized Politics? Strengthen Political Parties," *Washington Post,* February 6, 2014, http://www.washingtonpost .com/blogs/monkey-cage/wp/2014/02/06/how-to-fix-our-polarized -politics-strengthen-political-parties/.

14. Rauch, *Political Realism,* 739.

15. "The Living Room Candidate: Presidential Campaign Commercials, 1952–2012," Museum of the Moving Image, http://www.livingroomcandidate. org/commercials/issue/corruption.

16. Naila Awan and Liz Kennedy, "The Racial Equity Impact of Secret Political Spending by Government Contractors," Dēmos, September 2, 2015, http://www .demos.org/publication/racial-equity-impact-secret-political-spending.

17. Lawrence Norden and Daniel Weiner, "How to Shine a Light on Dark Money," Brennan Center for Justice, April 14, 2015, https://www.brennancen ter.org/blog/how-shine-light-dark-money.

18. Darrell West, *Billionaires: Reflections on the Upper Crust* (Washington, DC: Brookings Institution Press, 2014), 170.

19. Bright Lines Project, http://www.brightlinesproject.org/wp-content/uploads /2015/06/2014-11-15-draft-Regs-and-Cover-FINAL.pdf.

20. "Jeb Bush on Lobbying," C-SPAN, July 20, 2015, http://www.c-span.org/ video/?c4545207/jeb-bush-lobbying.

21. Will Tucker, "Bush Calls for More Regulations on 'Lobbying,' Whatever that Term May Mean," Open Secrets, July 20, 2015, http://www.opensecrets.org /news/2015/07/bush-calls-for-more-regulations-on-lobbying-whatever-that-term -may-mean/.

22. Jonathan Rauch, "The Case for Corruption," *The Atlantic,* March 2014, http:// www.theatlantic.com/magazine/archive/2014/03/the-case-for-corruption/ 357568/.

23. Jason Grumet, "How to Fix Congress: Bring Back Earmarks and More Privacy," *Christian Science Monitor,* November 4, 2014, http://www.csmonitor .com/USA/Politics/2014/1104/How-to-fix-Congress-Bring-back-earmarks-and -more-privacy.

24. Heath Brown, *Tea Party Divided* (Santa Barbara, CA: Praeger, 2015).

25. James Inhofe, "The Secret about Earmarks," *Politico,* November 12, 2010, http://www.politico.com/news/stories/1110/45023.html#ixzz3jx2DmUpv.

26. Zephyr Teachout, "The Anti-Corruption Principle," *Cornell Law Review* 94, no. 341 (2009): 413.

27. In order to examine this, in July 2015, I selected a random sample of 100 official House websites and coded each for any mention—positive or negative— of "campaign finance reform," "lobbying reform," or "Citizens United."

28. Jay Cost, "So, What About Money in Politics?," *Weekly Standard*, May 4, 2015, http://www.weeklystandard.com/articles/so-what-about-money-politics _928693.html?page=2.

29. Common Cause, "Unlimited and Undisclosed: The Religious Right's Crusade to Deregulate Political Spending," February 25, 2015, http://www.common cause.org/research-reports/unlimited-and-undisclosed.pdf.

30. Jay R. Mandle and Joan D. Mandle, *Change Elections to Change America* (Westport, CT: Prospect Press, 2014).

31. Jacob Hacker and Paul Pierson, *Winner-Take-All-Politics: How Washington Made the Rich Richer—and Turned Its Back on the Middle Class* (New York: Simon and Schuster, 2011), 305.

32. Michael Gould Wartofsky, *The Occupiers: The Making of the 99 Percent Movement* (New York: Oxford University Press, 2015).

33. Caroline Lee, *Do-It-Yourself Democracy: The Rise of the Public Engagement Industry* (New York, Oxford University Press, 2015).

34. Edward Walker, *Grassroots for Hire: Public Affairs Consultants in American Democracy* (New York: Cambridge University Press, 2014).

Index

Page numbers in italics refer to figures and tables.

About the Author

HEATH BROWN, PhD, is assistant professor of public policy at the City University of New York, John Jay College of Criminal Justice and The Graduate Center, New York City, NY. He is the author of *Lobbying the New President: Interests in Transition* (2012) and *Tea Party Divided: The Hidden Diversity of a Maturing Movement* (Praeger, 2015). He is also a reviews editor for *Interest Groups & Advocacy*.